THE COLOR
ORANGE

Also by Russell Martin

Cowboy: The Enduring Myth of the Wild West
Entering Space: An Astronaut's Odyssey
(with Joseph P. Allen)
Writers of the Purple Sage (coeditor)
*Matters Gray and White: A Neurologist, His Patients, and
the Mysteries of the Brain*

THE COLOR ORANGE

—

A Super Bowl Season with the Denver Broncos

Russell Martin

HENRY HOLT AND COMPANY
NEW YORK

Copyright © 1987 by Russell Martin
All rights reserved, including the right to reproduce this
book or portions thereof in any form.
Published by Henry Holt and Company, Inc.,
521 Fifth Avenue, New York, New York 10175.
Published in Canada by Fitzhenry & Whiteside Limited,
195 Allstate Parkway, Markham, Ontario L3R 4T8.

Library of Congress Cataloging in Publication Data
Martin, Russell.
The color orange.
1. Denver Broncos (Football team) I. Title.
GV956.D37M35   1987   796.332′64′0978883   87–11978
ISBN: 0-8050-0562-5

First Edition
Designed by Jeffrey L. Ward
Printed in the United States of America
1 3 5 7 9 10 8 6 4 2

ISBN 0-8050-0562-5

For my father

Football is many things, but mostly
it is a game of passion.
                    —Vince Lombardi

Acknowledgments

Unlike the Denver Broncos, who at long last have supplanted luck with excellence, I am among the luckiest of people. My good fortune began with Barney Karpfinger, my friend and agent, who agreed that after several forays into other fields we should tackle football players and their fans. My luck continued with Marian Wood, my editor at Henry Holt, who now knows that football is the game they play with the pointed ball, and whose support I cherish.

Jim Saccomano, the Broncos' director of media relations, immediately understood what I hoped to do when we met in the spring of 1986, and throughout the course of the long season that followed he met my constant requests with kindness, good humor, and with very specific assistance. I'm grateful to him.

The list of Coloradans who lent me their time and comments and conjectures about the Broncos and the particular kinds of passion they inspire includes Luther and Carole Allen, Pat Bowlen, Michael Dowling, Janet Elway, Barry Hawkins, Karen

Holmgren, Tom Jackson, Rulon Jones, Rich Karlis, Ann Lacy, Ilene Lehmann, Bob Martin, Tim McKernan, Gerald Phipps, Mike Spence, Frances Warner, Brad Wayt, Ron Zappolo, and many others whose names are not here, but whose help has been invaluable. It has been my great good luck to encounter them.

THE COLOR
ORANGE

Prologue

—

You really couldn't help but be impressed by the meteorological portent, by the way the weather presaged the start of the season. On Friday the city was hot and strangely still, the sky blue above the smog. Then on Saturday came a great drum roll of thunder and a spare and promising rain—the dark skies lowering the morning light, the chill wind abetting the nervous anticipation of the two hundred or so fans who milled, umbrellas open and jackets buttoned tight, at the edge of the turf at Mile High Stadium in Denver, waiting for a minor ritual to begin—the taking of the team photograph, annually executed the day before the Broncos' home opener, before new jerseys lost their luster, before injuries and expediencies inevitably began to change the faces in the photograph.

At last, large men in Popsicle-orange jerseys with white numerals wider than pie tins began to amble out of the locker room and onto the field. Helmetless, wincing against the weather and hunching their huge padded shoulders, they milled near the four rows of risers where they would pose, shouting "Sheee-*it*, it's cold," kidding each other about their ugliness, slapping each other's butts, and bouncing on the balls of their feet.

The fans, held at a distance by a harried team PR man, pulled cameras with long lenses from the cover of their coats, aimed them at the men in orange and chattered excitedly, the cold—at least for a few moments—no longer a concern. They watched and waited while Dan Reeves, the Broncos' forty-two-year-old head coach, took on the frustrating task that thousands of grammar school teachers know too well—trying to get his players to line up properly (in their jerseys' numerical order), to bunch up a bit, to move over this way just a little, to drop the rabbit-ears fingers they held behind each other's heads, to stop making silly faces. When Reeves made it clear that everyone could go back inside as soon as the photos were finished, his players quickly simmered down. They stiffened up and looked straight ahead, Reeves and his assistants standing attentively behind them now in matching sport shirts, nearly five dozen all told—players and coaches and trainers—hollering "Cheese" in the same instant, then "Cheese" three more times to be sure, before they bolted for the locker room, the fans breaking toward them then as if intent on some open-field tackling. But the contact was light, nothing more than the pressing of pads of paper into the players' chests, the fans—suddenly intimidated by the sea of orange and, *my God*, by the size of these men, and surely by their local celebrity—blurting only "Would you . . . ?" or "Please?" as they held pens up to the players' eyes.

I wiped the rainwater off an aluminum bench and sat down, the only spectator among 75,000 empty seats. I had never been in this place before, this colossal horseshoe painted in section-coded colors—yellows, blues, oranges, and reds—some sort of outsized theater in the round, all seats focusing on a distant stage that was simply a rectangular strip of grass, a place that, even in its emptiness, offered a vision of drama, a heady sense of coming attractions. Mile High Stadium, cobbled and riveted through four series of renovations since it first served as a base-

2

ball park in 1948, had been sold out for every regular-season home game of the Denver Broncos since the beginning of the 1971 season—fifteen years, 117 games, 120 if you count the three play-off games played here in 1977, 1978, and 1984. Tomorrow it would be sold out again as 75,000 blue-capped and orange-shirted football fans, no, *Broncos* fans, streamed into this stadium to pledge their allegiance, to scream their hearts out, to die with every Denver turnover, to know true exaltation if their guys were ahead at the end of the game.

The Broncos were my team, too, if the truth were told. After ninety-four years of American professional football, they were still the only team anchored between the Sierras and Kansas City—the only game in the Great American West save the teams scattered along the Pacific Coast, which somehow didn't count. Growing up in a rat-ass town located where the Rockies descended to the Navajo desert, I had become a Broncos fan in the years during which they were indisputably the worst team trying to play the game. They wore silly vertically striped socks, their helmet logo was a dumb cartoon depiction of a bucking horse, and, back then, a .500 season would have been something worthy of wild celebration. But the Broncos were likable. Actually, they were lovable, lovable in the way that a dog who just can't manage a trick is lovable. They reminded us of ourselves, I suppose—our unabashed optimism somehow always countered by a bare reality. Throughout the mountain West, the Broncos were the boys we worried about on tattered stools in small cafes, the team we lambasted on job-site lunch breaks, the team we coached brilliantly over beers and whiskeys, then gamely cheered through the subsequent losing effort. Perhaps we cared about them so much simply because they so often broke our hearts.

After eleven losing seasons (44 wins, 105 losses, 5 ties), the 1971 Broncos were nonetheless, and for no discernible reason, able to sell out every home game. To no discernible effect: The team barely mustered a 4-9-1 record that year.

In 1972, things began to get a bit better. In their first year under former Stanford University head coach John Ralston—a Dale Carnegie advocate and a shrewd judge of football talent—the Broncos went 5-9. Then in 1973, while the rest of the nation focused on a minor skirmish called Watergate, football fans in the Rockies reveled in—can you imagine it?—a winning season, 7-5-2. It had taken fourteen years to achieve, but we are a patient people, those of us who live in the American outback. Broncomania, the term for the condition that had afflicted long-suffering fans, came into common usage, and there was indeed a growing, nearly epidemic mania about this laughing stock football team that had finally found a way to win. Four years and three more winning seasons later, the meek inherited the earth and the 12-2 Broncos, coached by a fireplug named Red Miller, went to the Super Bowl. But because life has little meaning, the 1977 season ended in defeat. In Super Bowl XII, the Wild West Bowl, the Dallas Cowboys corralled the Denver Broncos, and 40,000 visiting Denver fans milled through New Orleans's French Quarter in dazed and dangerous post-game depression. Back in the Rocky Mountains, *everybody*—except those who were in comas and had good excuses not to have watched the game—turned off the television, sighed a great collective sigh, and averred in a voice sad and deflated, "Well, what'd we expect? Shoot, we're talking *Broncos*, after all."

Yet despite that game's bitter lesson, it was a kind of watershed. Never again could the Broncos simply be lovable losers. The very fans who had become devoted to them because of their strange socks, because of their succession of aging and unathletic quarterbacks, because of their penchant for snatching defeat from the pendulous jaws of victory, now demanded something better, more than mediocrity, something akin to excellence.

The national sports media, on the other hand, and football fans elsewhere in the country really didn't give much credence to the Broncos' ascendancy that year. They didn't suppose it would last long. One hinterland team or another always seemed to be able to pull off a Cinderella season. But for the Broncos' owners, coaches, players, and for their much-abused fans, .500

4

seasons would never again be adequate achievements. The vertically striped socks had long ago been burned in a pre-game ceremony. Now it was time to incinerate an image—one of a team, and a town, that simply didn't amount to much.

During the decade that followed the Super Bowl season, the Broncos were a good football team. Twice they won the American Football Conference's Western Division. They recorded at least ten victories per season in all but the strike-shortened 1982 season. Under current head coach Dan Reeves, the team had won forty-five games, losing just twenty-eight. Only two other teams posted better records during that decade. Yet at the start of the 1986 season, a remnant of the Broncos' first incarnation remained, some long-standing and latent suspicion of ineptitude: The Broncos had played in four post-season play-off games since that trip to the Superdome. They weren't super, or even adequate to the task, in a single one of them.

As the 1986 season was set to open, everyone's annual anxieties were compounded by a strange new reason to worry. In addition to all the usual concerns about the adequacy of the offensive line, and the utter absence of a running game, there was this to worry about: Five national magazines that are prone to make such prognostications had recently made the Broncos their pick to be representing the American Football Conference in Super Bowl XXI in Pasadena—a few months and a dozen and a half football games down the road. For crying out loud! Not only was the upcoming schedule a virtual mine field, not only was the running offense its usual suspect self, now there were these crazy expectations to contend with.

Sitting in the autumnal gloom on a hard seat in that silent stadium, I was eager for some football finally to be played, whatever the four-month succession of games might bring—a season unparalleled or a season like so many others. I had come to the city from the hard-scrabble sticks to observe firsthand what theretofore I had only gleaned from Sunday afternoon television and the sports pages of Denver's dailies. I wanted to

5

get some measure of what fed this football mania, to try to understand why this team could captivate so many dissimilar people. The Broncos were the great democratizer in Denver, the one safe but shared and passionate conversation between the rich and the poor and the sea of people in the economic middle ground, between people who were white and brown and black.

Still, football was only a *game*—a diversion, an entertainment, as simple and artificial and ultimately unimportant as a Saturday schoolyard match played between neighborhood boys. And this was what intrigued me. How was it that a series of games, of contests between mercenary athletes, which had no real or concrete connection to the lives of the rest of us, could assume such vital importance? Why did the weekly fate of Denver's football team—or of other teams in other cities—garner the kind of attention that might otherwise have been given only to a summit between the superpowers? What was it, for heaven's sake, that football offered us?

What follows are a series of reports from the city at the eastern flank of the Rocky Mountains, letters posted from a football town during the course of a single season, beginning with the long hot days of training camp in mid-July, climaxing in the emotional tumult of the play-offs in frigid January, and ending in a sun-drenched Pasadena Super Bowl. They are letters concerning this illness called Broncomania, letters about the relationship between the team and its city, its region—focusing in a kind of scattershot on the players who work wearing pads and plastic helmets, who are celebrated or ignored depending on what they have done for Denver lately; on the owner and his administrators and coaches, for whom football is big and serious business; on the beat reporters who cover the team as if the assignment were the State Department, and the television "talent" who stand in front of video cameras to record facile practice-field updates; on the bookies and bettors and the souvenir sellers; and, of course, on the fans—the fans who, over the cascade of years, have spent more money than they care to admit to buy tickets to more games than they care to remember, the fans who surely bleed in blue and orange, who root religiously for the home team, who are affected by its fortunes in ways that are not simple to explain.

What follows is a book about football—how the game on the grass (or on the imitation grass) is sometimes enlarged by us into something mythic, something hugely important, something that somehow gets under our skin each autumn.

The weather on Sunday continued wet and cool, but the stadium, filled with 75,898 people who doubtless didn't notice, now seemed smaller, almost intimate, a bowl of kinetic orange and blue. It was the most dramatic kind of opening day—the Broncos hosting their arch rivals, the Los Angeles, nee Oakland, Raiders, winners of the division championship the year before. This was a game that likely would figure prominently in the season's final standings come Christmastime, a game that a Super Bowl–bound team should certainly win. The Broncos got an early lead on an elegant touchdown pass from quarterback John Elway to wide receiver Steve Watson—the kind of play that makes the game seem more like splendid choreography than a contact sport—and the crowd erupted with a kind of jubilation that made you think nothing could ever go wrong, not today, surely not this season. But the Raiders were also ready to play; they, too, had aspirations—two quick touchdowns, a safety, and a field goal. The score was suddenly 19 to 7 and the second quarter had just begun. My God, it couldn't all crumble this quickly, could it? A row of seated players in orange jerseys stared stone-faced at the field. Dan Reeves, in a tie and a cheerleader's sweater, paced the sideline, dragging his headset's cord behind him. The people in the stands were apprehensive now, nervous. Some of them pulled coats close around their shoulders; all of them were quiet. They twisted their programs into tight rolls, and they worried.

July 28
———

Except for the times when it was derisively called "Cow Town," Denver, Colorado, used to be known as the "Queen City of the Plains," a name conjured up by some Chamber of Commerce booster, I presume, someone who noticed something regal about the place that the rest of us didn't see. It was true that Denver belonged to the sweeping, short-grass prairies that roll westward from the heartland. It was true that from the center of the city, the Front Range of the Rockies was only a low and distant mirage; ski lifts did not then and do not now rise from the bases of office buildings, as tourists are sometimes disappointed to discover. But if there was anything "queenly" about Denver back when that phrase was current—back when the Broncos had their humble beginnings—it must have been just that there was a rather matronly air about the place, the town a dowdy kind of dowager who still remembered the halcyon days of cattle barons and silver kings. Denver in the 1960s was a cow town in scope, a cow town in swaggering attitude. Its fledgling football team might have been named the Denver Dynamos—or the Roughnecks or the Miners or the Missiles—but it made perfect sense that it wasn't. Bob Howsam, the team's organizer and first owner, named his club after a rodeo mount, after a cantankerous cayuse with an independent spirit. You didn't name *anything* after cows, of course, but what could be more appropriate than a bucking bronco?

In 1986, however, Denver is a decidedly different sort of city. The National Western Stock Show, held during the coldest days of the year each January, remains a major event, but the energy and high-technology booms of the late 1970s have otherwise transformed the city. Skyscrapers have shot up like asparagus shoots; there was a joke for a few years that the Colorado state bird was the construction crane. Early in this decade, people poured into Denver from cities in the depressed Northeast, and dozens of bullish computer technology and oil companies built plants and office parks and set up shop. Today, despite the oil glut's depressive downturn, Denver remains a city on the economic make. It is still de rigueur to wear cowboy boots in the company of Christian Dior suits, but the city's movers and shakers bristle now at the suggestion that their town is Way Out West. Everybody drives Mercedeses and Saabs instead of Oldsmobiles these days; they eat croissants for breakfast and study wine lists like apprentice sommeliers at dinnertime. And if you were starting a football team today—well, you might be tempted to call it the Denver Metro Microchips.

If you wanted to find a true cow town in Colorado now, you'd probably do what I did this morning—drive northeast from Denver in the shimmering early heat, past vast fields of green potato vines, between more rows of feed corn than you can fathom, to Greeley, a pleasant cow-and-college town plotted on the table-flat banks of the South Platte River. Greeley is home to the state's principal teacher-training university and to Colorado's largest cattle-feeding and beef-packing conglomerate—a combination that is more amicable and complimentary than you might imagine. It is a sleepy, tree-shaded burg of 50,000 or so inhabitants (not counting the itinerant students or the bawling cows passing through to a better place) that was named after the nineteenth-century *New York Tribune* publisher Horace Greeley, who is supposed to have said, "Go West, young man." What Greeley actually had to say was a bit more wordy than that—he was a newspaperman, after all—but that was the gist of his statement; if your prospects weren't bright in the East, he opined, you should head out West to find your fame and fortune.

On the thick-grass playing fields at the University of Northern Colorado, it appeared as though Greeley's advice had been well heeded. But "Go long, young man" is what you might have heard instead, as dozens of rookies with raging dreams tried to do exactly as their coaches told them: "Run me a quick out and up, and when that ball comes by, you grab it like it's everything you own, Sucker. Let's see what you got now."

This was Monday of the second week of training camp, the third day since the veteran Bronco players joined the kids who are fresh out of college for a forty-day-and-night siege that resembles nothing so much as boot camp—Fort Ord without the haircuts, Camp Pendleton without the carbines. By 9:30 this morning, eighty-three players in pads and helmets and heavy adhesive tape were working in the ninety-degree heat. They ran sprints to "warm up," then the receivers ran pass routes, defensive backs covering them by running backward with astonishing speed, their arms pumping like pistons; linebackers endured lateral agility drills; linemen endlessly practiced blocking assignments; running backs took a succession of hand-offs, balls couched in their bellies, then planted their feet, made their cuts; punters sent footballs tumbling high into the clear sky; quarterbacks sent footballs spinning like fat brown bullets—all of them grunting, straining, swearing, as they exhaled hard breaths, their heads baking inside their blue helmets, sweat pouring from their determined faces.

This was one of summer's dog days—oppressive, anvil hot,

almost ugly beneath the sun's bright intensity. It wasn't football weather, wasn't weather for fifteen pounds of clothes and enveloping plastic hats. It was hard to imagine how the games to be played in six weeks' time—the season that seemed so distant—were worth this kind of punishment. This morning, like every other morning during camp, reveille was called at 7:00. Players who were under treatment for injuries had to report to the training room by 7:15. The mandatory breakfast (no meals can be skipped under any circumstances) concluded at 8:30, followed by an hour to don uniforms and to complete supervised stretching and warm-up exercises. Practice, a carefully coordinated series of drills and play formations and run-throughs, each one on the immediate heels of the other, lasted until 11:30. Media interviews took till noon, sometimes longer, then showers and lunch ate up an hour. Injured players were due back at the training room by 1:00; quarterbacks had a meeting at 1:30; and everyone else could either nap, if they needed to, or study their playbooks, if they were looking for job security. It was time to suit up again at 2:30, to warm up at 3:00, to practice hell-bent by 3:45. There were more media interviews at 5:30; dinner was served at 6:00, and a two-hour team meeting convened at 7:30. At 9:30, the players were on their own. They could do anything they chose to do; they could even drive downtown and very quickly try to get very drunk or to make amorous introductions. But they had to be efficient about it—curfew came at eleven.

Would you willingly submit to a similar summer schedule in order to spend each crisp autumn weekend being battered by 270-pound Giants and Bengals and Bears? Well, yes, you might, especially if base salaries and signing bonuses, options and inducements sufficiently sweetened the lure, especially if you loved to play the game, despite—or because of—its physical demands. Many of the hard-muscled men on the fields this morning have never done anything other than play football. Sure, some had summer jobs in high school, fewer worked during summer ses-

12

sions in college, fewer still have done any postcollegiate work other than to throw footballs or to catch them, to carry footballs toward distant goal lines or to tackle the men who possess that audacious ambition. These men, some of them just beyond boyhood, belong to a small athletic elite. Even the most marginally talented of them possess remarkable physical skills, and their skills are their professions, their livelihoods. They are prodigies, products of sophisticated interscholastic and intercollegiate football programs, young men who have always played football because they could always play it so well. And although they cuss it, they endure each training camp—a dozen or more of them for the longest-tenured veterans—because football, for now, perhaps for a lifetime, is the only trade they know.

There are six adjacent football fields on the broad expanse of grass at the southwest corner of the university complex, and the Broncos—the ten dozen players, one dozen coaches, "fluid technicians" (water boys), "ball boys" (ball boys), and assorted official hangers-on splitting up and separating by position and by assignment—practice on all six of them at once. Linebackers here, running backs yonder, quarterbacks and wide receivers working together, defensive backs working alone; offensive linemen and defensive linemen sharing the same field, sometimes lining up against each other instead of the tackling sleds; the punters and kickers, always the outcasts, working in isolation on the farthest field, staying out of the way, attending to the tedium of their single task.

Walking from group to group, it is easiest for me to identify with the kickers, perhaps because kicking the ball seems straightforward enough to understand, devoid of the complex machinations of running and passing plays, perhaps because the kickers' statures seem to mirror average proportions—mine, for one. Like golfers, the kickers come in several sizes. Punters tend to be long-legged, it's true, but not all of them are, and the several place kickers in camp seem to be six feet tall or less (downright

13

Lilliputian by football standards, but perhaps that is because two of the taller of them are masochists and kick the ball shoeless).

The men who practice the other positions seem far more uniform in size. The stout running backs are built like oatmeal boxes, their thighs as thick as their chests; the receivers are long and lithe and they can run lickety-split; the defensive backs—whose job it is to defend against them—are just the same. The quarterbacks are big—bigger than you would imagine—about the size of the linebackers, but the difference between them is this: The linebackers work themselves silly and their orange jerseys are soaked with sweat; the quarterbacks are seldom taxed, and their white jerseys stay dry. The defensive linemen are enormous and fast; the offensive linemen are enormous and slow.

Even the coaches seem to share a particular style. Today, all wear blue "coach's shorts"—except for assistant head coach Joe Collier, whose legs have never seen the sun, and each wears a white polo shirt with a Broncos logo where the alligator would otherwise go and a blue baseball cap with the words DENVER BRONCOS emblazoned on it. I am surprised to note that the coaches share similar limps. They are all former players, of course, and football players tend to destroy their knees; the coaches, almost to a man, walk as if they have sat in the saddle too long; they walk as if walking is a painful enterprise, and I suppose it probably is.

Some of the assistant coaches are shouters, barking complaints and encouragement like drill sergeants; others are soft-spoken, leaning toward an individual player when they have something to say, as if sharing a secret. Offensive-line coach Alex Gibbs, diminutive in the midst of his charges, hollers, "Come on, you assholes! You're pissing around pass protecting on a surge play!" Linebacker coach Myrel Moore shouts encouragement: "There! That's a head butt, Meck. Good head butt." Defensive-backs coach Charlie West, the only black assistant, is subdued as he sends passes that his players are supposed to tip or intercept. Head coach Dan Reeves—dressed like all the others, his limp perhaps the most pronounced—circulates among the groups, observing, saying little, asserting himself only with the whistle that signals the end of one drill, the start of still another.

On the sideline areas between each field, reporters and TV crews roam, relaxed, watching the uniformed men at work, chatting casually about who is looking mighty good and who will surely soon be packing, the camera operators aiming at groups of players whose drills have enough intensity, enough visual interest to make the evening news. Except for the television reporters, who wear oxford shirts and silk ties and who couldn't wear hats because they would crease their hair, the media people are dressed for the heat in shorts and sneakers or flip-flop sandals. Everyone wears a hat to protect against the sun; golf hats from local country clubs are popular, as are souvenir hats from major league baseball teams. In the interests of objectivity, no reporter would be caught dead wearing a Broncos hat.

Although they appear to be doing nothing other than burning the backs of their thighs, the sportswriters are actually working hard as they pace the sidelines in the sun. They are trying, desperately some of them, to turn the tedium and repetition of practice into story ideas, into something worth writing about, and that isn't an easy task. Often they simply have to resort to doing what the TV people do: escorting the players off the fields at the end of practice and asking them how they feel. The players always say it feels good finally to be at it again; it's hard and it's hot, but it's beginning to come together.

Against the long brick wall of the university fieldhouse, a row of motor homes and travel trailers are parked like a latter-day wagon train, each one sporting the call letters of the television or radio station to which it belongs. You wouldn't see similar rigs parked at most other NFL training camps, but they are an integral element here. They are the bases from which three Denver television stations, three Denver radio sports-talk shows, and scattered regional radio stations keep the rest of us abreast of who is about to be cut and who is playing up to his promise, up to the minute on whether the players are enjoying camp (they aren't) and whether they are hopeful about the coming season (they are). Each of the stations and each of the talk shows acknowledges that its coverage amounts to overkill, but none will be the first to limit itself. In the tough competition for audiences and advertisers, Broncos coverage, *exhaustive* Broncos coverage, is a proven and dependable draw.

There are a final group of people at this morning's practice, the largest of the several groups assembled, the one contingent that isn't working, isn't on hand because it has to be. Behind a thin polyethylene rope near the fieldhouse, near the electronic wagon train, three hundred or so fans watch the goings-on. They wear T-shirts that say things like CHARLIE IS A #1 BRONCOS FAN, and they are plainly enjoying themselves, recognizing the distant players by their numbers, telling each other whom they've spotted, watching the drills with surprising interest, clapping, cheering for long punts and for acrobatic pass receptions, pressing the ropes at the end of practice, shouting names, asking the sweating players to come give them their autographs. Several players oblige, signing their names a few times, a few signing dozens of times, before they head inside. The bravest fans ask the players how it's going as they wait for their prized signatures, but most are silent in the presence of these heroes. They wait till the players have gone before they shout "Shit! Incredible! I got Elway!" and "Hey, check it out! Here's T.J." When there are no more players on the fields and the souvenir stands have shut, they, too, leave, but they will be back in the baking afternoon.

The training camp press room is located in the basement of Turner Hall, a high-rise dormitory. Adjacent to the washing machines and the large industrial dryers, the room has no windows, only fluorescent strips for light, and today the beige walls are bare except for scattered posters of the coming season's schedule, photocopied lists of players who've been cut, and a notice of a Wednesday afternoon press members' golf tournament organized by the Broncos' media relations office, designed to help prevent the reporters from expiring from abject boredom. Copies of the Denver papers are scattered on a bank of desks punctuated by push-button telephones, and copies of three magazines lie there as well: *Street and Smith's Pro Football*, *Sport*, and *Playboy*, each issue of which includes that publication's predictions for the 1986 professional football season. The dog-eared copy of *Playboy* has been the most perused.

The magazines are like-minded in their conviction that the Broncos will win the American Football Conference's Western Division, a coincidence that seems more than a little arresting and which has caught the reporters' attention. Yes, the Broncos have had the third best win-loss record in the NFL over the past decade. Sure, only two other teams—Dallas and Miami—have had more ten-victory seasons during that span. But the Broncos are perennial bridesmaids; they are good but not great, perhaps not hungry enough, and, as virtually every prognosticator has noted (these fellows have favorite themes), Denver lacks a showcase, dash-for-the-cash kind of running back, the sort who sends you to the Super Bowl.

Yet two of the magazines go so far as to say that that's exactly the fortune that will befall the Broncos this year. *Street and Smith's* is a conservative, football fanatic's kind of publication, and it doesn't go so far as to guess how the play-offs will go; selecting the division winners is as long a limb as it is willing to climb out on. But *Sport* announces that the Broncos will meet the Chicago Bears in the Super Bowl; *Playboy* predicts the game will feature the Broncos and the New York Giants. The staff-written story in *Sport* says, "This year, the Broncos call all the shots," focusing its attention on the team's renowned defense, ignoring its suspect offense. *Playboy*'s Anson Mount, who has been making his magazine's fall predictions since the days when its playmates wore beehive hairdos, is downright enthusiastic:

> The passing game, with quarterback John Elway and receivers Steve Watson and Vance Johnson, is superb. The running attack needs reinforcements, but there are no other obvious deficiencies. The starting line-ups are stable, and if last year's crippling defensive injuries don't recur, this will be the best year in the history of the Denver franchise. The Broncos have been almost great for the past several years. We have a hunch that this season, they'll finally hit the jackpot.

But his royal "we" and his hunch notwithstanding, Mount says the Giants will beat the Broncos in that final game that so often isn't super. He doesn't elaborate. *Sport* says the Bears will be favored by four points over the Broncos. Take Chicago and give the points, it advises.

The consensus among the reporters who are drinking Cokes and staying out of the noonday heat in the air-conditioned dormitory press room is that well, yeah, these guys seem to have a certain confidence, a certain *spirit* out there on the university turf, but *Super Bowl*? Part of their reluctance to jump on the bandwagon, I suppose, is that to do so would run the risk of making them look like unthinking, blithering fans instead of objective journalists. Part of their reluctance has to do with their awareness of a kind of "Broncos jinx," which *Rocky Mountain News* columnist Teri Thompson—the only female writer from either Denver daily who regularly covers the Broncos—has written about:

> To say the Denver Broncos haven't had a storied, painful, checkered history would be sort of like saying Richard Nixon didn't have his ups and downs. They once went an entire game without a first down. Twice they've missed the

playoffs with better records than teams that made it. They've had their share of busted draft choices. For years they couldn't win on artificial turf. Their field goals hit uprights and crossbars. They have not scored in the third quarter in recent memory.

Somehow, the gathered press corps just can't imagine these orange horses at the top of the football heap. When the same reporters, working now, circle around Dan Reeves in the furnace heat of the afternoon and ask him his opinion of the national media who are at long last latching on to the Broncos, he replies in a Georgia voice that turns vowels into gooey substances, "Well, I'd sure rather be picked as a possible Super Bowl contender than be picked to finish last." Then he waits for another question.

There was a time in the annals of this nation when there was no Super Bowl, even a distant era when there was no NFL. If it hadn't been for a few testosterone-crazed Ivy Leaguers at the end of the nineteenth century, there might have been no football at all.

The game we call football—which should probably have some other name—derives from soccer, of course, and soccer, like golf and tennis and clubbings by fans, is a product of the British Isles. The game seems to have had its origins in the eleventh century when workers in England excavating a battlefield found a skull they took to belong to a hated Dane. The Danes had vacated Britain only some few years before, and the memory of their oppressive rule was still fresh enough that the workers kicked the skull back and forth between themselves to show their smoldering anger—as well as to avoid going back to work.

It was a lot of fun, except that kicking a skull with one's foot was painful enough that few were willing to give it more than a couple of licks. Shortly thereafter, however—and this discovery may indeed rival the wheel—someone experimented by inflating a cow's bladder with air and tying it off to create a

19

pneumatic sphere. The bladder would sail when it was kicked, and kicking it didn't induce pain. It was so pleasurable, in fact, that adjacent villages began to challenge each other in matches that were known as "kicking the Dane's head," a name that called out for a bit of abbreviation. Players would meet midway between their villages; the bladder would be thrown down as a signal for the game to begin, and then, with dozens, sometimes hundreds, of players taking part, the bladder was kicked, butted, swung at, and chased until at last one side had succeeded in advancing it into the portal of the rival village's parish church. The game was enormously popular among its players, but non-participants in the villages were terrified of the periodic on-slaughts; teams about to be victorious amounted to little less than invading armies.

The game needed some regulation, some standardization, and it got a new name: *futballe*. Fields with marked boundaries became the playing grounds; teams were required to have equal numbers of players; and points were awarded when the bladder or "ball" was kicked over the goal line of the opposing team. By the twelfth century, *futballe* was the most popular leisure activity in Britain; so many men were neglecting other essential tasks that King Henry II outlawed play, threatening imprison-ment for players as well as for landowners who allowed games to be played on their property.

King Henry's principal concern had been that the game's wide popularity would prevent the regular practice of archery, a skill he deemed essential to the isle's defense. His ban was remarkably successful, and the game was played only seldom and furtively throughout the rest of his reign and for the succeeding four hundred years. Enough clandestine football was played, how-ever, for the principles of the game to survive, and when King James I ascended to the throne in 1603 it readily gained currency again. Not only did James lift the centuries-old ban, he pro-nounced football a clean and honorable pastime, one that devel-oped strength and good character. Teams were formed in towns and cities throughout the realm, and the game was further refined

20

and standardized over the course of many years: Field dimensions were specified, goals were scored only when the ball passed between two posts instead of when it crossed an end line, and the use of hands and arms to move the ball was prohibited.

In 1823, William Ellis at Rugby College in Warwickshire was convinced that football would be much improved if players were allowed not only to dribble the ball with their feet and to kick it, but also to throw it from player to player and to carry it on the run. Ellis's version of the game soon had vocal advocates, but others remained staunchly opposed to this strange derivation of football. Teams who played by Ellis's rules called their sport "rugby," or "rugger." Their slang for the older, feet-only game was "soccer."

On November 6, 1869, twenty-five young men from Rutgers University met twenty-five others from Princeton at New Brunswick, New Jersey, to play the first intercollegiate football game in the United States. Played under the rules of the London Football Association, the game they played was "soccer." In the following few years, football teams were formed as well at Yale and Columbia, and representatives from the four schools met in New York in the autumn of 1873 to form the Intercollegiate Football Association and to draft its rules. Although invited, no one from Harvard attended the meeting because sportsmen at Harvard were convinced that *they* were playing a better game, one they called "the Boston game" for lack of a better sobriquet. The Boston game was played with an inflated round rubber ball, which could be kicked toward a goal line, but players could also pick the ball up with their hands any time the fancy struck them, then dash toward the goal. No one else played a game quite like the Boston game, although it had similarities to rugby, which was then being played in Canada and Britain. If it hadn't been for the rather haughty chauvinism of the Harvard players and their refusal to compromise their sport, the game Americans now know as football probably would never have evolved.

Since opponents were necessarily hard to come by, the Harvard players were happy to accept a proposal for a series of games wth McGill University in the spring and fall of 1874. The two schools agreed that the games would be played alternately under the loose rules of the Boston game and the rather more refined rules of rugby, a game already established at McGill. Under both sets of rules, it was agreed, there would be fifteen men on each side. But when four McGill players were unable to make the trip to Cambridge, the Harvard players agreed to limit their side to eleven men as well, a number now unchanged in more than a century.

The outcome of the Harvard-McGill series, apart from the forgotten scores, was that the Harvard players decided there were aspects of rugby that they liked very much indeed. They liked the egg-shaped leather ball; they liked the running that rugby entailed; and perhaps most of all, they approved of the gritty defensive business of *tackling* the ball carrier to prevent him from advancing toward the goal. But rugby really wasn't much of a kicking game, and kicking, too, was lots of fun. There was an easy solution, of course: the two games could be combined.

The new hybrid, no longer named for Boston, now called football or association football for lack of something better, as well as to emphasize that kicking was still a part of the contest, impressed many people—even those athletes at Yale and Princeton who theretofore had solely been playing soccer. It was a Yale player and coach, in fact, the legendary Walter Camp, who latched on to this new derivative of rugby and refined it into the game recognizable as American football. Camp created the scrimmage line, signal calling, the quarterback position, and he introduced the rule demanding that a team relinquish the ball to its opponent if it was unable to advance the ball at least five yards every four plays, or "downs." Camp became a member of the Intercollegiate Football Rules Committee, which worked to standardize the still-evolving sport, and he wrote the first football book, published in 1891.

Camp was eventually able to persuade the Rules Committee to allow tackling below the waist; he was convinced that if it was to be a truly excellent game, football had to be rough-and-tumble, it had to be tough. If broken bones were a by-product of play, well, sporting men shouldn't mind a fracture or two, should they?

By the turn of the century, football was becoming ubiquitous. Its popularity had gone beyond the Ivy League to include schools in the Middle West and California; noncollegiate "athletic clubs" had been formed in Pittsburgh, Philadelphia, Chicago, and Newark—some of which offered game-by-game fees to their players—and professional baseball teams like the Philadelphia Athletics periodically staged football exhibitions. But few baseball players were tempted to switch sports permanently: There wasn't any money in the new game. Although paying men to play baseball was considered a suitable enterprise in that era, the notion that you might similarly pay football players seemed a little unseemly. Baseball was a gentlemen's game; it had none of football's chaos or its battlefield casualties. Football players—even the Ivy Leaguers—were little more than thugs, went the popular conception, and their shenanigans surely shouldn't be encouraged with salaries or bribes or booty.

The game had become violent enough by the fall of 1905 that eighteen players were killed that season; more than 150 serious injuries were reported. President Theodore Roosevelt, a great partisan of the game, worried that unless the violence were curtailed, the sport itself would be jeopardized. At Roosevelt's urging, the Rules Committee tried to limit the game's basic brutality by allowing the forward pass, by prohibiting the then standard shove-and-pull mass plays, by lengthening the first-down distance to ten yards, and by discouraging both collegiate and athletic club teams from utilizing so-called tramps, mercenary young fellows who would gladly play for anyone and who seemingly lived to smash helmetless into the bellies of the boys on the opposite side.

The tramps never left the sport, but Roosevelt's game survived.

At 4:35 this afternoon, I saw for the first time, indisputably, that this is a brutal game, a *ball* game, yes, but more fundamentally, a blocking and tackling game in which bodies are battered and beaten and necessarily sacrificed. On the cue of Reeves's sharp whistle, the cadre of linebackers—more than a dozen of them, double the number that will ultimately make the team—join the seven running backs and a target quarterback in a pass rushing–pass blocking drill. Dozens of times in succession, quarterback Scott Stankavage took an imaginary snap and back-pedaled into the pocket, flanked by two running backs who had to try to protect his health. Each back—a sitting duck and delicate by comparison—tried to stop the charge, the single-minded, quarterback-seeking pursuit of the blitzing linebacker who approached him at full and unsympathetic speed. The running backs, each pair in turn, lowered their helmets as they braced for the first bite of contact—the spine-stinging blow—as the linebackers collided with them, then clawed to get away, to get around, to get on toward the quarterback. The *sound* of helmets and pads and upper torsos in collision was ominous from a few feet away—a loud popping explosion of plastic against plastic—always accompanied by desperate and straining grunts. The *sight* of each of these wrecks was stunning.

Whenever an orange-jerseyed linebacker escaped the block and rushed on to touch the quarterback, slapping his shoulder as a symbol of success instead of crushing him, the linebackers who were waiting their turns cheered and shouted encouragement. "All right! Yes!" they shouted. "Trap, Ricky, yes!" When a white-jerseyed running back somehow kept his defender at bay, far from the fragile quarterback, the encouragement from his fellow backs was more subdued. Each one knew he would soon be standing motionless in the path of a similar onslaught. There are moments, I now know, when there is no glamour in the backfield.

July 29

It wasn't all that different from the punt, pass, and kick contests the Ford dealers used to sponsor when I was a kid, the fundamental distinction being that we were ten-year-olds pretending we had futures in this game and they were twenty-plus-year-olds, one of whom would actually live out our fantasies as the Denver Broncos' punter. The three young men, a Georgian, a Californian, and a short, tow-headed kid from the Denver suburb of Northglenn, lined up side by side on the thirty-yard line of the central field. A crew of defensive backs, receivers, and the fleetest running backs—those who hoped and those who *knew* they would be punt returners—spread out about fifty yards downfield. The rest of the team, not yet under the coaches' scrutiny, was still running laps and doing stretching exercises.

Chris Norman, the Georgian, has been the Broncos' punter the past two seasons, but his job is widely considered to be in jeopardy. Although he has averaged a respectable forty yards per kick in each of his two years with the Broncos, he has always been erratic and he has never inspired confidence. Rick Partridge, from California, a free agent, has punted for New Orleans, San Diego, and for three franchises in the soon-to-be-defunct United States Football League. He, too, has averaged forty yards per kick as a professional. Jack Weil, the Coloradan, the *only* native Coloradan who might become a Bronco this year, had tryouts in 1985 with the Atlanta Falcons and the Houston Oilers, but did not survive with either team. As a collegiate All-American at Wyoming, he averaged 42 yards per kick. Norman and Partridge are tall and lanky, requisitely long-legged. Weil, significantly shorter of leg and of inches from

25

toe to crown, has the approximate stature of a fluid technician.

But Jack Weil was booming punts this morning. His kicks exploded off his instep into the morning sky, rising so suddenly that they appeared to be rocket-launched, then somehow spiraling as they reached the top of their arc, the balls gaining momentum as they spun, then finally losing thrust and descending sharply to the players who waited beneath them. Norman and Partridge are also capable of kicking footballs, of course; Norman occasionally put his foot into a monstrous kick—one went 63 yards before gravity got the better of it—but on this morning he was as erratic as his press clippings had made him out to be. His shortest kick, shanked off the side of his shoe, was a wounded duck that barely traveled 20 yards.

Partridge couldn't match Norman's longest kick, but neither did he embarrass himself. In fact, his hang times—the seconds between the moment when the ball is airborne and when it touches the returner's hands—appeared to be the longest, hence best, of the three. Although to my eyes Weil currently had the edge in this professional kicking contest, Partridge is evidently unconcerned. Last night after practice, he told KOA radio's Bob Martin and Sandy Clough that he was certainly the best punter of the trio. He cited his USFL experience, his athletic skills, and his concentration and said he wished the other two well, averring that he felt they might find employment elsewhere in the NFL. "But I'm going to be the Broncos' punter," he said. "I'm dedicating myself to it; I'm focusing on it, and I just feel strongly that I'm the best." Martin thanked Partridge for his comments, then, breaking for a commercial, he told his audience, "While you listen to this, we'll see if we can't get Rick Partridge to work on his confidence."

Each morning's punting contest is one of the few entirely objective evaluations that takes place on the practice fields, and the reporters are attracted to it for that reason. Bleary-eyed, still sleepy, and chronically sunburned, they amble out in surprising force to see the three punters in action, jotting numbers into their notebooks each time a punt is caught—the returners shouting "four nine," or "three seven," or whatever the punt's approximate yardage, to special teams coach Chan Gailey, who stands, clipboard in hand, beside the punters. Gailey measures each punt's hang time with a stopwatch and notes this as well as the distance, but the reporters record only the distance. They know that a good hang time gives the punting team an important instant longer to run downfield and to prevent a long and dramatic run-back. They know that no one whose hang times aren't respectable will be this team's punter this year. They know that, but their readers are not necessarily interested in such erudition. What their readers want to know is which of these three young fellows is booming the bejesus out of the ball, and tomorrow's editions will edify them: After fourteen punts this morning, Weil averaged 42.4 yards per kick; his longest was 59 yards, his shortest 36. Norman averaged 40.5 yards, with a long of 63 and a short of 19. The ebullient Partridge's numbers: 40.2, 52, and 33.

A group of veteran players got the chance to earn a little something extra, a bit of promotional booty, at the end of this morning's practice. Walking from the fields to the fieldhouse locker room, they were corralled by staffers from Denver's NBC affiliate, KCNC-TV, Channel 4, who offered each of them a navy-blue corduroy baseball cap emblazoned with the Channel 4 logo and the words THE BRONCOS' STATION if they would simply stand in front of a video camera and, hat on head, say once or twice or three times, "You're watching NewsCenter 4, The Broncos' Station." Can you imagine the players' delight? Nothing to it. No need to bullshit about how they were giving it 110 percent, no blithe comments about how yes, they sure were concentrating on the Super Bowl. Just a quick pitch and they could head for the showers, proud owners of new chapeaux.

It was a curious sight—two dozen jaded and surely sunstruck football players, each of whom had stood in front of television cameras more times than he could count during his career, waiting in a patient queue in order to do no more than plug the station that by virtue of a carefully worded contract and a stack of dollars of indeterminate height had secured the right to call itself the channel of the Broncos' choice. Each one took his turn with the brief station ID, carefully enunciating the seven words, and some, like linebacker and raconteur Tom Jackson, grinning broadly as they spoke them; others, like Karl Mecklenburg and Steve Watson—certified local celebrities—speaking so seriously you might have guessed this was some sort of screen test. And uncharacteristically, the players who waited their turns didn't kid, didn't heckle the one who was briefly center stage. They simply waited in silence, their uniforms dripping sweat, their helmets under their arms, their corduroy caps—now theirs to cherish in return for this impromptu promotion—spinning on their fingers.

It is Channel 4, by virtue of its NBC affiliation, that broadcasts almost all of the Broncos games. Under the terms of the NFL's contract with the three television networks (a contract that expires at the end of the 1986 season), NBC broadcasts games played between teams in the American Football Conference, CBS broadcasts the National Football Conference games, and ABC broadcasts the games played on sixteen Monday and three "Special Edition" nights throughout the season. Rights to broadcast interconference games go to the network that would normally cover the visiting team. When Denver, in the AFC, plays at an NFC city, NBC gets the rights to broadcast the game back to Denver (and elsewhere in the country, depending on the particular contest). The only time CBS covers a Denver game is when the Broncos host an NFC team at Mile High Stadium. During the 1986 regular season, NBC and KCNC—"the Broncos' station"—will broadcast fourteen games. CBS and its local affiliate KMGH, Channel 7, will broadcast two games. The Broncos will play twice on Monday night—ABC territory, KUSA, Channel 9 in Denver. If the Broncos make the play-offs, their game or games again will be broadcast by NBC; if they reach the Super Bowl (well, it *could* happen), CBS will carry the game because it is that network's turn in its year-to-year Super Bowl alternation with NBC.

What all this amounts to is that, without even trying, Channel 4 is the de facto Broncos' station. What Channel 4 purchases directly from the Broncos is a licensing agreement that allows it to broadcast four pre-season games and "The Dan Reeves Show," a thirty-minute interview and game-highlight program featuring the head coach, every Monday night during the season. What it gets as a bonus is a fall full of station IDs by camera-struck football players, IDs that none too subtly announce: *The Broncos are right here, so don't you dare touch that dial.*

Advertising revenue is the carrot, of course, and competition the prodding stick that account for the media madness, the overkill coverage of this training camp. For a full six weeks, four television stations, a dozen or so radio stations, three radio talk shows, and six daily newspapers maintain the sports equivalent of embattled foreign bureaus on this quiet campus only fifty miles from Denver. No single entity or issue in the Rocky Mountain region is as certain to be of vital interest to as many people as are the Broncos—not state or city government, not the economy or the crime rate, not skiing or the social scene or the vagaries of the weather, not the successful Denver Nuggets of the National Basketball Association, or the crowd-starved Denver Zephyrs of baseball's minor league American Association. The Broncos are a guaranteed draw, not only at the stadium gates, but in newsprint and on the airwaves as well. Advertisers understand that, even before the season starts, thousands of people will be poring over the sports pages as if they are treasure maps; their ears will be tuned to radios as though they are waiting for word from the battlefront; their half-closed eyes will stretch open again come the Broncos' segment on the late local news. And in order to attract more readers and viewers to entice advertisers further—to be able to up the marketing ante—the print and electronic media bar no holds when it comes to covering this camp.

Two beat reporters from the *Denver Post* and two from the *Rocky Mountain News* pack their bags and check into one of the dormitories for the duration, as do reporters from the papers in Pueblo, Colorado Springs, and Boulder—each of them filing daily pieces that are long on puff and necessarily short on meat and potatoes. Columnists, cartoonists, and sports feature writers make periodic forays up through the cornfields in search of story ideas—something exclusive, something overheard, something stolen, if it comes to that. "Give me a Greeley column for Friday," you know their editors have told them, and as they arrive you can see the look of dread through the dark lenses of their sunglasses.

In the talk-show trailers beside the fieldhouse, the search is not so much for story ideas as it is for callers and guests with healthy larynxes who speak something approximating the English language. Believe it or not, little KRXY, a station virtually without an audience except for its sports-talk show, broadcasts live from Greeley for *five hours daily*, Monday through Friday, from two in the afternoon till seven. Yes, the show has three hosts—longtime Denver sports pundits Irv Brown and Joe Williams, and hometown boy Dave Logan, who was a wide receiver for the Cleveland Browns and, briefly, for the Broncos—but five hours is a lot of time to bludgeon. As they take their turns in front of the microphones, the three hosts do their best to talk about the yawning pennant races, such as they are, in the major leagues; they gladly chat about golf when they get a chance—or tennis or rodeo or car racing—but virtually every caller brings the subject back to Greeley. "Yeah. Hi, Joe and Irv. Great show. Listen, I was wondering how Karlis is looking so far up there. Is he kicking any better?" the caller wants to know, and it's back to the Broncos again.

By 5:30 each afternoon, salvation comes in the large shape of a sweating football player or two who, begged or cajoled by the show's producers, sits down for a bit and fields questions from Irv, Joe, Dave, and from an occasional caller. Finally, after three and a half hours of the breeziest kind of chatter about whether Elway is the best quarterback in the league or merely one of the best, there is something a little more substantial. "How's it feel so far out there, Billy?" Irv is anxious to ask. "Well, it's coming together," responds veteran center Billy Bryan in a North Carolina accent you could whittle with a knife. Irv waits expecting more, but Billy Bryan is not exactly loquacious.

"As an offensive line," Dave now wants to know, a little more in depth, "what's going to be your primary goal this season?"

"Well, to protect John. Keep him healthy. That's got to be number one right there," Billy says. Irv takes a deep breath and tries again.

No one else has to keep the conversation up as long as the fellows in the KRXY trailer—and you can hear the competing talk show hosts knocking firmly on wood. "Sports Superstars" is the slightly unusual title for the KNUS talk show hosted by Mike Haffner and Jim Turner, both former Broncos, a receiver and a place kicker respectively, both of whom complain about the restrictions Broncomania places on their show, but both of whom can talk about the Broncos till they are blue in the face. Haffner and Turner don't start until three each day, but they, too, work until seven.

At KOA radio, the station that by licensing agreement broadcasts the radio play-by-play of the Broncos games, sports talk is much more an adjunct to the coverage of the team than the principle means of coverage. KOA's contract with the team allows it to do *live* reports from the sidelines of the practice fields—something the others dare not try—and throughout the season, Dan Reeves tapes an exclusive pre-game interview with KOA's play-by-play announcer Bob Martin. "Sports Talk" or "Bronco Talk," depending on the evening in question, the KOA call-in show hosted either by the twenty-three-year-veteran Martin or by wunderkind Sandy Clough, is a mere two hours of conversation and conjecture, six to eight, about—what else?—the Broncos.

Maybe it's because I secretly envy the fellows whose hair is held down with Final Net and who work in front of the Minicams, but whatever the reason, I'm convinced that theirs is the easiest kind of Broncos coverage. Their camera crews work a little harder than they do, but not so much harder that you think they ought to unionize. This is how it seems to go for them in Greeley:

About halfway through this morning's practice, men in cutoff shorts and giveaway T-shirts begin to pack cameras on tripods onto the playing fields, looking as though they might be a crew planning to survey this sweeping grassland. The cameras, of course, have numbers painted on them—a four, a seven, and a nine—and their operators aim them at the scattered action, shooting ten times the amount of tape that will be aired on this evening's news. Eventually, the people who work on the other side of the cameras arrive, wearing Ralph Lauren polos with the collars standing up, working in a way that is imperceptible. They carry no notepads, no mini-cassette recorders. They wander; they chat with assistant coaches; they kid with the print reporters and glad-hand among themselves. Occasionally they instruct a cameraman to be sure to get what footage he can of a particular player, and at roughly eleven o'clock, they hand a list of names to the team's media relations staffers—names of the players they want to interview when the practice comes to a close. The lists delivered, they and their crews adjourn to trailerside to set up cameras again and to wait for the requested players to appear. But all is not leisurely in that interval; there are tags and teases to get on tape. "When we return, a talk with starting guard Keith Bishop," KCNC's Ron Zappolo says into the camera three times before he is happy with his cadence. A trailer away, KUSA's Jim Celania—who had vowed when he came to Denver from San Francisco a year before that he would

32

do only studio work—now briefly questions cornerback Louis Wright, while a crewman aims a spherical light reflector at Wright's dark, wet face. Down the line, Gary Cruz, KMGH, speaks with veteran safety Steve Foley, rookie lineman Jim Juriga, and linebacker coach Myrel Moore, all in the span of thirteen minutes. When the interviews are finished and the players have disappeared, the cameras are packed into the trailers for safekeeping and everyone goes to lunch. There will be plenty of time to edit the tape after a little something to eat and maybe a short siesta. Then it will be work, work, work again at the end of the afternoon practice.

July 30

The Denver Broncos' 1986 collegiate draft garnered the team no superstars, no media darlings. The biggest story on draft day at the end of April was, in fact, a trade—the Broncos relinquished their second-round choices in 1986 and 1987 to acquire cornerback Mark Haynes from the New York Giants. Haynes, from the University of Colorado, had been a three-time Pro Bowler, but he had sat out much of the 1985 season in a contract dispute. The Giants had made it clear prior to draft day that the introspective, enigmatic Haynes was available for the right price, and Denver offered the Giants the draft choices they ultimately didn't refuse. Although the Broncos' defensive secondary was already one of the league's best, the Broncos crowed that with the Haynes trade they had effectively drafted an all-pro player, one who might immediately become a starter—something that is by no means assured on draft day.

Haynes made a media appearance at Broncos headquarters in Denver the day after the draft, announcing that he was happy to be back in Colorado, that the trade pleased him very much, and that he was looking forward to joining an already legendary defense. The television stations recorded the shy twenty-seven-year-old's remarks, filming him in his new orange jersey. The newspapers led their sports sections with stories about the Haynes trade, then analyzed the Broncos' other draft-day acquisitions and pronounced them adequate—solid, sensible choices all. But somehow, none of the new Broncos really captured anyone's imagination. There wasn't anyone remotely akin to John Elway, whose acquisition by trade in 1983 had made the mountains shake and the citizens see salvation. No, this crop of newcomers, including the veteran Haynes, were mere athletes—marketable, valuable football players, but little more.

It wasn't until late May that the media and the Broncos' fans found a freshman who seemed to have that ineffable something—a spark of individuality, a measure of personality and style that might sustain more than a single story, that might mean continuing fan interest and perhaps even celebrity. What they discovered at the Broncos' practice complex one bright spring morning was a Good White Hope of sorts, a scrappy running back named Joseph Anthony Dudek who hailed from Quincy, Massachusetts, and who seemed a bit surprised to find himself at the foot of the Rocky Mountains.

But this Joe Dudek, whose dark, angular features and quiet, self-effacing style made him seem like a football player from a different era, was not a totally unknown quantity. His friendly, Slavic, buck-toothed face had already appeared on the cover of *Sports Illustrated*, and he was a bona fide football star. As a Plymouth State College Panther, Dudek had set NCAA records for most touchdowns scored (79) and most points scored (474) during his four-year collegiate career. Now, tiny Plymouth State (in New Hampshire) doesn't include Penn State or Southern Cal on its autumn schedule, but nonetheless, those are impressive statistics. Even if you are playing for a Division III school where they patch up ancient equipment with nylon thread and duct tape, you have to be some kind of athlete to record those kinds of numbers. So said *Sports Illustrated*, and so echoed Denver's football reporters.

Although every NFL team had been aware of Dudek prior to the draft, none chose to spend a draft choice to acquire him. Very few running backs, very few white running backs in particular, ever make the long and rugged run from the NCAA's Division III to the backfields of the NFL. So even though he had set twenty-seven Division III records, Joe Dudek still wasn't given good odds of proving to be one of those rare small-college lads who could make it.

Undrafted, Dudek had been eligible to sign a free-agent contract with any team he chose, and he had accepted the Broncos' offer among the several he received because the Broncos—as everyone knew—were weak at running back. By the time the Broncos' rookie training camp opened in Greeley on July 18, Dudek had become the designated intriguing new kid on the block. His pass-receiving skills being his biggest shortcoming, Dudek had spent the two months between signing and camp at the Broncos' practice facility in Denver, standing for long, hot hours against a high wooden fence, throwing a plastic football secured to the fence by an elastic cord. Each day, Dudek threw the football into the air hundreds of times in succession. Each day, the boomerang ball snapped back to him a commensurate number of times. By the time he left for Greeley, the balls no longer slugged him in the nose or ricocheted off his shoulders, and the coaches and beat reporters were beginning to get excited.

As the *Rocky Mountain News*—the larger of Denver's two competitive dailies—began its annual flood of dispatches from the Greeley front, it initiated "Catching On: Joe Dudek Shoots for the Big Time," a regular series of reports on Dudek's progress written by *News* Broncos reporter B. G. Brooks. There had been "The Elway Watch" in 1983 when rookie phenomenon John

35

Elway arrived in camp, the young quarterback followed by a coterie of reporters from around the country which was about the size of the White House press corps. Come 1984, the national sports media no longer dogged Elway's every movement, but for Denver reporters, he still was *the* story. First-round draft choice Steve Sewell, a running back from Oklahoma, and wide receiver Vance Johnson, a personable little rocket from Arizona, had received special attention at the 1985 camp. This year, it was Joe Dudek's turn.

"Sunday offered precisely what Joe Dudek needed," wrote Brooks on July 22, sizing up his subject's first few days, "R & R & R. The free-agent running back . . . spent the first non-practice day for the Denver Broncos' rookies and free agents resting, recuperating and reading. . . . The playbook that he had received three days before begged for more study if Dan Reeves' offense was ever going to become comprehensible."

In examining his on-the-field performance so far, Brooks noted that he had been battered, but that Dudek seemed plenty tough. At practice the previous morning, "a trap play over left guard sent Dudek into the hostile embrace of six-foot four-inch, 240-pound defensive end Ray Phillips. After being hit, hoisted, and heaved, Dudek required several extra seconds to right himself." Following practice, Brooks asked running backs coach Nick Nicolau for his assessment of Dudek's prospects. "I don't care if a guy bleeds and wheezes when he's down," responded Nicolau, "just as long as he gets up. Dudek does." It was the kind of quote that makes a reporter salivate, and it looked to both Brooks and Nicolau at that moment as if Dudek might be catching on.

Six thousand die-hard football fans sat on the grassy slope above the southwesternmost practice field this evening and watched the first major scrimmage of the camp. There were no punts, no kickoffs, and there was no hated opponent on the field. They were all Broncos, or potential Broncos, out there—offensive players in white jerseys, the defense clad in orange. Team rosters cost a quarter, soft drinks were fifty cents, and those three or four people who didn't arrive in Broncos caps and T-shirts could have purchased them near the parking lots. The fans came on this still and sultry summer night to see the familiar numbers, the players who had thrilled them in the distant winter, but they also came to see the boys in the new numbers, the kids fresh out of college who just might help us out, especially this 32, this *Dudek*—if that's the way you pronounce it—the one who set so many records and who they say runs like a jackrabbit.

Joe Dudek did run tonight; against the veteran Broncos defense that was, well, a bit more imposing than the defenses he had challenged in Division III; he gained 54 yards on ten carries, including a long run of 18 yards. Churning into the line of scrimmage, his legs an unorthodox pair of rotors, yes, there it was, that uncoachable instinct to run, to escape, to break away at any cost. Say, maybe this kid had something, people began to say; they cheered from the grassy slope and, after his long run, they even chanted his name.

But on two of his ten carries, the young running back dropped the ball; he fumbled as he was hit and the defense recovered the prize. Twice he was the target of quarterback Gary Kubiak's passes, but only once did he cradle the ball. The second pass drilled his shoulder pads and bounced away as though it were the boomerang ball on the cord. At the end of the hour-long scrimmage, a dejected Dudek walked toward the locker room and told Brooks as he went that he was "terrible. If I keep doing that I'm not going to be around. I'm really P.O.'d at myself. I was tripping over white lines. It just wasn't working for me." Then Brooks sought out the quotable coach's assessment. "He didn't run all over the lot," Nicolau said when he stopped to talk with the soft-spoken, Tennessee-voiced reporter, "but you saw it again—those bolts of lightning. If he hadn't tripped over his tight end's foot on the sweep, he'd still be running."

The verdict on the grassy slope was even more encouraging

37

than the coach's. "Hey, he's got a lot to learn," said a man whose own legs were blocked from his view by his stomach, "but I'll tell you what, he can pick 'em up and lay 'em down."

I walked in a tight knot of fans toward the parking lot. "When was the last time we had a white running back?" someone wanted to know.

"Rob Lytle, I guess. Before that there was Jensen, Keyworth."

"Yeah, but they were just plow-ahead runners. This kid's got some sparkle. I think Reeves'll keep him. Reeves was a free-agent running back. I bet he's got a soft spot." The blond young man wore an orange T-shirt with the number seven on it, the name "Elway" printed above the number. He was clearly hoping the head coach would let nostalgia color his choices.

"Bullshit," said his friend, "Reeves would cut his mother."

"Not if she could run like that dude," said the blond, and the two men laughed, encouraged as they left the scrimmage.

The State Armory Bar is located in Greeley's marginally derelict downtown; it is housed in a building that indeed was once an armory and is the kind of establishment where an ancient airplane is suspended from the ceiling on cables, where the decor is a jumble of old Lucky Strike and Esso signs painted in enamel on broad tin sheets, where rusted license plates and shriveled shoes stand as knickknacks on every flat surface, where bartenders and waitresses come on like camp directors, where *fun* is the password and where—I had it on good authority—the Broncos choose to imbibe.

But at eight o'clock tonight, the State Armory was nearly deserted—the dance floor a dark ocean, vacant stools at the bars. A few cowboys, their hats on their heads and the ragged cuffs of their Wranglers scraping the floor, stood in near silence, waiting awkwardly for some kind of rodeo, something worth staying for. Uniformed softball players, some of them still in cleats, joked at a distant table, and a few coeds in shorts and cotton tops, their skin carefully tanned and smelling like sudden rapture, whispered near the disk jockey's stand. But there were no football players, no burly men in Fila cotton sweaters, no gold chains looped around their massive necks.

It was simply too early, I finally realized, as flocks of people began to file in past the bouncers—young men and women (and the coy college women were the majority now) who knew the Broncos' schedule and who were arriving just before the evening meeting ended and the players streamed for their cars. In a matter of twenty minutes, the State Armory went from silence to cordial chaos; the bartenders—all in T-shirts that read BRONCOS' CAMP, 1986—now were drawing beers at a frantic pace and, little by little, the dance floor began to fill.

At about 9:35, the first wave of players landed—big, broad-shouldered men in tank tops, young men who towered above the crowd that surrounded them—most of them rookies, most of them black, most of them unattached, all of them unattached for the evening. At the bar near the dance floor, the nine players, stunned by the size of the crowd, were offered free drinks and complimentary T-shirts like those the bartenders wore. They readily accepted both, unabashed to acknowledge that they were the evening's entertainment. Soon, the boldest young women, those who worked quickest and who knew precisely why they had come, walked up and asked the players their names, and standing nearby, you could hear the one question that certainly didn't need to be asked: "You're a Bronco, aren't you?" One woman said nothing while she stroked rookie linebacker Ray Phillips's strong ebony arm, smiling as she touched him, before she walked away.

A dozen more players were soon on the dimly lit, smoky scene, most of their faces still unfamiliar, their black skin and their enormous bodies nonetheless making their occupations unmistakable. They, too, got beers or Cuba Libres or gin and tonics on the house; they, too, rolled up free T-shirts and stuck them in their pockets. Larry Willis, a free-agent wide receiver, wearing needle-toed shoes and yellow suspenders, was quickly on the crowded dance floor, accompanied by a blonde woman who was deeply in love, and with whom he had obviously danced before. Then Gerald Willhite, the veteran running back renowned for his regular injuries, was dancing—seemingly without harming himself. Clarence Kay, the debonair tight end from Seneca, South Carolina, danced; defensive end Andre Townsend danced; safety Tony Lilly watched while he nursed his drink. Young Joe Dudek was inconspicuously absent, and it was safe to assume—no fainting spells apparent—that John Elway had yet to enter the premises.

By ten o'clock, there were half a dozen Broncos moving dangerously on the dance floor and more than a dozen Broncos standing passively by the bar. The cowboys and softball players and coeds with creamy shoulders crowded near them to observe the goings-on, sometimes shouting in the direction of a friend's ear to be heard above the din. By ten o'clock, the reporters—who had no curfews—were there; so were the talk show hosts and the television talent. The Broncos' media relations staff—numbering five—came in to celebrate a birthday, and a queue of dozens more cowboys and college students waited their turn at the entrance. In the restroom, farm boys who still seldom shaved joked about how they were big enough but not black enough to get laid later in the evening. And in long rows against the walls, nineteen-year-old women in shorts and with break-your-heart thighs debated which athletes they momentarily would ask to dance—maybe the next song; no, it was too slow; it would have to be the fast one that would follow.

By 10:30, a few phone numbers had been recorded on napkins and carefully secreted away—Saturday, the players' free night, was only two days away—and for some, the slow songs had assumed a kind of desperate importance in establishing relationships that might endure for forty-eight hours. On the dance floor, three players wrapped small, smiling women in their dark, enveloping arms, swaying with them, kissing their necks, their ears, telling them what a night it had been; saying yes, they

40

would see them on Saturday; saying sure, they had time for one last dance.

And then there was a sudden exit. The towering, imposing players—those who were romancing and those who were drinking because they weren't—touched each other on the arm and motioned toward the door. The several who had made new acquaintances said good-bye; the many who had not, sat their glasses on the bar. At 10:47, the reporters, the radio and television personalities, the cowboys, and the college kids were still settling into the boozy summer night, but by then, the bar was bereft of Broncos.

July 31

Although it is hard to imagine now, the game of football had a decidedly aristocratic image in the early years of this century. Its initial association with colleges and universities—and the universities of the Ivy League, at that—made it seem similar in those days to the way in which most of us nowadays perceive a sport like lacrosse, a rough-and-tumble contest played by the privileged kids, or so we tend to assume. By 1920, numerous semiprofessional athletic club football teams had been formed, but they continued to invite the scorn of the college-based coaches, who argued that men who played football for money were unable to maintain the honor and integrity they believed the game demanded. The college coaches so successfully inveighed against professionalism in football that spectators tended to stay away from the few professional games which were played in towns and cities scattered throughout the Northeast—the spectators assuming that the sport must be as crude and corrupt as, say, professional wrestling is today.

These informal sanctions against professional football might have succeeded in preventing it from ever becoming established if it weren't for the players themselves. College players, for the most part, had happily played the game for nothing, but were entranced by the idea that once their collegiate days were done, they might be able to play the game as a livelihood. Struggling professional organizations like the Canton, Ohio, Bulldogs, the Muncie, Indiana, Flyers, and the Rock Island, Illinois, Independents had little trouble attracting players with salaries and fees that reached as high as six hundred dollars a game. But fans—paying customers—were much harder to come by. A 1921 game between the New York Giants and the Chicago Staleys (renamed the Bears a year later) attracted only eighty spectators, just a couple of dozen people more than the players and coaches involved in the action.

Only four years later, however, a crowd of 70,000 people journeyed to New York's Polo Grounds to watch the Giants play a game against the same Chicago franchise. What had changed in that short span? Well, it was a simple matter of bringing a touch of celebrity to the sport. Harold (Red) Grange had become the nation's foremost football hero during his years at the University of Illinois. Known variously as the Wheaton Iceman, the Flying Terror, the Galloping Ghost, he was the most spectacular runner the game had yet produced, and, immediately following his graduation, Grange signed a playing contract with the Chicago Bears. The Bears, owned and coached by George Halas—a man who was somehow certain that the professional game could survive and thrive—quickly scheduled a fall whistle-stop tour in which the team played games in seven cities over a span of eleven days. In each city, people flocked to stadiums and ball yards to see the Galloping Ghost in person, and, in the process, they discovered that the money the men on the field received did not seem to taint the quality of their character or the caliber of their play. A year later, membership in what was now the National Football League had swollen to twenty-two teams.

Although professional football now seemed assured of a future, its future did not prove to be one of steady growth of profit or fan devotion. In 1932, when few fans could afford the frivolity of an autumn afternoon at the stadium, membership in the league shrank to eight teams, but the league somehow survived. By 1940, when the Mutual Broadcasting System paid the league $2500 for the rights to broadcast its championship game nationwide, ten teams belonged to the NFL and the game appeared to be on its way back, but its renaissance was cut short by the onset of World War II. Eleven years later, in 1951, when the league championship game was televised nationwide for the first time, there were just twelve teams playing professional football—two teams in both New York and Chicago, as well as teams in Cleveland, Washington, Philadelphia, Pittsburgh, Detroit, Green Bay, Los Angeles, and San Francisco. In that year's final game—seen by as much of the nation as had access to the television sets that were suddenly all the rage— the Los Angeles Rams routed the Cleveland Browns.

Come 1960, the NFL had grown by only one more team— an expansion club called the Dallas Cowboys. Indeed, the league had grown by only three teams in twenty years, and except for the new Dallas franchise and the two clubs that had moved to the West Coast in the late forties, professional football remained a game played only in the swarthy industrial cities that lay in the Rust Belt arc bounded by Chicago and New York City. And the game seemed to reflect its hometowns. The tony, upper-crust image that had once belonged to collegiate football was one that professional football never had. To the contrary, the mercenary game seemed to belong to the common people, the steel workers and longshoremen, meat packers and teamsters—working stiffs who could readily identify with the battles on the fields below them. Yet surely the game could appeal to a wider mix, could catch on elsewhere in the country, couldn't it?

But expansion was a risky business. It meant sharing television and radio revenues, the pieces of the finite pies becoming necessarily smaller. It meant increased travel expenses, smaller income from gate receipts in cities where the new franchises would inevitably have to struggle to establish themselves, to say nothing of the potential for meddling in long-established league policies by new owners anxious to show a profit. The safe thing to do was to stick to the status quo, to expand by a team or two when the new city seemed delirious with anticipation and the new owner's pockets were proven sufficiently deep. No, except for plans to follow the Dallas expansion with a club in Minneapolis–St. Paul, the National Football League was not in the market to acquire additional real estate.

It's doubtful that the NFL would even have been so bold as to expand into Texas and Minnesota had it not been for the intentions, announced a year before, of Lamar Hunt—youngest of the triumvirate of Dallas brothers whose oil wealth was so imposing that each of them *had* to be taken seriously—to form a second professional football league, which would be known as the American Football League and which was to include teams in Dallas, Minneapolis, Denver, Houston, Buffalo, Boston, New York City, and Oakland. Hunt's new league wasn't given much chance of succeeding by the press and pundits of the sporting world—and the NFL's subsequent two-team expansion did mean that an AFL team in Minnesota never materialized—but despite the new NFL Cowboys in Dallas, Hunt forged ahead with the formation of his own AFL Dallas Texans, and teams—to use the word in its most generous sense—got off the ground in each of the other AFL target cities. On September 9, 1960, a ragtag group of journeymen football veterans and thinly talented rookies who went by the name of the Denver Broncos defeated the Boston Patriots in Boston in front of a crowd of 21,597 people—the first regular season game of the new American Football League.

The eight AFL teams struggled to survive against the established league. Even in cities like Denver that had no NFL competition, tickets weren't easy to sell. And in Dallas, Hunt's 8-6 Texans proved no match at the gate for the 0-11 Cowboys; the Texans ultimately played three seasons—and won an AFL championship—before Hunt moved them to Kansas City and renamed them the Chiefs. The New York franchise, the Titans, was renamed the Jets, but no other AFL team ever moved and none disbanded—Hunt's audacious scheme having proved marketable and financially successful. The AFL signed a national television contract with NBC in 1964; it added a Miami franchise in 1966, and a Cincinnati club became the tenth AFL team in 1968.

The event that more than anything else signaled the AFL's legitimacy was the NFL's agreement that its 1966 championship team would meet the AFL champions on January 15, 1967, in Los Angeles in a game that Hunt himself dubbed the "Super Bowl." Hunt's Chiefs were ultimately trounced by the Green Bay Packers in that game, but it proved pivotal nonetheless. Eight months later, the lowly Denver Broncos defeated the Detroit Lions in a pre-season game in Denver—an AFL team's first victory over a team in the NFL. In January of 1969—in a game that turned a kid from Beaver Falls, Pennsylvania, named Joe Willie Namath into someone called Broadway Joe—the AFL New York Jets defeated the NFL Baltimore Colts, 16–7, in Super Bowl III (the Roman numerals somehow considered appropriate for that now-annual football contest, as well as for the quadrennial Olympics and the occasional world war).

Following its first Super Bowl victory, the American Football League played only one more season before the two leagues merged into a two-conference league that went by the older league's name. The Pittsburgh Steelers and the Baltimore Colts of the old NFL joined the rest of the original AFL teams in what was called the American Conference; the NFL's thirteen other teams made up the National Conference, the two conference winners meeting in the season's final game. The Colts celebrated their realignment and the merger of the two leagues by beating the Dallas Cowboys in Super Bowl V. The Denver Broncos' first year in the new combined league wasn't the stuff of heraldry, on the other hand; the boys from the Rockies, who had finally shed their strange socks and the cartoons on their helmets, nonetheless finished the year 5-8-1.

Few of the fans who watched the Broncos practice today—four or five hundred of them secured behind yellow ropes—remember the early-day Denver teams, the calamitous football club that drew fans because it somehow lost so charmingly and with such predictability. Oh, some of them remember, those who sat in lawn chairs on the Greeley grass, whose sunglasses are bifocaled by now and whose hair has begun to gray. But most of these training-camp fans are too young to have memories of those years of fond ineptitude. Many of them know the stories, the tales that have firmly entered the folklore, but to them, they seem ancient history.

The view of the practicing players from the area cordoned off for the fans is a poor one. Only the offensive and defensive lines normally practice on the field immediately adjacent to them, and it is only scintillating for so long to watch linemen bash into each other. To get a good look at John Elway and his catapult arm requires binoculars and abiding patience; the wide receivers are similarly distant, the running backs way over yonder, and the famous defenders like Tom Jackson, Karl Mecklenburg, and Rulon Jones are nothing more than distant runners. The fans do get a good look at the legion of players as they walk out of the locker room to run a warm-up lap; they see them again as they go into the fieldhouse to stretch and as they walk out again to go to work. The fans are close enough at that point, crowding into the ropes, that they can even call a player's name, profess love or long support, and sometimes get a wave or a "How ya doin'?" in return. But in terms of watching the rudiments of football, the specialized skills that inhabit the sport, their seats—although free—are so poor as to be not worth bothering about.

Yet the word doesn't seem to get out. When I joined them at 9:30 this morning, numb from a night of research at the State Armory saloon, a regiment of fans had already staked its territory along the hundred yards of yellow rope—young mothers in cut-off jeans and halter tops toting kids in football uniforms; shirtless men sporting tans and strange tattoos; exhibitionist couples in the briefest kinds of bikinis (often orange), sprawled in the sun as if spending a day at the beach; retired men and women who had arrived with baskets and the requisite picnic gear; and a few men in ties and short-sleeved shirts, salesmen, no doubt, who had dropped by for a bit between appointments. They were a happy crowd, unhurried by their schedules, pacified by the blazing sun, catered to by souvenir stands and soft drink vendors, the sweet smell of suntan lotion wafting in the air.

After the players retreated to the distant fields to practice, the fans returned to the spots they had earlier claimed to watch the action as best they could. They cheered on the rare occasions when something happened near enough to them that they could be sure of what had transpired, but there was nothing akin to stadium pandemonium. Old men chatted with each other in their chairs, mothers dozed, kids tried to mimic the men on the fields, teenagers flirted, a few adults flirted as well. "No, I've never come to camp before," said a woman in white bib overalls who sat on a beach towel that featured the visage of Snoopy. She had driven from nearby Longmont with her son and a neighbor's son. "We thought the boys would enjoy it. That's them over there." She pointed to two four-year-olds in orange T-shirts and miniature football helmets who were having little luck throwing a foam rubber ball. "It's a nice break for me, too," she said. "Shoot, I'd rather be doing this, which is nothing, than cleaning my dirty house."

As I walked, I heard a man in his mid-twenties remark to his friend, "They look littler than on TV, don't they?" The friend took a sip of his beer and said, "Hey, you get up next to one of them and I bet you'd shit your pants." I swear I heard a sixty-year-old woman in beige Bermuda shorts say to the woman who sat beside her, "I get real excited by these big hunks of manhood." Her friend said nothing in reply, but she grinned in naughty agreement and chuckled beneath her breath.

Then a diminutive Japanese-American man, also in his sixties, stopped me and asked why, with my press pass, I was staying behind the rope. His name was Tom Mishuna and he had been born in Denver, the son of truck farmers. He had moved to California's Central Valley in his early twenties and still lived there, in Bakersfield, but his brother had remained in Colorado and Tom visited him for a stretch of weeks each summer. "We always come watch the camp a day or two," he told me. "My brother's a big Broncos fan. I like them okay, but the Raiders are my team. I always get to give him trouble because the Raiders are always better."

We stood silently for a moment and watched the linemen go into a three-point stance, then on signal, bear into each other like butting rams—all deep thoughts and determination. Then Tom Mishuna asked me a surprising question. Had I noticed, he wanted to know, "how many Negroes there are on these teams?" I said, well, yes, they probably did outnumber their percentage of the general population. Or something like that. And I asked him why it had crossed his mind. "Well, I was just wondering if they are really better at it than white people, or if maybe they get more opportunities in football than in other things," he said. I told him I wasn't sure—and I wasn't—and I asked him why so few Asians seemed to play the game.

"Too little," said Tom Mishuna, "way too little and too smart. I like to watch, but I wouldn't want to go out there and get beat up."

Tom Mishuna's comments about the racial makeup of the team were not as immediately interesting to me as was the mix of the fans themselves. On this team, black players did slightly outnumber whites, though that was not necessarily the case on every NFL team; there were no Hispanics, no Asians under contract, not even a token Samoan—the massive Polynesian nose tackles and blocking backs with commensurately enormous names who have become common on team rosters in recent years. The Broncos were simply, plainly, black and white, and so far, the similarities between the two groups of players seemed much more obvious than did their dissimilarities.

These fans, on the other hand, were a curious blend of ethnic groups and classes—though people out West tend to like to pretend that the distinction called class is nonexistent. Among the five hundred or so fans with whom I watched practice today, a fifth, perhaps a quarter, were Hispanic—men and women, young and old, who follow the Broncos with a particular kind of passion. Hispanics make up about 10 percent of Colorado's population; 15 percent in the city of Denver, perhaps 20 percent in the farming environs surrounding Greeley. Denver's black population is small—only about 5 percent—and Greeley's is smaller still, and I saw few blacks behind the ropes. Tom Mishuna and his brother were the only Asians I encountered.

Although obviously dedicated to the Broncos, it seemed likely to me that the large majority of this group of fans would not possess a similar devotion to, say, the University of Colorado Buffaloes or the Colorado State University Rams or even the University of Northern Colorado Bears. The three schools had their maniacal supporters, to be sure, but their fans tended to be alumni, old grads who went to the games in wool trousers and belted trench coats, and undergrads so deliriously drunk that the games resembled a fraternity rush. These professional football fans, on the other hand, probably had few collegiate allegiances, if any. I would guess that only one or two of them had degrees in finance or foreign relations or even physical education; some would no doubt say they came from the school known as Hard Knocks; most had probably attended the one called Meager Income.

Just as the earliest professional teams had depended for their survival on the industrial cities' working classes, so it seems that the current generation of professional football franchises finds its truest fans, its firmest partisans, among that amorphous group called the common people. That isn't to say that the Broncos can't count lawyers and lithographers and licensed physical therapists among their ardent followers. They can count them by the carload. It's just that when you get down to the dividing line between those fans who are willing to risk sunstroke to see rookies and free agents have their face masks ground into the summer grass and those who offer the Broncos little more allegiance than ten or twelve autumn afternoons in front of the television set in the den, you find that the truest believers—the people who stand in line for autographs and who shout their support in bold letters printed across their orange chests—are people with little social pretension, plain people who are unabashed about their bold emotions, who give the Broncos their die-hard devotion because the Broncos give them something to cheer for in return. And opportunities to cheer are few and are damn near precious.

My informal study of T-shirt slogans this afternoon noted three rather distinct approaches to professing team allegiance. By far the most common kind were the shirts that simply said DENVER BRONCOS, many of which included a favorite player's number. Then there were the shirts that either rated the Broncos number one or vowed, more specifically, that they are Super Bowl–bound this year. The third kind of slogan brought attention to the wearer's own credentials as a Broncomaniac. I saw several I'M A BRONCOHOLIC shirts; I suppose there was no intended irony in the stretched and distorted SUPERFAN written across an obese woman's chest; and there were half a dozen shirts that spelled out the theme most succinctly: IF YOU AIN'T A BRONCOS FAN, YOU AIN'T SHIT. It wasn't the sort of shirt you'd see your accountant wear, but then, your accountant probably didn't even care enough to drive up to Greeley for the day.

August 3

This is Sunday, the end of the second week of camp for the rookies and free agents, the first week for the veteran players, a day off for all of them before the long week that precedes the first of four exhibition games—the league office likes to refer to these as "pre-season" games, thinking that without the word "exhibition" involved, fans are somehow fooled into thinking the games have some significance.

A few veteran players whose jobs seem secure went fishing today; some went out to golf courses to humble themselves as amateurs; others went home to Denver to mow lawns and reacquaint themselves with wives and children; there probably were one or two who didn't go home, but who called with carefully composed excuses. Rookies and free agents tended to stay in camp—nursing headaches acquired from overservice at the State Armory, studying playbooks in dark dorm rooms, running laps, lounging in the shade with stereo earphones in place to block out the intruding silence, reading the accounts in the Sunday papers of yesterday's big scrimmage.

It wasn't the scrimmage itself that was a big event—just the offense having a go at the defense for an hour and a half or so, nothing you could remotely call a game. But the Broncos and the university charged three dollars per person (splitting the take in half) to see the short display of football at Jackson Field (UNC's ten thousand–seat stadium), and the fans filled it to overflowing.

Saturday began for the players with a mandatory mid-morning brunch, the eighty-strong bunch of them joining an intimate group of five hundred at the University Center ballroom. KCNC-

TV had invited fifty of its closest friends to break bread, as had the Public Service Company of Colorado; there were university administrators and Greeley politicians and even a candidate running for Congress. But fully half of those dining on a buffet of breakfast steaks and scrambled eggs belonged to the Denver Broncos Quarterback Club, "the official fan club of the Denver Broncos," an organization that team administrators long have acknowledged is a bit of an albatross, the club doing virtually nothing to encourage fan support: In a city where sixty thousand people are already waiting patiently (their chances almost nil) to purchase season tickets, the Quarterback Club is costing the team time and money for nothing tangible in return.

But the four busloads of clubbers who headed up from Denver at eight that morning didn't see it that way at all. They are, they were all too happy to tell you, the Broncos' biggest, best, and most stalwart fans. They have stuck with this team through thick and through very thin; they have played a definite role in making the Central Rockies the Broncos-mad region that it is, and in return, they deserve to meet the players personally and to pat them on the back, to pose for pictures with Dan Reeves, to firmly grasp his hand and tell him he's doing a hell of a job.

Beer and Bloody Marys were the refreshments on the bus ride north, and by the time the clubbers were seated in the ballroom they were feeling festive. Two players were assigned to every table—many of them shy and seldom speaking, others, like the grandfatherly Barney Chavous, working their tables like politicians, circling from seat to seat, shaking hands and squeezing shoulders. The clubbers all wanted to know how camp was going and the players reported that camp was going pretty good.

After a quick bite to eat, Dan Reeves rose and flattered the city of Greeley, flattered the university, praised the contributions of the Quarterback Club, then introduced his assistant coaches, each of whom in turn introduced the players under his tutelage—players like Louis Wright, who had been through a bevy of these breakfasts in his long tenure with the team, and players like Larry Willis, Ken Bell, and Joe Dudek, who might not be

Broncos much past Monday. Guard Paul Howard, defensive end Barney Chavous, and linebacker Tom Jackson—the three already four-year veterans when the Broncos had their Super Bowl season in 1977—were acknowledged for their remarkable longevity. In a sport where the average career is just four years long, each of them was enduring his fourteenth training camp. The expected jokes about how their tenures reflected on their intelligence followed their introductions. But the Quarterback Clubbers, nothing if not appreciative of long and faithful service, gave them loud and warm applause.

When John Elway was introduced by quarterbacks coach Mike Shanahan as "The Franchise," the crowd roared its approval; no one seemed reluctant to single him out of six dozen other players, and the players applauded him as well. The Broncos are basically a team of equals, was the message, but at least one Bronco plainly has no peers. Elway, fair and mop-haired and wearing a madras shirt, stood at his table near the dais and offered a quick and deferential wave in response to the applause, then—as Dan Reeves announced that the players had to leave early to get ready for the scrimmage—he made a beeline out of the ballroom.

The stadium was full by a few minutes after noon but the scrimmage wasn't scheduled to begin until 1:00. Kids gulped hot dogs and stood in long lines for soda pop. Parents drank beer out of plastic cups and had hot dogs as well; some unwrapped home-made burritos and sandwiches from covers of aluminum foil. The souvenir stands sold Broncos pennants, Broncos pins, Broncos dolls, footballs, scarves, T-shirts, key chains, rings, belt buckles, bumper stickers, wristbands, paper plates, pens, as well as the "Denver Broncos Trivia Game," and the pre-game business was brisk. On the slope behind the stands, the Mizuno sports shoe company was giving away John Elway posters to kids under twelve—a photograph of a sweating, uniformed Elway, looking far more hunklike than usual, which was captioned, "You Should Be In His Shoes." Kids who were over twelve were busy bribing their juniors to get in line a second time to secure a poster for them. Kids who were over thirty were making similar deals.

In the tiny press box whose walls were unpainted plywood, places were marked with name cards—four seats for KOA radio, which would broadcast the exhibition; three seats each for the *Denver Post* and the *Rocky Mountain News*; two apiece for the *Colorado Springs Gazette-Telegraph*, the *Pueblo Chieftain*, and the *Greeley Tribune*; only a single seat for the reporters from the *Boulder Daily Camera* and the *Fort Collins Coloradan*. The television talent and the television crews would roam the sidelines.

At 12:30, the Broncos arrived in buses, and the crowd cheered as they took the field. By 1:15 some football was finally played: seventy-six plays from scrimmage, to be exact, most of them running plays designed to test and compare the talents of new running backs Ken Bell, Tony Boddie, and Joe Dudek, only one of whom will likely make the team. Although the fans, to no one's sudden surprise, seemed predisposed to favor Dudek, it was Bell, a free agent from Boston College—so far virtually unnoticed by the media magnifying glass—who recorded the impressive statistics: 52 yards on nine carries, compared with Dudek's 21 yards on seven carries. Boddie, a refugee from the USFL's Los Angeles Express, really didn't get a chance to compete; he gained 4 yards on only two tries.

Like the Wednesday evening scrimmages, this one included no kickoffs and no field-goal attempts, but the three punters got their practice. And in an attempt to make it something of a contest on this Broncos versus Broncos afternoon, the defense was awarded points for pass interceptions, fumble recoveries, and forced punts—but the ten thousand–strong fans seemed a bit confused about whom to root for, given the fact that their guys were on both sides of the line. A completed pass was guaranteed to bring an ovation, but a pass knocked away by a cornerback somehow didn't elicit the same response. The occasional ten-yard run got the crowd clapping, but a tackle for no gain was hard to cheer for. In the end, the defense had the better day, at least on the scoreboard, "winning" the scrimmage 29–18, and the fans got what they came for—a smattering of August football followed by a fifteen-minute autograph session, fully half the crowd streaming onto the field at the conclusion of play, darting from player to player, garnering what scribbled signatures they could, their eyes scanning the white and orange jerseys for the famous numbers, the few familiar faces.

One boozy fan chose to discuss the starting lineup with the head coach rather than to seek out valuable autographs. "How come Sammy Winder is still starting?" the forty-year-old shouted in Dan Reeves's face. "There's no way he should be in the starting backfield!" Winder, a Pro Bowl running back two years before, had had an appendectomy in 1985 and had not repeated his 1984 performance.

Reeves didn't bother to offer a defense of his running back or of his decisions in general. "I don't need your help, partner," the preoccupied, now slightly aggravated coach told him. "If you don't like what we do, then you can take it on down the road."

"Winder's just not good enough to start," said the fan, softening his charge, but still intent. "That's just my opinion."

Reeves had turned to walk away, but he stopped. "You're entitled to your opinion," he offered philosophically. "Opinions are like assholes. Everybody's got one."

Up in the creaky press box, *Denver Post* columnist Buddy Martin's young son asked his father, "Do you have to write about this now?"

"He doesn't want to, but he has to," quipped Channel 4's Ron Zappolo, finishing his stint as the scrimmage's public address announcer, getting up from his microphone, leaving Martin to search his notes for something from the afternoon that he could flesh out as a Sunday column.

In the stands, a farm worker from Mexico in a broad-brimmed hat was puzzled that it had all ended so soon. As team owner Pat Bowlen made his way from the press box to the fields, the young, bronze-skinned man stopped him to ask, "It's over?"

unaware that the man he was addressing was as wealthy as the state of Sonora or that he was the person responsible for the afternoon's extravaganza.

"That's it, man," Bowlen said as he hurried by, en route to congratulate his employees. "It's over."

The first name of the Broncos' president and chief executive officer is Patrick, but consider that privileged information. His biography in the team's media guide simply calls him "Pat," and the Denver press has understood since he purchased the Broncos in 1984 that the diminutive form of his name is the one he much prefers. Pat Bowlen. One of the boys.

The Broncos have had five owners or groups of owners since they were founded in 1960, the first three all Denverites, the most recent two out-of-towners. When longtime owners Gerald and Alan Phipps decided to sell the team in 1981, their buyer was Edgar F. Kaiser, Jr., heir to the California aluminum fortune, an absentee owner who was widely presumed to have put the team back on the market just as soon as the ink on his purchase contract was dry. Kaiser headed the franchise for only three years before he sealed the sale to Bowlen.

The current owner—and, he says, the owner for decades to come—is a native of Prairie du Chien, Wisconsin (a Canadian born just across the border because his American mother wanted it that way), who received degrees in business and law from the University of Oklahoma where he tried unsuccessfully to make the football team in the mid-1960s. It was in the oil and gas industry and later in real estate in Alberta, Canada, that Bowlen made his economic mark, but, he told me in his modest Broncos office in Denver, his long-range goal had always been to acquire the resources that would allow him to purchase a football team.

Bowlen, forty-two, blond, tanned, cut from Robert Redford's bolt of cloth, met me wearing a powder-blue polo shirt with a Broncos logo above the pocket, a gold chain visible through its open placket. He apologized for the conflict that had led to the cancellation of a previous appointment, then spelled out an immediate ground rule—he wouldn't discuss his wife, children, homes, or personal life, nor would he even affirm whether he possessed any or all of the above. The family of his friend Peter Pockington, owner of the Edmonton Oilers Hockey Club, Bowlen explained, had been involved in a bizarre break-in and hostage-taking a few years before. That incident ended without tragedy, but it had served to make Bowlen extremely cautious about his new role as a very visible and obviously wealthy Denverite.

"Another thing to make clear," he said with a face so stern I thought I was in serious trouble, "is that I'm not a businessman who happens to own a football team on the side. This, operating the club, is how I spend my time. It's my principal responsibility, and it's what I want to be doing."

Bowlen said he spent several years quietly shopping for an NFL franchise, and at one point he looked rather specifically into the purchase of the then-for-sale Dallas Cowboys. But it was the potential availability of the Broncos that ultimately captured his attention. "Comparing Denver with Edmonton, the two cities seemed so much alike—both located where they are near the Rockies, both growing, developing, the oil and gas influence. I knew I could be very comfortable in Denver and I knew this was already a good organization. I can't really imagine now a club I'd rather be involved with."

Bowlen's first act as the team's new owner in March, 1984, was to assure his employees and the people of Colorado that he would be making no sudden changes. He certainly wanted Dan Reeves and his coaching staff to stay on board; he made no dramatic changes in his administrative staff; and yes, he assured everyone, he was committed to do—and to spend—whatever it took to make the Broncos a championship football team. "I realized very quickly that people here consider the Broncos *their* team. I sort of have the team in trust. They're willing to let me manage it, let me pay the bills, but absolutely, this team belongs to Denver."

And Pat Bowlen quickly understood as well that the Broncos' fans would be suspicious of another absentee owner. "I heard stories that Edgar was the kind of guy who would fly into town on the weekends and arrive out here to the offices or to the stadium in a limousine. Then he'd be gone in a day or two. I don't have any criticism of that, I don't mean to imply that, but among people here, there was obviously some resentment of it. And I knew that wasn't going to be my style. I wanted to be a part of this club on a day-to-day basis."

Bowlen's first year at the Broncos' helm was a spectacular introduction to the NFL. The team won the AFC Western Division, finishing the regular season with a 13-3 record, the most single-season wins in the team's history. And the Broncos sold out 75,000 season tickets at Mile High Stadium—every seat for every home game (750,000 in all) purchased by early summer—for the fourteenth consecutive year. The new owner was indeed pleased with his purchase.

I couldn't be sure why, but Bowlen relaxed after we had talked for a while. He even smiled and began to pepper his comments with jock talk and an occasional four-letter word. And he began to explain what it's like to operate a professional football team. "It's a business with two separate aspects to it. One is the business itself, the effort to keep it viable and to try to make some money. The other is to be competitive on the field. The two are related—one affects the other, obviously—but they aren't the same thing. When I took over, we were fortunate that we didn't have to worry immediately about how to fill the seats in the stadium. As you know, people have been very supportive of this team for, God, twenty years or more. But that doesn't mean we can assume that those same people will want to come to watch the Broncos forever. To keep them, we have to field a team that's exciting, competitive, fun to watch. We can't take the fans for granted. God, no. They're critical to us.

"A football team only generates revenue from three sources— tickets, television, and Kewpie dolls. That's it. The Kewpie dolls— souvenirs, game programs, and so forth—are important, but they are obviously the smallest of the three. We share the television revenue equally with all twenty-seven other NFL teams. It's substantial, but it's a fixed amount. It's your gate that can really fluctuate. And if you put a shitty team on the field, it isn't going to be too long before people stop coming to see it."

I asked Pat Bowlen why Denver's fans have been so maniacally supportive for so long. "I think we have two kinds of fans," he said, making it obvious that he had considered this issue before. "There are the people, the old fans, who have been loyal to this team since it was first organized. They loved the Broncos when they were terrible and, of course, they continued to love them as they improved. That Super Bowl year was a dream come true for them. Then there's a second group of people, newcomers, people who are new to Denver who see the Broncos, the successful Broncos, as being representative of the new Denver. The Broncos began to get good in the mid-1970s, at the same time that Denver was becoming a major, important city. People wanted to identify with the image of a thriving, exciting city and not with a cow town, and for some reason— the Broncos' success against other teams from other cities, I guess—we, the team, sort of began to represent that new era. So, very fortunately for us as an organization, we have strong support from both the old Denver and the new Denver. It's great, but, as I said before, it's something we can't just assume we'll always have."

The Denver Broncos and twenty-six other clubs in the National Football League carefully guard their financial facts and figures. Only the Green Bay Packers, a public corporation, must open their books to nosy scrutiny. But despite the cloistered accountancy, a few general assumptions can be made about the league's—and its member clubs'—finances, and a few round numbers can be penciled in.

According to figures the league was required to supply to Congress in the spring of 1985, its twenty-eight teams generated combined revenues of $711 million in 1984–85, a figure that would place the league 377th in the *Fortune* 500 standings for that year if the league were a single enterprise. It is not, however. It is an uneasy, sometimes warring confederation of separate franchises—separate profit-motivated businesses governed by a not-for-profit association. Assuming that the NFL's figures for Congress were substantially correct, the twenty-eight franchises would have averaged $25.4 million in revenue in 1984–85, an amount that would keep each franchise well away from the *Fortune* 500, but that is still a good bit more than is annually generated by your average family shoe store.

In the case of the Denver Broncos, a 1985 estimate of NFL income by *Regardie's* magazine estimated that the team was a good bit better than average at putting dollars into the till. According to estimates garnered from confidential sources, from official NFL data, from comparison with the Packers' annual statement, and from estimates made by the National Football League Players Association, the Broncos brought in $27,429,424 in 1984–85, the third highest income in the league that season, behind only the Los Angeles Rams and the Minnesota Vikings. Like every other NFL team, the Broncos received $13.9 million in revenue from the league's regular-season contract with the television networks and $800,000 in shared revenue from the end-of-season play-offs. In addition, *Regardie's* estimated, the team generated $1.4 million in pre-season revenues, $800,000 from local radio and television contracts, $200,000 from licensed use of the team's name and logo on authorized souvenirs and products ("Kewpie dolls"), $1 million from the annual rental of private stadium boxes, $2.3 million from the team's 34-percent share of the gate at its road games, and $7.1 million from its 66-percent share of the gate receipts at Mile High Stadium.

These figures have to be considered crude estimates, but they are close enough to the mark to allow some obvious conclusions to be made, the first being that the most important people in the stadium on any given Sunday are those who operate the television cameras. The second simple conclusion is that $27.4 million is enough money to allow you to field a decent football team: 1984–85 was the year the Broncos were 13-3. Yet a quick look at the revenues of the other NFL teams shows that while high-end revenues *can* correspond with a winning season, they generally have nothing to do with win-loss records. The wealthy Los Angeles Rams made the 1984–85 play-offs as a wild card team but were promptly eliminated; the revenue-rich Vikings finished the season 3 and 13. On the other hand, the San Francisco 49ers, the eventual winners of that season's Super Bowl, finished the year in twentieth place in the league's financial standings. The 49ers finished the regular season with a 15-1 record, but they earned more than $3 million *less* than the lowly Vikings.

If a team like the Broncos brings in a tidy $27 million each season, where does the money go? Well, not surprisingly, the Broncos aren't saying. But in order to placate pestering reporters, the NFL has provided some general figures on the expenses incurred each year by an average member franchise. Fifty-four percent of the total outlay, $13.5 million or so, goes toward player salaries, bonuses, and benefits. Team costs—coaching, scouting, traveling, equipment, facilities—comprise about $4.5 million, 18 percent of the total. Administrative costs consume 15 percent, about $4 million. Stadium rentals vary widely but average just under $1 million annually, say, 3 percent of the outlay, and NFL membership currently costs $600,000, 2 percent or so. If you've been keeping track, that leaves 8 percent unaccounted for, and that's the share that, on average, is entered in the profit column—but not for every team, not in every year. In fact, the Broncos are widely rumored to have *lost* a little money during the year they were 13-3 and finished number three in the income standings.

Pat Bowlen was reported to have paid Edgar Kaiser $60 million for Denver's NFL franchise. Let's assume—and this is wild speculation, not educated guessing—that Bowlen paid $20 million down and financed the remainder. If some institution financed a $40 million note at 10 percent over twenty years, the owner's annual amortized payment would be $4.1 million. It's true that the interest would be tax deductible and his players would be depreciated right along with the locker room and the uniforms, but the point is, you probably don't get rich by owning an NFL franchise. As Edgar Kaiser knew, you get rich by selling one: Kaiser purchased the team in 1981 for $35 million. If Bowlen did, in fact, pay $60 million for the team three years later, Kaiser's profit represented $8.33 million in annual appreciation, a 71-percent return in no time at all.

The Dallas Cowboys were purchased for $72 million in 1984; the substandard New Orleans Saints brought $70 million in 1985. If Pat Bowlen wanted to cut and run, he could already make a handsome profit. But that seems unlikely to happen. Bowlen knows that the Broncos are similar to the Frederick Remington bronze sculptures he collects—the sculptures bringing in nary a dime while they sit on display in the elevator foyer of the team's stadium penthouse suites, but gaining value in daily gallops nonetheless. Yet there is clearly another, more pressing and personal reason why this businessman wants to retain his football team. Bowlen, a former marathon runner and triathlete, is a competitor, the kind of person who is stirred by nothing so much as the challenge to try to win. "I'm going to consider myself a failure here if I'm unable to keep Dan Reeves for the length of his career, if the Broncos don't become known as one of football's great teams, one of the best organizations," he told me, leaning back in his leather chair, determination rising audibly in his throat. "Sure, I want this club to make money, but by God, I'd also like a Super Bowl—or several."

But nothing is likely to be simple for Pat Bowlen or for his football team in the year or two to come. Super Bowls may well remain as scarce as they always have, and, together with the twenty-seven other owners of NFL franchises, Bowlen will soon face a host of issues that seem certain to complicate the prospects for a bright financial future. Sometime after the end of the coming season, and before a down of football is played in the fall of 1987, the NFL must renew its contracts with the three television networks as well as with the NFL Players Association. Because of sagging ratings and soft demand for commercial minutes, the league will have to struggle just to maintain its current television income, and a players' strike seems very possible given the likelihood that they will be demanding a bigger share of the owners' potentially smaller pie. And although financial disaster would have come their way had the United States Football League been awarded substantial damages in its recent antitrust suit with the NFL, if the courts eventually award damages in the Los Angeles Raiders' suit concerning that team's right to summarily pack up and move from Oakland, it could cost Bowlen and his fellow franchise owners millions of dollars each.

Yet despite the promise of contractual and legal wranglings which may make the football games themselves seem pacific in comparison, Pat Bowlen has found a business in which numbers are not the sole measure of success, a complex and inherently risky enterprise that also values that thing called victory, so alluring and so elusive.

August 15

The Broncos drove down to Denver on Saturday night and played sixty minutes of miserable football, losing to the lowly New Orleans Saints (5-11 last year; never better than 8-8) in a game whose 10–7 score made it seem far more interesting than it was. Although the defense played respectably, Denver's offense managed only a single touchdown against a New Orleans team that ranked twenty-fourth in the NFL in defense last season. But the loss was a secondary consideration. The only real purpose of the exhibition game was to give the two teams' coaches a chance to see their rookie prospects in game situations, to test their combat mettle, and to compare them with the veteran players, who are not exactly willing to surrender their roster spots. And the Broncos' coaches did not like what they saw from the sidelines Saturday night, nor did the videotape of the game show them pretty pictures.

"Well, welcome to reality," Dan Reeves told the assembled reporters in the Broncos' locker room following the game. But you could see right through Reeves's thin veneer of disappointment. You could tell that it suited him just fine for his boys to get a quick comeuppance. You could tell the early talk of Super Bowls scared him silly.

On Monday afternoon, in the midst of the final round of the PGA golf championship being telecast on Channel 9, the staccato beeps coming from the television set sounded like a tornado warning. Then these words crawled portentously across the bottom of the screen: THE DENVER BRONCOS HAVE WAIVED 14-YEAR DEFENSIVE END BARNEY CHAVOUS AND SIGNED FREDDIE GILBERT OF THE USFL NEW JERSEY GENERALS. Chavous, who had played in a club-record 182 football games spanning thirteen years, who was revered by teammates, coaches, reporters, and fans, who had the visage of Moses and the countenance of the Virgin Mary despite his awesome size, had been dumped by the team to whom he had been so dedicated for so long. It was a shocking story, a distressing one to everyone for whom Barney Chavous represented the epitome of the big and bighearted football player—and it was a story that wasn't quite true.

Chavous had indeed been absent from training camp on Monday afternoon. Dan Reeves confirmed that he had discussed Chavous's future with him in recent days, but he refused to explain why he had excused him from practice to go home to his wife and family in Denver "for personal reasons." Reeves simply wouldn't discuss what was at issue: "If I told you that," he said, "it wouldn't be personal." Yet there was quick speculation among players and reporters and assorted Greeley cognoscenti that Chavous had been told by Reeves, defensive coordinator Joe Collier, and defensive line coach Stan Jones that his chances of making the 1986 team were slim and that perhaps he should consider retiring now rather than risk being waived later. It was certainly no secret that Barney Chavous was not at work on the playing fields, and most of the reporters guessed that a retirement announcement would be forthcoming the following day.

Somehow, Channel 9's Jim Celania—who had come to Denver from San Francisco amid great promotional fanfare a year before, and who had made no secret of his disdain for the sportscasting ordeal in Greeley—got word that Chavous had indeed been waived, and, on his 5:00 P.M. Monday sportscast, he reiterated the story that had crawled across the golf match a couple of hours before, adding that "five Broncos players" had confirmed to him that Chavous had been cut. He did not explain how he was sure that the team had signed former New Jersey General Freddie Gilbert—and, in fact, Gilbert had not yet even talked with the Broncos' management. Although Jim Saccomano, the Broncos' director of media relations, had called Channel 9 soon after he heard about the "crawl" vehemently denying that Chavous had been waived or that Gilbert had been signed, Celania persisted. He was sorry if he had "stepped on any feet," he said, "but we had to go with the story we thought was newsworthy." Never mind that neither aspect of the story was correct.

By Tuesday morning, the Broncos' hierarchy was hopping

mad at Celania and Channel 9. "That's a bunch of crap," Broncos' general manager John Beake said of the report that Gilbert had been signed. "There's absolutely no truth in that. He has not signed. We have never even talked to him." About the Chavous story, he said, "They're really going way off base. They're really way out of line on this one. I don't know where they got their information."

In his *Rocky Mountain News* column, Dick Connor, the city's senior sportswriter, was outraged:

> Chavous became the victim of the media wars, the ones that dictate that first is best. . . . The Broncos had attempted to allow their veteran defender to go with some style, still draped in the almost Biblical dignity that has marked his career. . . . The Broncos apparently were willing to arrange a retirement announcement, let it be Barney's decision, with lights and cameras and maybe a tear or two. It's the way athletic warriors should end it. It should be signaled with trumpets and garlands, not ignominious little beeps. Channel 9 robbed him of that.

At the *Denver Post*, columnist John McGrath was a bit more circumspect. "It says something about both Chavous and the city he has represented on the football field for fourteen years that the first—and only—instance his name appeared in a TV bulletin was at the end. 'Chavous waived,' the bulletin on Channel 9 cried. (And lied.)"

Then in the Broncos' press room in the basement of Turner Hall, adjacent to the loud drone of the dryers, Dan Reeves settled the speculation. Yes, he said, Chavous had called him from Denver late Monday night to say that he had chosen to retire. Reeves said he urged Chavous to hold a press conference to announce his retirement, but that Chavous—private above all else—had declined. "Hopefully, he'll change his mind," said the coach who had regretfully recognized that the warm and gentle man incongruously nicknamed "Yard Dog" could no longer compete with players ten years his junior. "As I told him, when you think of the Denver Broncos, he's one of the first guys who comes to mind."

Before he left for the practice fields, Reeves acknowledged that in a team meeting Monday night he had let his players know that he was, well, *displeased* about the leaked information that led to the Channel 9 story. Yes, he said, he assumed that it was one or more players who had given Celania or someone at Channel 9 information that led to the incorrect conclusions.

At Channel 9, no one seemed contrite. "It's just semantics," said executive producer Patrice Jordan. "It now looks as if the Broncos asked him to retire or be waived. Whatever, Barney is not going to be with the Broncos." Celania said nothing more.

On the playing fields after practice, a legion of reporters sought out the reactions of Chavous's veteran teammates to his departure. "It gives you kind of a sick feeling," said guard Paul Howard, who, like Chavous, had completed thirteen seasons with the Broncos. "It makes you wonder about your own situation. It's going to happen to every one of us." Linebacker Tom Jackson, another thirteen-year veteran, said, "This is business. It's fun, it's a good profession and a great livelihood. But it also has a great deal to do with business. This won't be the first time or the last time that anything happens to a ballplayer . . . I will say this, I've never been on a football field professionally and not had Barney Chavous be there, too."

Rubin Carter, Chavous's longtime roommate, a team member for only eleven years, said simply as he made his way to the locker room, "All I know is that Barney is feeling good, so I'm feeling good," sounding as if his friend had gone to some kind of football heaven. And although there were no indications that he harbored ill will toward anyone, Barney Chavous, suddenly unemployed, was hugely silent.

August 19

They are down to just five dozen now—Barney Chavous retired, a few young players already injured and placed on season-long reserve, sixty others dropped unceremoniously from the squad, their football careers likely at an end. Virtually every morning since camp began, defensive line coach Stan Jones has waited near the door of the players' and coaches' cafeteria, the bearer of bad tidings. Jones is "The Turk," the unlucky staff member whose job it is to tell one and sometimes several players that Coach Reeves would like to see them in his office and, yes, would they please bring along their playbooks? Each has just eaten his last breakfast as a Denver Bronco, and each one knows he's history when Stan Jones greets him at the door. "Everyone knows why I'm sitting here," Jones said as he waited this morning. "I'm sure a lot of them dread finishing breakfast and taking the chance of walking past me."

The Broncos, always efficient, have a seven-step system for sending young men home, beginning with the trip to chat with Reeves, who makes the severance official, and followed by:

2. Report to Carroll Hardy [director of player personnel], Travel Arrangements, Room 3A.

3. Out-Going Physical, Steve Antonopulos, Training Room.

4. Check In Equipment, Dan Bill, Equipment Room.

5. Return to Room and Pack.

6. Report to Carroll Hardy, Room 3A, Return Room Key and Await Transportation Instructions to Denver.

7. Leave from Front of Lawrenson Hall, Transportation to Airport.

And then they are unemployed, most of them without good prospects for finding future work, either with other football teams or in unrelated endeavors, all of them already pariahs in the eyes of the players who will still report for practice, who see them carrying the orange checkout cards that list steps one through seven, who sense in the pits of their stomachs that tomorrow morning The Turk might talk to them.

The two players cut this morning to reach the league-mandated sixty-player limit were veteran tight end James Wright and cornerback Eric Riley. Yesterday, eleven players received their orange cards and were waived—seven rookies and four veterans, including wide receiver Butch Johnson and tight end Mike Barber, each of whom played ten seasons in the NFL, Dean Miraldi, a tackle who played for four, and linebacker Aaron Smith, whose career has ended after two. "I just think it's a young man's game," Dan Reeves said after the cuts were announced. "We're hoping we've got some young people who are going to come through and play a little better for us."

Reeves's point was drastically understated; it is a *very* young man's game. Mike Barber is thirty-three, Butch Johnson thirty-two, both of them graybeards now, slower, weaker, more easily expendable than the young bucks who beat them out; Dean Miraldi turned twenty-eight four months ago; Aaron Smith, washed up, was twenty-four last week.

August 26

The pre-season hasn't been going quite as planned. True, another magazine, this time *Sports Illustrated*, has declared that the Broncos will play in the Super Bowl. But after a trio of exhibition games, this team of supposed destiny is a paltry one for three, having lost for the second time on August 16 in the Hubert H. Humphrey Metrodome in Minneapolis, falling 29–27 to the rebuilding Vikings, before finally winning a game three evenings ago, beating the San Francisco 49ers 14–9 in front of a packed house in Denver.

Sports Illustrated's renowned "Dr. Z," Paul Zimmerman, considered by many to be the most insightful pro football writer in the country, surprised many readers by jumping on the Broncos' bandwagon in his magazine's annual football preview issue, published this week. "Yeah, we know, it's a reach," wrote the Doctor, "picking the Broncos to make the Super Bowl. They're not a perfect team. Their offense is flawed by the lack of a big name running back, and the opposition can figure out what's going on by noting which backs are in the game." But like everyone in the Western Hemisphere (and not a few fanatics of American football in Britain), Dr. Z is impressed by Denver's defense. "There's another reason I like the Broncos," he wrote, "and it's a bit more nebulous. You just have the feeling the Broncos are doing things right. When was the last time you heard of a holdout in Denver? When was the last time a player seriously ripped Dan Reeves, the coach? There are so many wacko outfits around that it's a breath of fresh air watching the way the Broncos operate—maybe Pasadena air."

Pasadena will be the site of this season's Super Bowl, and

you can bet that Dr. Z will be in attendance, watching the Boy Scout Broncos battle the New York Giants, assuming his picks are correct, watching one or two other teams if his guesses miss the mark.

There are fifty Broncos now, ten fewer than a week ago. Chris Norman, the team's veteran punter, is gone; Rick Partridge, the punter so sure of his future, is now a thing of the past. Joe Dudek, who didn't so much as get a chance to show what he was worth against the 49ers Saturday night, seemed certain to be a casualty as well until he appeared yesterday morning at the Broncos' practice facility with his arm in a sling to protect a mysteriously sprained shoulder that, ironically, may have saved his football career.

Dudek, the Good White Hope, the Slavic steamroller, did survive the Greeley front; he was still a member of the active squad when the Broncos pulled up stakes, packed their shoulder pads, and left Greeley for good last week. But if the 49ers game highlighted a rookie running back, it was Ken Bell from Boston College, who gained 28 yards on four carries and who now seems likely to make the final forty-five man squad, one of only five running backs.

Dudek, despite his promise and his popularity and the newspaper series subtitled "Joe Dudek Shoots For the Big Time," seemed destined for oblivion until the Broncos' trainers discovered an injury that Joe himself seemed to know little about, and the team subsequently placed him on injured reserve—meaning that he can remain employed by the team, that he can return to practice after a minimum of four weeks' rehabilitation, and that sometime, most likely next year, he will again be eligible to gain a spot on the active roster. Compared to the alternative—being cut from the squad and set adrift from football—Dudek seemed delighted when he talked to a circle of reporters and camera people this morning. "This is the first time an injury might have helped my career rather than hurt it. The Sunday nights and Monday mornings were getting to me," he said, referring to the anxious hours that led up to August's weekly cuts. "Now, at least, I know I'm going to be around a while. In a situation like this, time is the best thing for me."

And what about his injury—the one that no one, Dudek included, seemed to notice during his kickoff returns against the 49ers Saturday evening? "I've got it written down," he said with a straight face, ready with the medical terminology. "It's a shoulder sprain and an impingement." He explained that the injury first occurred during training camp, that it wasn't severe enough for him to miss any practice time, but it had been aggravated Saturday night. Was his shoulder painful? the reporters wanted to know. "There's some pain," said the nearly jubilant running back, now assured of not being cut, assured of buying some time. "I have medication for it."

In the last of the *Rocky Mountain News* articles covering Dudek's camp and his attempt to make the team, B. G. Brooks quoted Reeves on the injured player's prospects: "Joe's a guy who competed in small-college football, and when he came in, I think he was a little bit awed by the situation. But he saw that he could compete. This year could possibly give him a chance to develop and become certainly a candidate to make our football team . . . because he's got that kind of talent."

Joe Dudek, his picture now out of the papers, the articles called "Catching On" at an end, will nurse his arm for a few days—until the trainers pronounce the impingement passed, until the reporters no longer trail him—then he'll go back to the fence at the south end of the practice field. He'll throw the boomerang ball through the long weeks of the fall; in a month, he'll begin to practice with the team again, his legs churning through holes in the offensive line to assure the coaches that they were wise to keep him around, but he'll spend each game in the stands at the stadium, unrecognized by even the most ardent fans who sit beside him, who won't have any idea that the buck-toothed boy who is cheering himself hoarse is employed as a football player.

September 6

The season is seven weeks old now. After seventy practice sessions, three scrimmages, and four pre-season games—the final one of which the Broncos won convincingly, with John Elway and wide receiver Vance Johnson shredding the Los Angeles Rams' defensive secondary, the orange horses at last appearing to have an offense—the games that matter, that will be tallied and kept track of and bet on with very big money, will now begin. And tomorrow's contest—played at home against the Los Angeles Raiders, arch-rivals, arch-enemies, arch-nemesis, perennial wreckers of Bronco dreams—should be a spectacular football game.

But today, there is a cold and steady rain and it is hard to summon excitement. Dressed in their brand new uniforms, their white Lycra pants so tight they define each player's femoral muscles, their jerseys a bright and edible orange that pays no attention to subtlety, they sit uncomfortably in the drizzle to have their pictures taken, all of them together, a team at last— one owner, one general manager, nineteen coaches, trainers and equipment managers, twelve players on injured reserve, forty-five players who will suit up on game days and "get after it," as they say.

John Elway is in the photograph, of course, number 7 in the front row, indistinct from all the rest unless you're a fan and you're sure he hung the moon. Jack Weil is there, 13 his lucky number, the player who survived the punting contests, the rawest kind of rookie, a punter Dan Reeves admits he's taking a chance on, the only native Coloradan on the squad, the only

73

one a Broncos fan since birth. There is cornerback Louis Wright, number 20, five times a Pro Bowler, a sage in the defensive secondary and a survivor from the Super Bowl year; Sammy Winder, his shoulder pads distorting his 23, once a Pro Bowler, the team's best hope for controlled explosions at running back; and Joe Dudek, number 32, suited up only today, who might explode in a year or two. Tom Jackson, number 57, smiles at the end of the second row, the oldest linebacker in the NFL, still buoyant and intense about the game of football despite the injuries and the atrophy of thirteen seasons. Jim Juriga, number 66, pale, sullen, and stone-faced, sits in the middle of the third row, the cast on his leg hidden by the players sitting in front of him. Juriga, the team's first pick in this spring's draft, had won a starting position at left tackle until his knee collapsed in practice ten days ago and the promise of his rookie season went sour. Behind and above him is Karl Mecklenburg, number 77, a national media star as the season opens, a star in last season's Pro Bowl, a roving defender who has played as many as seven positions in a single game, sharp as a physicist, blond as an albino. And in the same row are Steve Watson and Vance Johnson, the starting wide receivers, biracial Mutt and Jeff, the lanky Watson, number 81, nicknamed "Blade," a young and pass-catching Cary Grant; Johnson, 82, small and compact, legs like pistons, his hair hennaed and trimmed in a flattop, a pass-catching El DeBarge. Pat Bowlen grins from the center of the coaches' row at the rear, proud of the talented people he has assembled; Dan Reeves is sober standing beside him, staring into the camera as if to acknowledge that this season, the real season at last, may be a son of a bitch.

Fifty yards away, two hundred fans shiver beneath the stadium's south goalpost, taking photographs of the taking of the photograph, unaware and uncaring that in their midst are the senior Broncos beat reporters for Denver's two major newspapers—the *Denver Post*'s Joe Sanchez, a ten-year veteran of the football wars, and the *Rocky Mountain News*'s Steve Caulk, on the

Broncos beat for four years. Locked in a circulation war—the *Post* the longtime leader on Sundays, the *News*'s lead seemingly secure on the weekdays—the two papers have chosen their sports sections as principal battlefields, their Broncos coverage the heavy artillery in boldface, 48-point headlines. Although it is hard to imagine either sportswriter making much of a feature out of the taking of the team photograph, here they are, covering the cold morning's activities, just in case.

"Why in the hell are you here?" The question is from Charlie Lee, the team's director of player and community relations, the man charged with keeping the fans at bay. He directs it at Caulk, his arms crossed to shield against the cold, Sanchez a pace or two away.

"Because he's here," Caulk says, pointing toward Sanchez with a nod and a thrust of his nose.

"So why are you here?" Lee asks the *Post*'s reporter.

"Because he's here," Sanchez responds, grinning, his thumb poking against the pocket of his wool jacket, poking toward the competing paper's scribe.

The three of them briefly share the humor before Lee hurries away. "Well, whatever," he says as he goes, "it's y'all's project."

September 7

Two weeks ago, the entire issue of *Empire*, the *Denver Post*'s Sunday magazine, was devoted to the Broncos, something of a pre-season tradition at the beleaguered magazine. 26 YEARS OF BRONCOMANIA, rang the orange headline on the cover, inside of which were color-illustrated stories on highlights of the Broncos' history, renowned Broncos of yesteryear, the Broncos' toils in stormy weather, the new penthouse suites high above Mile High Stadium from which corporate, deep-pocket Denver will now watch the Broncos' games; profiles of John Elway, newcomer Mark Haynes, and the whole of the Denver defense; a piece predicting a terrific 12-4 season but declining to be clairvoyant about the play-offs; and features on two superfans—County Judge Francis C. Jackson, who spends his summer vacation as a volunteer assistant to the Broncos' equipment manager at training camp, sorting dirty towels and jock straps, and Charlie Goldberg, "Charlie Bronco," a retired businessman and twenty-six-year supporter and defender of the team, who says, "I love this city. I want to make it great. When the Broncos came of age, nationally, Denver started to rise out of the ashes and become a real city. The people of Denver owe whatever they have to the Broncos." And so, it seemed, does *Empire Magazine*. The Broncos issue of *Empire* was fat, full of advertising worth hundreds of thousands of dollars to its parent newspaper, many of the ads touting the Broncos more heartily than pitching shoes or window shades.

But this morning, *Empire* is defunct, its fate parallel to that of other Sunday magazines at city newspapers across the country, many of them the victims of the predominance of television as an advertising medium, of reduced competition in cities where often only a single newspaper remains in business, and of readership surveys that contend that people today have no time to read long, comprehensive articles—even in their Sunday papers. In recent months, *Empire*, never strongly supported by the management of the Times Mirror Company, owner of the *Post*, grew thin as a coupon insert; six weeks ago, the *Post* announced that the decades-old magazine was at an end, including in the announcement a catalog of other Sunday magazines that no longer roll off the presses, rather than acknowledging that *Empire* just wasn't one of the paper's current priorities. As they cleaned out their desks and unplugged their word processors, some of them moving to other departments at the *Post*, you could imagine *Empire*'s staffers lamenting, *If only we could have done a Broncos issue every week. . . .*

But don't assume that the *Denver Post* ignored the Denver Broncos on this Sunday when the season began, when the black-and-silver Raiders came to town and the two teams mixed it up. Drinking coffee in a dreary hotel restaurant at eight o'clock this morning, I flipped first to the *Post*'s sports section—as any certified fan would do—and perused these several stories:

• A feature on the few wayward souls in the city of Denver who *hate* the Broncos and whose club of choice seems to be the Raiders. "I grew up in Denver," barber Juma Archuleta told sportswriter Mike Monroe, "and I get tired of all the Bronco hype. And yes, I relate to the outlaw image of the Raiders. But after all I've been through in my life, football isn't that important. It's just a game."

• Columnist Buddy Martin's prediction that the season will bring the Broncos only moderate success: "The Broncos get a wild-card berth and beat the Dolphins in Miami, but lose the next week to the Jets, winners of the AFC East with a red-hot 13-3 season. Eventually, the Jets win it all, beating the Bears in the Super Bowl."

• The results of a poll commissioned by the *Post* and Denver's Channel 4, indicating that only 28 percent of all Coloradans believe the Broncos will make it to the Super Bowl, yet 78 percent of them think the team will survive into the early rounds of the play-offs.

• Letters to the Broncos written by students in Roseanne Bradbury's third-grade class at Cimarron Elementary School. Tim Eberly, eight, admonished the team: "You have got to win the games and the Super Bowl. If you do I will jump in the air and touch the ceiling."

• A column purportedly by John Elway, ghostwritten by the paper's beat reporters, eschewing complex sentences even though Elway is a graduate of Stanford University: "One thing we learned last year, though, is that the way to win the division is to beat the Raiders. So let's buckle up. Everybody put on that orange and let's go get us a Raider."

• And, believe it or not, the first of what are promised to be weekly columns by psychic Lou Wright, whose vibrations or female intuition or cosmic insight foretell a so-so season. And as for today's game: "The Raiders offense will feature lots of running. The signals I get are that it will be a *faster* kind of running game, if that makes any sense."

To top it all off, the *Post*'s readers were titillated with a special reason to buy tomorrow's paper—not simply its clear and insightful coverage of the clash with the Raiders, but also a free-wheeling piece by novelist Leon Uris, a resident of Aspen, Colorado, and the most rabid kind of Broncos fan. Uris had accepted the *Post*'s invitation to wax novelistic about Sunday's game (Raiders fan Louis L'Amour regretfully declined a similar invitation), and tomorrow's front page would tell Mr. Uris's tale.

My coffee tremor vibrating me into something approaching consciousness, I plunged on through the sports pages of the competing *Rocky Mountain News* before I bundled myself up against the cold and the Sunday drizzle and made my way to the sacred stadium.

The big, boxy motor homes had begun to pull into the parking lots at the south rim of the stadium at about eight o'clock. By eleven, the rain had diminished to mist and the lots were a sea of white and silver aluminum, each rig parked only inches from the next, doors propped open, the smoke from charcoal briquettes rising from portable barbecues, people milling with Bloody Marys and bottles of beer, shunning rain gear in favor of Broncos shirts and hats and sweaters.

Many of these folks were old friends—not neighbors or business associates or social companions; they knew each other from dozens of seasons of Sunday mornings, remembering faces if not always names, asking each other if they were still out in Lakewood, or was it Westminster? If they still had that body shop, and didn't their daughter get married? They spread the Sunday papers across the small tables inside their RVs, some of them staying out of the weather. Outside, a few boys threw orange foam-rubber footballs. Men with gravelly voices stood in small groups, grinding cigarette butts into the pavement and wondering if Steve Sewell was going to turn into a by-God football player this fall, if Tom Jackson had one last season in him. Women in outlandish homemade hats, some replete with players' pictures, talked about how exciting it was to get to start against the Raiders, to get to pound them into the rainy turf as the season's first official act. A man hoisted a big Broncos flag on a pole atop his motor home, and the crowd that could see him do it gave him a cordial cheer.

South of the stadium, south of adjacent McNichols Arena, where the Denver Nuggets play, under the Colfax Avenue viaduct, a younger, nattier, yuppier group of fans poured into Brooklyn's, a popular sports bar housed in a historic building that has served over the past century as a saloon and brothel, a halfway house for Eastern European immigrants, a fish market, and now as a watering hole with satellite receivers stationed out back and a bevy of television screens on the walls, one visible from virtually every seat in the house. Named for the neighborhood in which it resides, Brooklyn's otherwise tends to attract relative newcomers to Denver who still keep track of the Cleveland Browns, Chicago's Bears and Bulls and Blackhawks, or Detroit's cowardly Lions, and who are willing to stare through the smoky haze at a distant TV to keep their credentials as fans, their hometowns in their hearts. But it is Broncos fans who really pack the place, arriving, as they did today, three hours or so before a home game kickoff, casually eating Sunday brunch if they are lucky enough to have secured reservations, otherwise standing cheek by jowl throughout the joint, discussing with total strangers the problems that will be posed by the Raiders, comparing the seat locations of their season's tickets, buying each other drinks, exchanging business cards on occasion, making an amorous dinner date or two, assuring each other that ass will be kicked come the middle of the afternoon.

By noon, traffic on Interstate 25 began to clog at the stadium exits, and arterial streets in the near westside neighborhood were festively, buoyantly bumper to bumper. People bestrewn in orange and splattered with royal blue, carrying stadium seats and blankets, carrying thermoses filled with Fuzzy Navels and concealing flasks filled with American vodka, ambled in groups of two, four, sometimes ten or more, converging on the stadium from every direction, the gray skies unable to dampen their spirits.

At a souvenir stand on the edge of Seventeenth Avenue, a Raider was hung in effigy from a high bamboo pole, and people beneath him crowded in close to buy banners and T-shirts, jackets and sweatshirts, assorted styles of Broncos caps and strange, flat, foam-rubber hands, huge and orange, of course, the long index fingers, bigger than bananas, thrust out to signal Number One. On the west side of the stadium, in contrast, people whose orange attire was decidedly subdued, who wore tweed sport coats and pleated wool skirts, who wore orange sweaters if they bothered to come in any kind of a costume, large rocks on their left ring fingers, were handed complimentary glasses of champagne as they entered the elevator foyer for the long ride up to the "penthouse suites" atop the stadium, far from the gladdening crowd.

At half past twelve, Pat Bowlen, his wife, Annabel, and their guests arrived in a handsome Mercedes still bearing Alberta plates, parking in a reserved spot so close to a ticket gate they barely got to stretch their legs, declining as they passed through the turnstile the orange paper sacks with eye holes provided to all comers compliments of the soft drink Orange Crush. The idea, it seemed, was for everyone in the stadium to pull the sack over his or her head each time during the game that the Denver defense sacked the Raiders' quarterback, the 75,000 shameless "Sack Maniacs" shouting in joyful approval. But there evidently would be few sacks covering heads and expensive hairdos in the owner's suite this afternoon. Bowlen, dressed in a dark Italian suit, white shirt and orange tie, pushed past the sack suppliers, vendors, and ticket takers, walking up the short ramp to his suite, his party close behind him.

In the nearby press box—renowned as among the NFL's smallest, most cramped, most uncomfortable, but offering the three dozen reporters in its front row perhaps the best football vantage imaginable in this sharply tiered stadium—nearly three hundred media people—reporters, photographers, radio and television personnel—ate a complimentary buffet of roast beef, Italian sausages, and salads (something similar is provided for them at every stadium) before they spent the afternoon and evening at work watching football and describing what they saw. They renewed old acquaintances as they ate, as they milled in a narrow walkway, talking shop and telling tales, uneager to squeeze into their folding chairs, their portable computers forced up near their faces, where they would be held captive until halftime briefly set them free.

The irony of the many dozens of men and the half dozen women who worked as football journalists in that cramped and uncomfortable place was that, on the face of things, virtually everyone else in the stadium and thousands more scattered throughout the region envied them their jobs. What could be a better way to earn your pay than to watch the Broncos from summer to the frozen end of the season? Yet what most of those fortunate sportswriters yearned for, the thing that seemed like something approaching bliss, was to curl up on a couch on a Sunday afternoon with a bag of potato chips and several bottles of beer, watching the Broncos—or, better yet, two teams they barely followed—transform football back into a game for them, making it recreation instead of occupation. A few reporters would even opt to spend the games in the stands, but only a few of them. Most of them knew that the stands were a chaos best left to the most courageous.

At one o'clock, forty-five players suited in orange and blue filed through a padded door beneath the stadium's south stands and the 30,000 or so fans who were already in their seats greeted them with wild abandon—at long last they had indisputable evidence that the Broncos would play football this fall—their cheers startling the flock of black starlings that inhabit the stadium, sending them spiraling into the sky. When the forty-five men in black and silver emerged from a tunnel in the northeast end of the stadium a few minutes later, the reception was not quite as cordial. Boos echoed off the empty seats and seemed to swirl as buoyantly as the birds; the enemy had emerged from its shelter and evidently deserved a reminder that it had come to Colorado.

While the two teams went through calisthenics and warm-up drills at separate ends of the field (this one true turf, maintained by horticulturalists instead of by plastics technicians, acknowledged as one of the best playing surfaces in the NFL), the fans began to stream into their seats, spreading cushions and blankets on the bare aluminum, unpacking tote bags and uncorking thermos bottles, readying themselves for the ritual events of the afternoon. Curiously, as the stadium filled, it grew smaller, seeming almost intimate by the time it teemed with people—75,898 of them in the space of two contiguous city blocks, fivefold more people than inhabited the large, rural county where I lived, more people, as my father used to say, than you could shake a stick at.

At about twenty minutes before two, both teams retreated to their locker rooms, and the University of Colorado's marching band briefly took the field, ignored by all but those who had once been members of marching bands themselves, a quick, time-killing interlude before the boys went at it, all asses and elbows and enthusiasm. The huge animated scoreboard above the south stands welcomed the band, then welcomed "Bucky Bronco," a small Munchkin-like horse in a football helmet, the Broncos' official mascot, the sort of cuddly character that loiters at Disneyland. Little Bucky ran onto the field with a wave of his little front hooves—and was absolutely ignored, everyone suddenly deaf and blind or simply supremely uninterested, and he bounced his way to the sidelines. Another horse, unannounced, this one immobile, stood atop the scoreboard—the stadium's high figurehead, a huge plastic animal rearing on his hind feet, his front hooves pawing the sullen sky, a supposed white stallion that had been gelded in the interests of family entertainment.

You could see the white horse shake as the crowd roared when the Broncos returned to the field, 150,000 feet stomping their unison approval, their excitement, their anticipation, stomping, screaming as the Broncos won the coin toss and chose to receive the kickoff, the stomping subsiding through the playing of the "Star Spangled Banner," then beginning again when it was a few bars away from ending, roaring—the entire place in tumult—as the two teams took the field, stomping (our catastrophic deaths seeming certain now, the vibrating stadium surely about to collapse), stomping more intently still, frantically waving their orange sacks in the cool September air, the noise so thunderous it seemed the world was ending—or maybe was beginning again in ecstasy—as the ball settled into the sure arms of kick returner Gene Lang and the season was under way.

"On each and every down, we're going to be laying fingerprints all over those guys' anatomies. It's academic," Lester "The Molester" Hayes, the Raiders' aggressive cornerback and intimidating talker, had said a few days before the game. "Our forte is playing tight man-to-man coverage. We're going to bump them in the 5-yard bump zone. As far as freedom in the 5-yard zone, Vance Johnson and Steve Watson shall not see freedom. That thought is null and void. They could line up King Kong Bundy and Andre the Giant out there and we're going to bump the shit out of them, too. It doesn't matter."

As far as Hayes was concerned, Johnson, the Broncos' sensational second-year wide receiver, certainly could be contained by close man-to-man coverage and by a game-long series of hits each time Johnson accelerated off the line of scrimmage. And there was one more thing. Hayes wanted Johnson to know that he would not tolerate it if Johnson tried to take him out of each play with a cut-block—a legal but disliked and potentially dangerous move in which the receiver tries to "cut" the defender's legs out from under him prior to running his pass route. "There is a pre-game pact that states the receivers do not 'cut' me," Hayes explained, "and I will not jam them in their face area."

But Vance Johnson, it seemed, hadn't paid attention to the admonition. On the Broncos' first play from scrimmage, Johnson gave Hayes a cut-block as he left the line of scrimmage, then caught a 21-yard pass from John Elway, immediately giving the Broncos good field position and convincing Hayes that Johnson had to be taught a lesson. On the next play, a 4-yard reception by Johnson this time, Hayes rolled him to the ground near the sideline, stuck his knees in Johnson's ribs, reached inside his face mask and gouged his eye with his fingers, drawing blood, causing Johnson's eye to quickly swell, his vision to become blurry. "Jesus, look what you did to my eye," said Johnson as he got to his feet.

"Hey, I'm sorry," Hayes told him, "just stay high in your blocks, okay?"

"You want me to stay high in my blocks? Look what you did to my eye!" Johnson shouted incredulously before he went back to the huddle. Somehow, no official had seen Hayes's foul, and his flagrant act of violence went unpenalized.

Despite the blood and the blurry vision, Johnson caught two more passes—halfway through the second quarter, the Broncos trailing 19–7—before he was tackled following a 7-yard reception, one knee buckling as he fell to the ground. Two plays later, he had somehow recovered enough to reenter the game, and once again Elway rifled the ball into his arms. This time, Raiders cornerback Sam Seale made the hit, and this time Johnson did not get up.

Vance Johnson, his prospects for stardom exceedingly bright, had played less than half of a football game and already his season was in jeopardy, already this combative contact sport had robbed him of the same physical talents that had given him such promise and that made him such a pleasure to watch in action. The face-lacerating, eye-gouging incident with Hayes was inexcusable by any count, evidence of how rough and necessarily aggressive play too often crosses the boundary into barbarism. The knee that was strained, then its ligaments torn apart by Sam Seale's clean and legitimate tackle, was simply sad evidence that human knees were not designed to play this game, that injuries are its damnable downside, that yes, it offers some of its participants financial security, a sense of purpose, and true pleasure as few other occupations can, but that too often young men leave football badly wounded.

"It's a very interesting game," Soviet hockey coach Viktor Tikhonov reportedly said after he had seen an American football game for the first time. "They have big bears up front and little rabbits in back. The idea is for the bears to protect the rabbits." That's a fair enough synopsis of the sport, but the irony is that it isn't just the rabbits who need protection; the big bears who work the offensive and defensive lines are battered and bruised and beaten in almost equal measure. Football, for players at every position, is synonymous with injury, and unwarranted violence—the demented need of a few uniformed thugs to make the field the scene of their crimes—makes injury all the more commonplace.

A study conducted by the NFL Players Association found that there were an average of 102 serious injuries a week during the 1984 season, meaning that over 8 percent of the league's 1,260 players were injured on a weekly basis, meaning that, on average, every player experienced at least one significant injury during the course of the season. Injuries are attendant to every sport, to every form of strenuous exercise, but why are they so rampant in football? At least one answer is obvious: Blocking and tackling, the game's fundamental offensive and defensive maneuvers, are brutal business. Both require one body to smash headlong into another, often at harrowing rates of speed. And the hard suits of armor that protect each player also inevitably act as weapons of sorts, aimed at the opponent with whom the player comes in crashing contact. Helmets are missiles, shoulder pads broad battering rams, forearm protectors virtual brickbats. As protective equipment has been improved over the years, injuries have not subsided, in large part because any piece of gear hard enough and strong enough to protect against injurious blows is almost certainly able to do damage in its own right.

Yet during the same years that the quality of the players' protective uniforms has been at least marginally improved, the quality of most of the fields on which they play has been dramatically reduced, a decline that began with an artificial playing surface dubbed "AstroTurf," developed in the mid-1960s by the Monsanto Corporation for Houston's Astrodome, the nation's first domed stadium, a place inside of which—it was discovered after construction was completed—grass simply wouldn't grow. Today, seventeen of the NFL's twenty-eight teams play on rugs known variously as "AstroTurf-8," "SuperTurf," and "TexasTurf," all of them providing too little cushion and too much traction, a combination that results in greater numbers of skin burns, muscle bruises, compression injuries, and a few totally new injuries such as the now common toe dislocation known as "turf toe," as well as the aggravated, season-ending knee and ankle injuries that result when shoe soles stick to the carpet as if cemented in place—even when the legs to which they are attached are being violently whipped and contorted.

If artificial turf has a virtue—other than the fact that little or no money needs to be spent on it for maintenance, a virtue, I guess, in the eyes of general managers—it's that it is a virtual racetrack. It allows receivers to run faster routes than grass does and, if their knees survive the ligament-tearing torque, it lets them make quicker cuts and changes of direction that result in more completed passes, more touchdowns, more money come contract-renewal time. But artificial turf allows *everyone* to run faster, not just those receivers who are built in the image of antelopes. The 240-pound linebackers in bad moods who bear down on darting receivers in the defensive secondary are also moving fractionally faster than they would on grass. Colliding cars are crushed in direct proportion to the speeds at which they are traveling, and the physics are the same for football players.

Adding to the odds of gridiron injury is the statistical fact that players grow bigger and stronger by the season, some of them solely by means of diet, weight training, and conditioning, others with the illicit assistance of anabolic steroids—synthetic variants of the hormone testosterone, which stimulate muscle growth, cause weight gain, and increase aggression. What "roids" also can do are cause liver and prostate cancer, high blood pressure, sterility and atrophied testicles, and abnormal breast growth. If that list isn't indictment enough, it seems certain that steroids increase on-the-field injuries by adding muscle mass to skeletal systems that can't support it, as well as slowing the normal recovery time from all types of musculoskeletal injuries.

Anabolic steroid use is widespread, in part because the NFL has yet to make the problem a priority. While the league officially prohibits the use of steroids by its players, it does not test for steroids, as it does for illegal street drugs. And although officially frowned on by the league, if a player is in possession of steroids prescribed to him by a doctor, he is breaking no law of any kind. While few, if any, players are willing to defend steroids or admit that they personally use them, Raiders defensive end Howie Long has estimated publicly that they are used by "at least fifty percent of the big guys. The offensive line—seventy-five percent. Defensive line—forty percent, plus thirty-five percent of the linebackers. I don't know about the speed positions, but I've heard they're used there, too." The

Broncos' head trainer, Steve Antonopulos, says he believes his team is steroid-free. Although that seems unlikely in the face of fairly rampant steroid use by the team's competitors, it may be true: The current crop of forty-five Broncos, crowded together on the same scale, are the lightest team in the NFL.

The irony, however, is that Vance Johnson wasn't injured by a blow from an industrial-strength helmet, his knee wasn't shredded on a Monsanto carpet, and at 185 pounds he can hardly be suspected of steroid use (although his calves do belong on a person roughly twice his size). Vance Johnson's knee "blew out" because football—being tackled in particular—puts lateral stresses on legs that knees, no matter how well protected or conditioned, cannot always withstand. Knee injuries, it has to be presumed, are here to stay, as much a part of the game as screaming coaches and end-zone celebrations.

If sports medicine can claim one positive change with regard to knee injuries, it is that although it can't prevent them, it can now repair them and rehabilitate them in a fraction of the time it used to take. Outpatient arthroscopic surgery, in which a probe inserted into the knee allows a surgeon to see and repair damage without making a full-fledged surgical invasion, has cut recovery time by more than half. Before the third quarter had ended this afternoon, word came from the trainers and physicians in the Broncos' locker room that Johnson had torn the posterior cruciate ligament in his right knee and would require arthroscopic surgery tomorrow. He would play again this season, the trainers assured his coaches, teammates, and the fans—in six weeks, seven or eight at the outside.

Johnson's eye will recover more quickly, of course. Lester the Molester succeeded in doing little serious damage. But surely the eye gouge is the shocking injury of the two that Johnson suffered. "The main thing that happened was what Lester did to my eye," Johnson said standing on crutches after the game, his right leg in a splint cinched tight with Velcro straps. "That was the worst thing that happened to me through the whole day. Why does he have to try to pull my eye out?"

In the visiting team's locker room, tucked under the stands at the opposite end of the stadium, Lester Hayes was unrepentant. "Vance Johnson is telling an out-and-out lie," said Hayes, his eyes sparkling like a showman's. "I am a gentle Texas A&M Aggie, and I would never gouge his eyes out. I would never do that. I am very fond of Vance Johnson. I was actually trying to get a speck of dust off his eyebrow. There was a speck of dust on his eyebrow, and I was being a nice Texas A&M Aggie. So be it."

Hayes could afford to be flip about the incident. He hadn't been penalized following its occurrence, and despite Johnson's and the Broncos' protestations, there was little chance that the league would fine or suspend him for the flagrant act that videotapes of the game so clearly verified. Although the league claims to stand foursquare against the intentional attempts to maim known as "cheap shots," it is a rare one that results in the $1,000 or so fine, which is little more than beer money to most players. Only very rarely has a player been suspended for so much as a game for inflicting a criminal hit. Lester Hayes, unwanted by the authorities, flew home to Lala-land confident that he had taught a kid a lesson.

Beneath the stadium's south stands, adjacent to the Broncos' coaches' locker room, two dozen reporters waited in a makeshift conference room at the game's conclusion, waited to hear Dan Reeves's comments, then to question him on the particulars of week number one. Weary after the long game, but their real work yet to begin, the reporters chatted quietly, joked with each other, and each one scribbled "Reeves" onto a blank page in his or her notebook. "What do you bet he'll open with 'Well, you have to be pleased any time you beat the Los Angeles Raiders?' " asked the *Rocky*'s Steve Caulk. It was a good guess; it would be classic Reeves, and the head coach had proven his press-conference predictability during his five previous seasons in Denver. But when Reeves made his way to the podium, still wearing the cheerleader's sweater emblazoned with BRONCOS

89

that had been the subject of extensive sartorial discussion in the stands during the game, he had a quip up his sleeve. "You didn't like that one," drawled the coach, feigning the farm boy, "I guess you just don't like football."

And it was a wonderful game, far better than the sloppy, tentative sort of contest you'd expect at the start of the season. But then, this was a Broncos-Raiders game, and anything less than a three-and-a-half-hour free-for-all would have seemed like kissing your sister. During the 1980s, each of the twelve games the two teams played against each other was decided by less than a touchdown. The last three games between the two ended in overtime. Today was no exception to the wild and wooly tradition, but it seemed—at about the time Vance Johnson was assisted off the field—that it might be, that finally a game between these old AFL enemies would be merely football instead of the stuff of folklore.

The Raiders quickly stole Denver's early seven-point lead, tying the score with a 24-yard touchdown pass from quarterback Marc Wilson to running back Marcus Allen, following three minutes later with a four-play, 75-yard drive and another touchdown, this one an end-zone catch by tight end Todd Christensen. When the Raiders defense forced a scrambling-for-sanctuary John Elway out of the back of the Broncos' end zone for a two-point safety at the close of the first quarter, the score was 16–7, and the fans were feeling peculiar. Hadn't these street toughs from south Los Angeles read that the Broncos were Super Bowl–bound? The season's script had called for a glistening string of victories, for a divisional championship to be stuffed into three million Christmas stockings, and a first-act defeat by the Raiders simply wouldn't do.

When Los Angeles kicker Chris Bahr added a field goal in the opening seconds of the second quarter, the score now 19–7, you could see dreams die throughout that horseshoe stadium; you could watch as visions of glory slipped into the rainy skies. But then—oh, we weren't really worried—the Broncos, too, proceeded to play. Starting from their own 23-yard line, they needed six plays to reach the Raiders' 23. Next they razzled the Raiders and dazzled everyone within eyeshot when running back Steve Sewell took a hand-off from Elway and started to sweep right before he stopped, cocked his arm, and launched a spiraling pass back to Elway, who was headed downfield like a pigeon-toed wide receiver. The ball settled into the quarterback's hands and he ambled untouched into the end zone. Paid—and paid rather handsomely—to throw footballs, Elway hadn't caught one since his preteen, Pop Warner days in Missoula, Montana, but he somehow remembered how the feat was accomplished and the Broncos were back in business.

The Raiders scored another field goal before the Broncos—thanks to an end-zone pass-interference penalty against the Raiders that came as a bit of a gift—found themselves a yard away from another touchdown. With a minute and seven seconds left in the half, Gene Lang lumbered across the goal line, Rich Karlis kicked the extra point, and the Broncos—back from their nap—had narrowed the gap to a point. Raiders 22, Broncos 21 at half-time.

The two teams tallied three touchdowns in the third quarter, just to keep up the offensive extravaganza, just in case anyone was tempted to beat the traffic and make an early exit. First the Raiders scored on a 2-yard Marcus Allen run, then, a series later, Broncos linebacker Ken Woodard scooped up an Allen fumble and carried it 16 yards for a touchdown. Four plays later, the Raiders had breathing room again when Wilson completed a 57-yard pass to receiver Rod Barksdale, a spectacular touchdown strike that seemed to herald the Raiders' superiority—at least on this September Sunday. At the end of the third quarter, they led by eight points and the Broncos' offense had seemingly sputtered to a halt.

But you play four quarters in a football game, and the Broncos were alive again when Karlis kicked a 51-yard field goal, the longest of his career, as the quarter opened. Then Raiders returner Napoleon McCallum fumbled the ensuing kickoff and the Broncos had the ball again on the Raiders' 39-yard line. The

91

stands erupted with delight, with hope at last that the game wasn't lost, and, nine plays later, Gene Lang caught Elway's 7-yard touchdown pass. Karlis's extra point put the Broncos ahead by two with ten minutes left to play.

But, my God, there was no end to it. The Raiders seemed certain to score, to take the lead again, when Dokie Williams caught a 10-yard Wilson pass on the Broncos' 16-yard line. Then, as Williams spun toward the goal line, he fumbled the ball and Denver's Dennis Smith fell on it; the Broncos had dodged a very black and silver bullet.

With just three minutes to go in the game, the Broncos tried to maintain possession of the ball and the fragile lead. They managed three first downs, but then the Raiders forced them to punt. With the ball on their own 20-yard line, the Raiders had 42 seconds to score; a field goal would be enough to give them the game. On two quick and surgical pass completions, they reached the Broncos' 45; ten more yards and they would be within Bahr's kicking range. With twelve seconds to go, Wilson dropped back to pass again, desperate to find a receiver near the sideline. But he was smothered by Broncos defensive end Rulon Jones before he could get the ball away. Wilson was sacked for a loss of 13 yards and the Raiders—out of time-outs—were beaten, but only barely. Jones raised his arms in triumph, his teammates and coaches streamed jubilantly toward the locker room, but in the stands, the fans seemed more to sigh than to celebrate. Their team had won, the scoreboard certified that, but the Broncos had to scrap their way to the win; they had to struggle to beat a team that seemed—admit it—a little better. On the long ramps that led from the stadium's upper levels, spirits were high in the growing twilight, but this wasn't the ecstasy that accompanied the opening kickoff. Headed for home, headed back to Brooklyn's or to neighborhood haunts like the Log Cabin and the Bonnie Brae Tavern, headed for pizzas or redfish or Sunday-night bowls of cereal, the fans now knew what they relearned again each autumn, that the game on the grass, my God, could drive you crazy.

September 27

—

The skies had cleared on the Monday after the Raiders game; summer had returned to the Rockies, the Raiders had been beaten, if not routed, and all was well with the Queen City— except in the sports department in the basement of the Channel 9 studios, where a palace coup was in progress. Jim Celania, the station's $100,000-a-year sports anchor, had arrived at work to discover that he was being bumped from that night's newscast, offered a couple weeks of unexpected holiday to be followed by the sort of apprentice reporting assignments that perchance would make him choose to resign.

According to Ken Tonning, the station's vice-president and general manager, Celania would be replaced by Mike Nolan, the anchor who had been dumped in favor of Celania just a year before. The sudden change in the starting lineup was being made, Tonning said, "to realign our sports department and make it more aggressive. There was no single factor for making the change." What Tonning didn't say was that Celania had been an experiment that did not pan out. Imported to Denver from San Francisco, Celania's arrival had been promoted in the fall of 1985 as if he were the epicenter of American sports journalism. Young, urbane, more than a little acerbic, and with the kind of dark-eyes-aimed-at-the-camera good looks that television producers die for, Celania replaced the older, old-school, midwestern Nolan, who, the station soon discovered, had been surprisingly popular.

It was an almost impossible task for Celania to live up to his billing; he hadn't hung the sportscasting moon, it turned out, and Channel 9's largely conservative viewers made a habit of writing and phoning the station to announce that they missed Mike Nolan. Then Celania made the mistake of riling the Denver Broncos.

Soon after his arrival, Celania had aired videotape that his crew had filmed at a Broncos practice. It was of a flea-flicker pass play the Broncos were planning to try out on the San Diego Chargers. The Broncos' media-relations rules have for years allowed attendance by local media at team practices, but specific coverage of play formations—either in print or on television—is akin to treason. Celania, either ignorant of the rule or not heeding it, thought his viewers would like to see the fancy play. When members of the Broncos' coaching staff saw a piece of their game plan played out on the evening news, their shouts echoed off Mount Evans.

Then Celania embarrassed the station in the Barney Chavous affair. Although Channel 9 maintained publicly that the error was a simple matter of semantics, the station plainly had egg all over its face. It would be one thing, say, to report erroneously the results of a mayoral election, but you just don't mess with the Broncos or Barney Chavous, and it seemed certain that the blunder was at least partly responsible for Celania's removal from his anchor spot. "I think we might have mentioned that it was a mistake," Tonning said about his dismissal conversation with Celania. "We were discussing a lot of things. We're not doing this for the Broncos, although they are fans of Mike Nolan and had a good working relationship with him."

But Celania himself didn't see things quite that way. As far as he was concerned, the Broncos had railroaded his departure. "I understand they were active in expressing their displeasure with me," he told Clark Secrest, the *Denver Post*'s television editor, and his accusations were trumpeted in the paper's Tuesday sports section. "Everybody's in bed with the Broncos," Celania said, "and everybody wants to be on their good side. There's not a station that would deny that. I come from a market where the media doesn't bow over to the pro sports teams. It's done here quite frequently. It's a sad state of affairs when a football team is that powerful, that they can get ahold of the media like they do in this market."

Did the Broncos force Channel 9 to change its lineup? Not according to Jim Saccomano, the Broncos' director of media relations. No one in the Broncos' organization had gone seeking Celania's head. But yes, he said, it was no secret that the Broncos had been very unhappy with Celania on two occasions.

The issue of who was or was not in bed with whom heated up a degree or two come Wednesday, when the *Post*'s sports columnist Buddy Martin took rather personal issue with Celania's charges. Martin acknowledged that it is common practice for players, coaches, and management personnel of professional sports teams to punish reporters with the silent treatment when they publish critical pieces, but he said he knew of no case where the Broncos had seen to it that a member of the sports media who had fallen from grace was axed. "I resent the outrageous statement by Celania that the Denver media is 'in bed' with the Broncos. The reputations of a lot of good, honest, hard-working journalists have been impugned by such a remark. I know a lot of professionals in TV, radio, and newspapers took heat from the athletic establishment for having the guts to pursue tough stories and ask tough questions long before Celania showed up here with his lantern, looking for an honest man."

As far as Martin was concerned, "The Broncos didn't get Jim Celania dismissed, Jim Celania got Jim Celania dismissed. . . . Celania never worked hard at his craft until it was too late. . . . He always seemed to be gliding above us, as if he were simply passing through town and, frankly, a little too hot for this market."

On Thursday in the *Rocky Mountain News*, television editor Dusty Saunders's column carried Celania's response: "My comments about Channel 9 being in bed with the Broncos were taken out of context," Celania told Saunders. And as for Buddy Martin's comments about Celania's comments about the Broncos: "The column was vicious, indicating that I didn't work at my job. That's not true. I have been screwed royally in print. . . . I never intimated that team officials were responsible for my firing. The Broncos and Channel 9 are professional organizations. The Broncos wouldn't demand my firing nor would Channel 9 be badgered by any such threats."

Although Saunders editorialized that Celania had probably been "the wrong man for the wrong job even before he moved in front of the cameras," he didn't speculate about why Celania's appraisal of his ouster had changed so radically in two days' time. Whatever his true feelings, Jim Celania was California-bound by Saturday, and the Broncos, still protesting their innocence, were off on Sunday for Pittsburgh and a Monday night football game, with Channel 9's repatriated Mike Nolan in tow.

The Broncos had not one but two good trips to Pennsylvania. They recorded their second win of the season on September 15 in front of a sullen Three Rivers Stadium crowd and a national television audience, defeating the Pittsburgh Steelers either 28–10 or 21–10, depending on who was counting. Six days, two plane rides, and a touch of jet lag later, they returned to the Keystone State to beat the Philadelphia Eagles in a most unbrotherly fashion.

The Pittsburgh game marked the first controversy of the season involving the NFL's new instant replay rule, which was undergoing a one-year trial. Accordingly, a "replay official," sitting in an isolated booth in each stadium's press box, has the option of overturning a decision made by officials on the field if he believes the videotape replay shows "indisputable visual evidence" that the call should be changed. When the experiment was approved by the NFL's owners in March, the Broncos were one of only four teams to vote against it, believing, according to owner Pat Bowlen, that the system would put too much pressure on the officials, both on the field and in the booth. Perhaps one of the problems Bowlen envisioned when he voted no was the one his team faced in the second game of the season. Midway through the fourth quarter on that Monday night, with Denver leading 14–10, the Broncos began a drive on the Steelers' 21-yard line. On the first play from scrimmage, John Elway dropped back to pass, threw the ball to his left and behind him to running back Gerald Willhite, who faked a run, then passed the ball downfield to receiver Steve Watson, who caught the ball at the Steelers' 45-yard line and ambled untouched into the end zone. But the play was quickly called back. According to referee Bob McElwee, Elway's pass had not been thrown behind him as a lateral; it was a forward pass, and two forward passes during the same play are illegal. Nice and simple. No controversy. Loss of down and a 10-yard penalty; second and twenty. What McElwee didn't know was that the play was under review in the booth, and despite the gnashing of teeth from Elway and the rest of the Broncos' offense (as well as a highly exercised Dan Reeves) that the play had been legal in every respect, the referee told them to get on with the game; there was nothing to discuss. After the Broncos ran another play, replay official Paul Trepinski, who had been studying the videotape and hadn't noticed that the game had gone on, called down to referee McElwee to say that the call should be changed; the first pass was a lateral, sure enough, and the touchdown should be counted. Then both men remembered that one of the replay rule's stipulations was that you can't reverse the call on one play after a second play has been run, and, well, rules are rules, and it was a fun play, but Denver was ahead anyway, so what the heck.

Cries of "Kill the Zebras!" crescendoed in bars and living rooms throughout the Rocky Mountains; Dan Reeves looked apoplectic on the sidelines, and in the visiting owner's box high above the Three Rivers field, a furious Pat Bowlen was even more convinced of his position. "That's why I voted against instant replay in the first place," he said after the game, speaking in clipped and contemptuous sentences. "It was clearly a mistake, it didn't benefit us, and it made the referees look like fools."

The Broncos eventually scored another touchdown, one they

were allowed to count this time; Pittsburgh didn't score again, and the final score was officially tallied at 21–10, a touchdown shy of the proper score.

The game in Philly was a sleeper, free of controversy, virtually free of the Philadelphia Eagles, whose somnambulistic performance in front of their hostile hometown fans made the Broncos look like world-beaters, even like a team with a running game, and the final score, 33–7, made the game seem a little closer than it really was. The season was three weeks old and the Broncos were 3–0, the team's best start since—yes—1977, the papers gleefully pointed out.

Sometimes relationships just go sour. Even though Jim Celania is a safe three states away in the City by the Bay, even though dry, dependable Mike Nolan is sitting at the Channel 9 sports desk, despite the fact the Broncos are undefeated, the team's management has once again come to blows with Denver's embattled ABC affiliate. And these were not good days to begin with at KUSA, Channel 9. The station has lost its longtime, once invincible ratings lead to the city's NBC affiliate; it has been forced to revamp a sports department in disarray; former ABC powerhouses like "Good Morning America" are only shadows of their former selves, and "Moonlighting" is the only prime-time ABC show that has ever been watched by anyone in the continental United States—and its episodes are always repeats. Now, to make matters even worse, the Broncos have informed Channel 9 that its crews are no longer allowed to fly to road games on the team's chartered plane. The expulsion began with the Philadelphia game, and now it's official policy.

No other television station, radio station, or newspaper has ever been banned from the team charter before; many TV and radio reporters routinely fly with the team and are billed by the Broncos for their seats. The reason for the surprising expulsion seems to stem, at least in part, from Broncos' general manager John Beake's concern that Channel 9's weekly half-hour Broncos show, "The Denver Huddle," is infringing on the exclusive licensing agreement the team has with Channel 4, "The Broncos' Station." "The Denver Huddle," aired each Monday night prior to ABC's "Monday Night Football," hosted by Nolan, reporter and former Bronco Butch Johnson, and current Broncos safety Dennis Smith, doesn't use the team's name or official logo, but it is similar in format to Channel 4's officially sanctioned "Dan Reeves Show," which it is currently trouncing in the ratings race.

It's hard to know if Beake would have chosen to lock horns yet again with Channel 9 if "The Denver Huddle" hadn't been doing so well. "I'm just saying I have a license agreement with KCNC, Channel 4," Beake said after news of the ban became public, "and there are certain rights that are afforded to those people because it's our club, it's our name, it's our game, and it's our logo." And it's their plane.

Yet according to Ken Tonning, KUSA's general manager, his sports crew was given a different reason. "They told us basically that they have a shortage of available seats due to the situation they have with the skybox owners." Included in the contractual agreement with each person or corporation who leases one of the Broncos' new luxury "penthouse suites" atop the stadium is a complimentary trip for two on the team plane to a road game, meaning that the team will indeed now carry far more guests to road games than it has in previous years. Yet Tonning was suspicious that Channel 9's decision not to lease a skybox of its own entered into Beake's decision. "All I'm saying is that it was within a day or two after we turned them down on the skybox that we were informed we wouldn't have access [to the plane]."

Channel 9 currently leases a $30,000-a-year loge-level box at the stadium, and it had considered upgrading to one of the new $60,000 or $80,000 suites, but decided it couldn't justify the extra expense. According to Tonning, "It came down to an either-or situation where the Broncos finally said, 'What's it going to be?' We said, 'We can't do it.' " And then, coincidence or not, John Beake leveled his ban. "The down side of all this is that we've been denied some pretty good coverage of the players and coaches on the return flights," Tonning told the *Denver Post*'s Broncos' beat reporter Michael Knisley—who virtually never flies with the team, if for no other reason than that he and his print media comrades are still stuck in some distant-city press box writing game stories while the Broncos and the sanctioned TV and radio personnel are winging back to Colorado.

At Channel 4, the supposed victor in this scrap over who can and cannot get a seat in tourist class, sports anchor Ron Zappolo was disturbed. "My initial reaction is that I think they should reinstate Channel 9," he said. "I think it reflects badly on the other television and radio stations. People think we might have had something to do with it, when in reality we had nothing to do with it. It was all the Broncos." It was just a football club flexing the muscle that, two weeks before, it had insisted it didn't have and wouldn't use.

September 29

I had seen glimpses of him for years, usually during games played in the midst of swirling snowstorms, when the television cameras would pan the stands to find him, this middle-aged man in an orange cowboy hat and orange boots and wearing only, well, a *barrel* in between. This loony guy, leading the legions in cheers, was always easy evidence to display to the TV audience that people in Colorado weren't just crazy about their football team; they were crazy as well about rather more fundamental issues like survival. Yet there was something intriguing about this fanatic fan, this naked extrovert who roamed the stadium aisles, shouting "DEFENSE!" above the din, exhorting the crowd into chaos. He had to be a bit of a nut, didn't he? Wasn't he probably the sort of Broncomaniac who has a hard time naming the opposing team, who revels in the spectacle, the P. T. Barnum ballyhoo of it all, but who doesn't know a screen pass from a butter sandwich? Surely you're a little unstable, aren't you, if you go to a Broncos game in a barrel?

I met Tim McKernan, "The Barrel Man," yesterday morning, four hours before the Broncos played host to the New England Patriots, and we talked inside his motor home, parked in an ocean of other RVs, a few feet away from the south-stands entrance to Mile High Stadium. Big, potbellied without his barrel, his hair and beard salt and peppered, his voice sandpapered by his chain-smoking habit, he curled himself in the driver's seat and described himself as a "superfan—the kind people either love or hate. They either think it's great that I make it into their section, that they can give me a high five or a slap on the back, or they think I'm some kind of lunatic."

A mechanic for United Airlines, McKernan, forty-six, has been moonlighting as the man in the barrel since a Monday night game against the Chicago Bears played in Denver in October, 1978. He wore his barrel to that game on a dare, and enjoyed the experience so much that he's worn it, rain or shine or subzero wind, to every home game during the subsequent eight years. But his attendance at Broncos games isn't perfect; he has missed six away games, six out of sixty-six, during those seasons. Although he isn't an official Broncos cheerleader—and isn't connected to the team in any way—the Broncos are helpful, he said, in acquiring away-game tickets for him, tickets for which he pays. He has been a season ticket holder at Mile High Stadium in Denver since 1968, but his seat is always empty. "I'm always counted as a no-show," he said, "which kind of bothers me, because, of course, I'm there."

McKernan is always there somewhere in the frenzied sea of

fans, making his way from tier to tier, shouting into his orange megaphone, initiating the "wave" of fans who stand up in the section-by-section unison that has become virtually obligatory at stadiums around the country, starting the "Go" and "Broncos" cheers that are screamed in a kind of competition across the open stadium, east stands trying to outshout the west; south stands besting the north. "There's no question that the team draws energy from the crowd. I think their level of play sort of matches the emotion of the stands. The crowd, the fans, become part of the game, and we're famous for that here, of course. The only other stadium in the country that's as loud—and it's probably louder—is the Kingdome in Seattle, but that's because it's got a roof over it. If there was a roof here—my God, it would be incredibly noisy." Yes, a sort of three-hour sonic boom.

I asked him if he got a chance to see much of a game in progress. "I doubt I miss more than ten plays or so in a whole game because I'm heading to a new section. I never start a cheer during a play itself; I always watch the play and I do my best to stay out of other people's lines of sight. No, I wouldn't do it if I couldn't enjoy the game. But it's work; you're pretty damn worn out after a game. And it's funny, the cold is really easier to handle than the heat. On a real hot day a few years ago, I lost eighteen pounds. I thought I was going to die. It can get pretty chilly, too, of course, but as long as I keep moving I seem to do all right. I think the coldest it's ever been here was about one below zero. Not too bad. But in Kansas City a couple of years ago, we had a game where the windchill was forty-one below. I remember that real well. I think my body temperature was something like eighty-nine degrees after the game. They had to warm me up real slow to keep me from breaking."

McKernan estimated that he spends about $2,000 a year on his football habit, and that, with the addition of occasional special appearances, he sometimes devotes as many as twenty hours a week to his barrel. "It's kind of a second job—one that I pay for—but it's also a hobby. Hell, it's a love affair."

Was it an affair that has ever lost its luster? "I'm an alcoholic," he said. "I stopped drinking on March 17, 1982. The first year or so that I did my thing without anything to drink, I'll be honest with you, was a little rough. But by now, I have a lot more fun doing it sober. I really do. Now, the only thing I can't quit is the Broncos—that and these things." He held up the cigarette he had just lit. "I don't know. It's kind of amazing. I guess it's sort of a religious cult when it comes down to it— all these people living and dying for this team. You know, I really am pretty down for a day or so whenever we lose. It's like that song—have you heard it? 'When the Broncos lose, I've got the mile-high blues/But when the Broncos win, I can breathe again.'"

Tim McKernan smiled broadly, as if the song lyric was exactly right. Then it was time to leave him alone, this man who had surprised me with his soft-spoken devotion to the thing that gave him his fondest identity. He had an orange barrel to get into, then he would head into the stadium to stroll the walkway that encircled the field, chatting with fans, sharing handshakes, gearing up for the afternoon, while the Broncos and Patriots warmed up on the manicured grass. He would stand, as he always did, on the roof of the baseball dugout just beyond the north end zone during the playing of the National Anthem and until the opening kickoff, then, the game at last underway, he would work the stands, filled with people as happy as he was.

In his office at Mile High Stadium, Broncos' ticket manager Gail Stuckey keeps a numbered list that is some 15,000-odd names long, all people who would like to purchase Broncos season tickets; virtually every one of those names represents a request for four or more tickets. If the Broncos' current season ticket holders, all 75,000 of them, somehow vanished into the thin, high-prairie air, Stuckey could, in all probability, replace them in the time it would take to mail the congratulatory letters. And with word that the wait had finally paid off, another 20,000 or so would probably stampede to Stuckey's office to get their names near the top of his new list.

In a metropolitan area of 1.8 million people—only the twenty-second largest in the nation—more than 10 percent of the population is already on record as being willing to spend relatively big money to attend Broncos games in person, and fully half the population might do so if it somehow had the opportunity. The other half, presumably, is made up of misanthropes, plus those who know that television—although unable to hawk hot dogs—provides a better-than-average vantage point.

It would be a mistake to imply that Denver is the only city in the country where people are funny about football. Robert F. Kennedy Stadium, the home of the Washington Redskins, has been sold out as long as Mile High Stadium has been; fans are legendary as well in cities like Seattle and Dallas; Giants Stadium in East Rutherford, New Jersey, fills to overflowing with fans of *two* football teams. Yet Denver is perhaps the perfect example of a town where football is, if not life itself, then the thing that life is worth living for.

There are no easy answers to explain the sport's popularity, the genesis of this devotion to a privately owned team made up of mercenary athletes, all but one of whom come from somewhere faraway, and who average only about four years in the orange uniform before they are replaced by other, still higher paid athletes from still other distant locales. There is no question that a kind of civic boosterism is part of the fundamental process of falling in love with a football team. These boys belong to us, after all, no matter where they come from; they do battle for us, they represent us to the nation, and somehow—yes, damnit, absolutely—their successes belong to us, too. When they win, when the network sportscasters have to acknowledge that, by God, the Broncos, the *Denver* Broncos are a fine football team, they praise as well the people who literally (via the ticket window) and emotionally (in the shape of their orange T-shirted devotion) give the players a reason to play. There is a kind of solidarity in that support, a collective identity shared by those 1.8 million people who are a part of this cow town metamorphosing into a city, by all three million who claim Colorado as home, and by the six million in total who live in the long shadows of the Rocky Mountains, people who ultimately share little more than the fact that they set their watches to an otherwise forgotten time zone—that and a kinship to orange horses.

There are those who will tell you that the real lure is the opportunity to observe violence, controlled and sanctioned violence. It isn't a sport, it's a war; look at the terminology, after all—passing attacks, offensive strategies, traps, trenches, gunners, assassins, bombs, blitzes, blowouts. Football is so feverishly popular because the chance to experience violence vicariously is almost irresistible, as difficult to deny as it is to drive by an automobile accident without slowing for a moment to take a look. And isn't there a kind of healthy catharsis involved? Each time you do a bit of symbolic bloodletting as the opposing quarterback is sacked, his helmet smashed into the turf, don't you spare your wife—or husband—a cruel and frustrated slap?

Then someone else will tell you that, no, the game isn't about anger so much as it is about the acquisition of property, the gaining and losing of ground, good old American capitalism reduced to a hundred yards of real estate. Or perhaps football is freedom, the most exhilarating kind of liberty—backs breaking free of what appear to be certain tackles, finding holes in knots of linemen, finding daylight, running alone on open ground.

Let's make the case, too, that art is what it's all about. Brilliant physical performances are nothing if not aesthetic—the precise choreography of teamwork, a spiraling pass thrown to a streaking receiver who cradles the ball into his arms without breaking his stride. It seems possible to me that a football game is the only circumstance in which many fans, perhaps most, are able to observe something being done as beautifully as it can be.

Or is participation more the lure than observation? Is watching a football game an act of fantasy? Do we, too, somehow throw the passes that thread needles at 30 yards, make acrobatic end-zone catches, return punts for 90-yard touchdowns? Yes, of course we do, whether or not we understand, in the celebratory seconds of slapping friends' backs and embracing wives and children, the complexities of our feelings, and of our boyish fantasies.

Interwoven with all of these facets of what is at the core of the phenomenon, and perhaps employing them all, is the possibility that professional football has emerged as a kind of worship, the secular mix of feast days and mourning, pageantry and ritual, laity and athletic saints. The word "fan" is a diminutive of "fanatic," derived from the Latin *fanum*, meaning temple. Fanatics, fans, are zealots, the people of the temples, and it would seem silly to deny that the term, as we use it today, remains somehow true to its roots. The sweep of events, of pageantry on the field and ritual responses in the stands above it, are nothing if not a civic Sunday service, the game itself a kind of grace.

Yet what was curious when I asked people in the stands yesterday why they had held tickets for twenty years, why they decked themselves out like hunters, in orange from head to toe, why these coaches from down in the Bible Belt and these players from scattered strange universities mattered to them so much, they deemed the questions ridiculous. *Because we're Broncos fans, for God's sake*, was a standard sort of reply. We're here because we haven't missed a home game in eleven years, said those who were proudest of their longevity. Because John Elway is fantastic and Tony Lilly, oh, he is so rad, said the teenaged girls. Because we like to get fucked up and scream our heads off, said the young men in need of an excuse to party. Because this team has done so much for this town, said a man in a porkpie hat who didn't seem to own anything orange. None of them wanted to talk about common identities or violence or freedom or religious fervor—it wasn't as complicated as that. There wasn't any need to get highfalutin about it. No, they just knew there was no better place to be.

106

This Denver Broncos team that inspires such ardor is now the only undefeated team in the American conference, and it leads its western division by a game over Seattle and Kansas City. But if you were only able to watch the first half of yesterday's game against the Patriots, the defending AFC champions, that news will come as quite a shock.

For two quarters yesterday afternoon, something almost unheard of happened at Mile High Stadium. Those very fans who bleed with the Denver Broncos, who admit such allegiance, showered them with boos, bombarded them with boos, cursed their beloved quarterback, then made their half-time trips to the beer stands shaking their blue-capped heads. It wasn't just that the fans were feeling cantankerous; it was that the Broncos were soiling the carpet. They were flat, they were sluggish, they were slipshod, and John Elway, as he acknowledged himself after the game, was playing worse than he had ever played—ever. Since the beginning of time. He threw passes that sailed over receivers' heads, that hit them in the shoes, that veered first 5 yards to their right, then 10 yards to their left. He did hit one player right in the numbers, but that was New England's Lawrence McGrew, who returned the interception to the Broncos' 5-yard line, from which location the Patriots needed just two quick plays to score. The Patriots also had two Tony Franklin field goals in the half, and were on the verge of scoring a second touchdown when safety Steve Foley interrupted the day's incompetence by intercepting a Craig James halfback-option pass 3 yards from the Broncos' goal line, and the Broncos were lucky to escape with just a 13–3 half-time deficit.

It may have been Foley's interception, or it may have been that the impostors were wrestled out of their Broncos uniforms and the forty-five men who usually play came out for the second half. But whatever the reason, the second half was a Denver showcase—error-free, virtually perfect football in so distinct a counterpoint to the first half that the fans forgave and forgot. Elway completed eleven of fifteen passes in the second half and threw for one touchdown; Gerald Willhite and Sammy Winder ran for one apiece, Rich Karlis kicked his second field goal of the day, and Denver's defense allowed New England nothing but aggravation and a consolation score as the game came to a close—Broncos 27, Patriots 20. Dr. Jekyll and Mr. Heart Attack.

Standing near his locker after he had shaved and showered, surrounded by reporters who outnumbered by three times the Patriots he had had to face, Elway said repeatedly that the first half was not a lot of fun. "I was wondering if I shouldn't just go back into the locker room, then come back out and start all over," he said amid the scribbling. "I never expected anything that bad. The harder I tried, the worse I got. Then finally I said to myself, well, shit, things could be worse. I could be in Israel getting shot at. At least I'm not going to die." And they say football players don't pay attention to current events.

When he was asked if he was bothered by the boos that cascaded down on him during that frightful first half, he said with a smile, "Nothing hurts my feelings anymore," not even the spite of the fickle fans, the people who were so enamored of him at the start of the game, and who loved him like a prodigal son at the finish.

October 4

The game against the Patriots—last year's AFC entry in the Super Bowl, still regarded by some as the conference's best team—was one of those contests with inherent sex appeal, at least as far as NBC was concerned. The network sent its first-

108

string commentators, Dick Enberg and Merlin Olsen, into town for the broadcast, and the game was aired across much of the country as the second half of an NBC doubleheader. Back in Boston, where they pay passing attention to football, at least before the Celtics start their season, overnight Nielsen ratings gave the game a 20.7 rating with a 41 share, meaning that just over a fifth of the city's television sets were in use on Sunday afternoon, and less than half of the sets that were on were tuned to the Broncos-Patriots contest. In Denver, on the other hand, on a gorgeous autumn day when suntans could still be procured, the television numbers were a 46.1 rating and an 85 share. Slightly less than half of *all* the television sets in the Queen City were spewing microwaves on Sunday afternoon, and *85 percent* of those were tuned to the events at Mile High Stadium. We can presume that porno tapes were being played on the inattentive 15 percent.

But if last Sunday's game was a big one, today's is simply gargantuan. It is an opportunity for Dan Reeves to post his fiftieth career victory, a chance for the Broncos to go 5–0, and to remain atop the AFC West. But those are just sidebars. The real story is that, for the first time, Reeves will face his old mentor, the legendary Tom Landry, head coach of the Dallas Cowboys since 1960—back when the franchise first rented office space. Reeves spent eight years playing under Landry as a free-agent running back, then ten years as an assistant coach and offensive coordinator before he came to Denver as head coach in 1981, a job that, despite his repeated denials, some say is just an apprenticeship before he one day returns to Dallas to replace a retiring Landry. "It would be nice to beat the guy I learned everything from and owe everything to," Reeves said this week as he sat in front of the Pepsi machine in the press trailer at the Broncos' training facility. But he didn't want to dwell on his personal interest in winning the game. "It's a long season," he said, "and this is just one more game you've got to win if you want to have a shot at the play-offs. The Cowboys are a football team that a lot of people like. If you can beat the

Cowboys, it's a nice feather in your cap, and I think our players realize that."

The people in the city of Denver and the state of Colorado probably wouldn't have put it quite that way. Beating the Cowboys, a club that somehow dubs itself "America's team," that represents a state whose caravans of citizens literally invade Colorado to ski and to hunt and to purchase real estate, that trounced the Broncos back in Super Bowl XII, wouldn't be so much like putting a feather in your cap as like putting the bastards back in their place. When it comes to the Cowboys, Broncos fans hold a grudge roughly the size of the Royal Gorge. Both go deep, one into physical, the other into psychic bedrock. To make the play-offs, the Broncos' primary goal is to beat the teams in the AFC West—the Raiders, Seattle, San Diego, and Kansas City. Beating the Cowboys would bring a richer pleasure—revenge. Never mind that the Broncos did beat the Cowboys 41–20 in Mile High Stadium in 1980, during Reeves's last year as a Dallas assistant. To avenge the Super Bowl loss in 1978, the Broncos will need to beat the Cowboys about seventeen times before the score is settled.

Given the magnitude of tomorrow's game, it isn't surprising that tickets have become so valuable they could be traded on the commodities market; good seats are going for about a hundred dollars, five times their face value. "It's amazing," says ticket manager Stuckey. "You can't imagine the number of calls we've gotten. There are more requests for tickets for this game than for any game since the Super Bowl season."

And CBS knows a hot item when it sees it. The network has sent its number one crew to Denver for the broadcast—play-by-play announcer Pat Summerall, plus former Raiders' head coach and current Lite beer pitchman John Madden, who will offer witty and insightful analysis of the contest—what is known behind the cameras as "color." Not only is CBS coveting the ratings it is virtually assured of getting in Colorado and the Lone Star State, this game has the makings of one they'll watch all the way from Sagaponack to Sausalito. CBS has made the

Cowboys the most widely watched team in professional football, and the network isn't about to lose ground tomorrow.

The Broncos' offices, training facilities, and practice field are located in unincorporated Adams County, just a long John Elway pass from the northern limits of the City and County of Denver, hard by Interstate 25, known hereabouts as the Valley Highway, in a part of town filled with furniture warehouses and the city's merchandise mart. Although it wasn't wilderness when the Broncos moved here in the early 1970s, the area was pastoral compared with its current heavy habitation by the Home Pride Bakery and Port-A-Built Barns & Cabins, the Colorado Remnant King, the Denver Tool Crib, and an enterprise called Randy's VW Stuff, to name a few of its better businesses. It isn't among the city's correct addresses (and Pat Bowlen is known to be looking for land in Denver's sprawling, mirrored-glass, glossy southeast sector, a former prairie where trees still look like novelties), but somehow the Broncos seem to belong in this working-class warehouse district where pretensions are few and aesthetics are simply unheard of.

The team's administrative offices are housed in an unassuming flat-roofed, cottonwood-shrouded, dark-brick building, its door suitably stained orange, its reception area containing the plaque signed by NFL commissioner Pete Rozelle certifying that the Broncos do indeed belong to the league. Across a quiet street is the huge, white, air-suspended bubble inside of which the team practices when the weather warrants; the long, metal prefab building, painted a Broncos blue, containing the players' lockers and the training room that looks like a little hospital; the two-story, burnt-orange brick building sporting a nightlighted, two-dimensional Broncos helmet and the words DENVER BRONCOS FOOTBALL CLUB on the side that faces the freeway, inside of which are the coaches' offices, the film facilities, the meeting rooms that make the place seem like a school, and the weight room, where a lot of iron is annually pumped; and the single-wide, wood-sided trailer, complete with picture windows, that is used exclusively by the press, but which was furnished and is maintained by the Broncos—a year-old arrangement that provides reporters with working space, as well as serving to keep them at bay. The players' and coaches' buildings and the press trailer shield from public view two 60-yard practice fields which are kept in immaculate shape by a full-time grounds-keeper, and that are the scene of suited-up, sweated-out practices on Wednesdays, Thursdays, and Fridays, and the scene of something that resembles recess on most Saturday mornings.

This morning, the players and their coaches met inside, as usual both in position groups and in a full-team meeting, the two sessions lasting from 8:00 until 10:30, when it was time to bust outside and get physical. As is their habit, the defensive players went to the far field and played a quick and sporting volleyball game, the defensive line versus the secondary, a derivation of the game played without a net and with an NFL football. The offensive players, still mindful of the sport they were paid to play, took things a little more seriously—Jack Weil, the punter, playing quarterback, heaving wounded-duck passes to anyone willing to break into a bit of a run; Jim Ryan, a linebacker, comically trying to make 20-yard field goals.

A few minutes later, with Pat Summerall and John Madden looking on in bemused amazement, Dan Reeves called both squads together and, with all the intensity of a substitute teacher, called for the members of a variety of special teams to take their positions—the field-goal unit, the punt-return unit, onside kick-off, onside return. Once that bit of rote business was out of the way, there was little left to do. The players circled around him and Reeves bade his men good-bye, then he asked them before they left to please "give something back to the community"— a ritual reference to the three hundred or so fans who waited behind ropes to be allowed to stream onto the field for the customary Saturday autograph session.

Virtually all of the players obligingly turned to walk toward the fans; then the fans were loosed and the two groups merged into a kind of feeding frenzy. John Elway was surrounded; Rich

112

Karlis, Tom Jackson, Steve Watson, and Ricky Hunley were in high demand; but surprisingly, it was John Madden, former head of the dreaded Raiders—these days seemingly second in sales pitches only to Ed McMahon—whose signature was the most sought after. Children and adults encircled him with great excitement, and he seemed to scribble his name very willingly, doing so until the field was empty of players and he and Reeves were the only two autographs still attainable. It was a curious sight—two men who a few years before would have been capable of drawing death threats in this city, each of them employed by hated rivals, now giddily celebrated where they stood on the Broncos' own north Denver turf, one a welcome visitor, the other a resident, a man who could win a mayor's race in a walk.

When you make a list of the famous sons of Sumter County, Georgia, I suppose you have to put the thirty-ninth president of the United States somewhere near the top. But leave room for Dan Reeves, whose red-dirt background is similar to Jimmy Carter's, yet whose success at the pinnacle of his profession has lasted a little longer. Reeves, forty-two, grew up on a 275-acre peanut, cotton, and corn farm outside Americus, Georgia, a family operation that required the young man, weakened by rheumatic fever, to learn how to work at an early age. "I'd get off the school bus and have to go plow for the rest of the evening," Reeves remembers. "That's the reason I played all three sports—so I wouldn't get home from school too early. I would have played more if there were more sports to play. I liked the farm life—I still do—but I knew I didn't want to be a farmer all my life."

The "All-Americus boy" played quarterback on his high school team, and was a good enough prospect to interest the legendary Paul "Bear" Bryant at Alabama—the dream coach of every scrappy southern kid who ever touched a football. Reeves also captured the attention of coaches and scouts from Georgia, Florida, and South Carolina. He ultimately signed a letter of intent with South Carolina because, well, they were the first to ask, and he was the Gamecocks' starting quarterback for four years. But if the college scouts had seen something in Reeves that interested them in 1961, the pro scouts were unimpressed in 1965, and his phone didn't ring on draft day.

But Reeves was driven to compete; he loved "anything where you have a winner and a loser." He signed a free-agent contract with the up-and-coming Dallas Cowboys, and he somehow made the team, not as a quarterback, but as a running back with speed that could only charitably be called moderate. What Dallas coach Tom Landry saw in Reeves was not only his toughness— he once practiced the morning after a bone chip had been removed from his knee—but also his uncanny understanding of a game that can be maddeningly complicated. "He thoroughly understood the concepts of what we were trying to do, more than just at his own position," Landry explained. "Very few players understand more than their own positions."

It was Reeves's savvy, his clear, analytical mind that kept him on the Cowboys' roster and that in 1970 helped make him a player-coach after a series of crippling knee injuries (and a rookie-of-the-year named Calvin Hill) had benched him as a first-string running back. When Landry passed over Reeves for the job of offensive coordinator in 1973—"Danny wanted too much too soon," said Landry, "he wanted to move too fast"— Reeves spent a year in the dangerous world of Dallas real estate. Then, more convinced than ever that football held his fortune, he returned to the Cowboys as a special-teams coach. By 1977, at age thirty-three, he had become Dallas's offensive coordinator and Landry's right-hand man, and it seemed certain that it was only a matter of time before someone snatched him away from the Cowboys to become a head coach himself. "He's always gotten the most out of what he's had," averred Landry of his prodigy with the Georgia accent. "He's got a great mind for football."

When Edgar Kaiser bought the Broncos in 1981, he shocked the followers and fans of the team by firing popular head coach

Red Miller as his first official act—a coach who in four seasons had done little more than lead the Broncos to an AFC championship, a division championship, and a wild-card playoff spot. But Kaiser wanted his own coach, someone whose tenure would be no longer than his own, and he promptly made Dan Reeves the youngest head coach in the history of the NFL by hiring him to captain the Broncos.

It wasn't surprising that the Broncos soon began to resemble the Cowboys—Reeves instituting in Denver an offense brought north from Dallas that was roughly as complicated as the theory of relativity, and managing the team with a stern and paternal style that reminded a lot of people of Tom Landry. Though he perceived himself as a players' kind of coach, he discovered that his particular brand of sidelines dictatorship didn't go over well with some of his lads on the field. "I'm extremely competitive," Reeves says in retrospect, "and I do a lot of hollering. When I was a player—and I was not a great player—if I was doing something poorly, I started hollering at myself. That's the way I did the players when I first got here. I guess a lot of them took it personally." Personally enough, it turned out, that veteran cornerback Louis Wright was eventually asked by his teammates to have a talk with the coach, to ask him to lighten up a little bit, and to explain that some of the younger players were actually afraid of him. Reeves did more than a little hollering at Wright during their meeting, but he also listened, and their interchange led to a kind of mellowing that has, after five seasons, made Reeves an effective and successful mentor, one whom his players like very much, even if few of them invite him over for backyard barbecues. "That meeting helped me understand that I wasn't exactly the way I perceived myself. Some of the players felt they couldn't come in to talk to me. You tell them your door is always open, but that doesn't mean much if they're afraid to come in. The biggest thing that meeting did was have me look at myself. I don't know how many people have actually sat down and evaluated themselves, but there's an awful lot of things you don't necessarily like. But football, to me, is a game of emotions. Somebody hits you hard, you get mad, you come back and hit them harder. Football's a game where you can get mad and still execute. That's the reason I love it."

And Dan Reeves, despite his fiery outbursts, or because of them, has been successful in Denver coaching the game he loves. Going into the Dallas game tomorrow, he is the most successful coach in Broncos history (winning forty-nine games, losing twenty-eight, a .636 percentage; Tom Landry's career percentage with the Cowboys is .639, so Reeves still has something to shoot at), and he has coached the Broncos longer than anyone else. "I think I learned from a great teacher," Reeves adds, "not only the X's and O's, but making executive decisions, handling things with dignity and class and building the respect of people across the country. I spent sixteen years with a great coach, and I think I got a great foundation."

Beginning last season, Reeves brought Landry to mind again when he began wearing sport coats and ties on game days, sometimes even wearing a suit, rivaling Landry for the first position on the NFL's best-dressed list. Reeves decided to spruce up his sidelines look as an experiment to see if nattier attire would help him keep his temper in check. By all indications a year later, you can dress Dan up, but you can't quiet him down—yet he seems to have grown comfortable in the guise of a stockbroker with a subscription to Gentlemen's Quarterly.

And Reeves has become comfortable in the state of Colorado. He says with some regularity that he believes he has the best job in the NFL; the region has enough golf courses to feed his off-season habit, and he is amassing a small fortune as a television adman, pitching Ford Broncos (get it?) and a line of Western wear regionally, as well as an antiperspirant in commercials aired around the country: "Never let the press pick your starting quarterback. Never take a last-place team too lightly. And never let 'em see you sweat."

The lines were written by a New York advertising agency, but they might have come from the private diaries of Dan Reeves. A man who prides himself—and with reason—on his organizational abilities, Reeves is a master of analysis and planning. He wants his players to "get better yesterday," yet he says that if he has to give them Knute Rockne speeches to do so, either he or they are in the wrong line of work. He is often disarmingly charming; he is warm and witty in private, but he can occasionally be as taciturn and stubborn as the Georgia mules with whom he was once well acquainted. He is endlessly willing to let reporters pester him with questions, but if the subject is one that irritates him, he is very likely to make the questioner feel like a fool. And despite his sartorial good taste and his square-jawed good looks, he is driven by a down-in-the-dirt competitiveness, by the kinds of anxieties, demands, and desires that can make less prepared people perspire.

October 6

It is a lesson of sport, and I suppose of life itself, that events that seem downright stellar in anticipation, often prove earthbound in actuality. This showdown in the Denver autumn between the undefeated Broncos and the 3–1 Cowboys, between the niggardly Denver defense and a Dallas offense that had scored at least thirty points a game so far this season, between the game's longest-tenured head coach and the Georgia farm boy in whom he had seen something special twenty-one years before, turned out to be nothing more than a football game, a lopsided scrap that made the Broncos look appealing and the Cowboys look appalling. It was one of those games in which the Broncos appeared so deceptively good that you'd think Pete

Rozelle ought to save us all a lot of trouble by giving them the Lombardi trophy a few months early, and in which the Cowboys seemed so deceptively bad that you'd think the once mighty "America's Team" shouldn't really claim much more geography than, say, suburban Irving, Texas, where the Cowboys play their home games.

This is the way Skip Bayless reported from the front in this morning's editions of the Dallas *Times Herald*:

> "Dynasty" is better than "Dallas." The Broncos have too much that the Cowboys don't—an orange blizzard of a rush, and a halfback of a quarterback, and a healthy, unheralded dream backfield, and a crowd and momentum that echoes through the Rockies. . . . Mile High Stadium is three decks built steeper than Pikes Peak, and Sunday's record 76,082 booed the 46 no-shows and stomped thunderously and took your breath like the snow-capped panorama with their love of the Broncos. The overall impact was awesome. The Cowboys didn't have a prayer.

What Bayless couldn't have known is that the fans *always* boo the no-shows; it's one of the rituals they delight in the most, when the official paid attendance is announced and they get their turn to shower their disdain on the scum who actually *had tickets* but didn't bother to come out to the ballpark. And those forty-six who were berated yesterday were the smallest number in history—that's how big this game seemed before it started. But when you stop to think about it, those forty-six fans probably deserve some sympathy. If you take any random group of 76,000 people on any random day, can't we assume that some of them are taken into police custody? Aren't some of them stranded by car wrecks? Surely some give birth, and more than a few have heart attacks. Some, no doubt, succumb. It seems, as a matter of fact, that, given the odds and the mere forty-six no-shows, a large number of people attended yesterday's game under some very trying circumstances. But there you are. When the Broncos have an opportunity, at home, to cream America's team, well, broken bones simply take a backseat.

By halftime, the score 22–0, with the Cowboys' star tailback Tony Dorsett standing on the sidelines in street clothes and starting quarterback Danny White watching the action with a badly sprained hip flexor, both of them injured the week before, the Dallas offense was faced with a pretty tall order. If they were going to score thirty points again this week, it would soon be time to get started. Yet backup quarterback Steve Pelluer, getting his first start, had never played this much professional football in his life, and you could tell he was considering a career change during the first two quarters, when he was relentlessly blitzed by defensive ends Rulon Jones and Andre Townsend, linebackers Ricky Hunley and Karl Mecklenburg, and safety Randy Robbins.

The Broncos did not exactly put on an offensive extravaganza themselves in the first quarter, getting nothing from three possessions. But in the second quarter, they broke open the corral gates, scoring a safety and three touchdowns, each of the touchdowns scored by Gerald Willhite, the fifth-year running back who first played football as a college freshman and who's beginning to look like he's getting a knack for the game. Willhite scored once on a single-yard run that followed a 50-yard pass reception by Mark Jackson, and caught two passes of his own for touchdowns, the second coming just before the whistle that signaled the half.

The Broncos blew cold again in the third quarter. Dallas managed a touchdown on a 3-yard ramble by Heisman Trophy–winner Herschel Walker midway through the period, but the Broncos increased the lead to 22 again early in the fourth when Gene Lang caught Elway's third touchdown pass of the day. The Cowboys came back with a final touchdown with five minutes to go in the game, but that was all they could muster before Louis Wright intercepted his second pass of the day, Mike Harden his first, and the Cowboys were down for the count.

Dan Reeves ran to the middle of the field and exchanged a few quick words with Tom Landry, then jogged away toward the locker room, raising his arms en route to celebrate the victory with the fans in the south stands who seemed to know what it meant to him. Reeves's players offered him a game ball in honor of his fiftieth win when he joined them in the jubilant locker room, and he told the massed reporters a few minutes later that "I've never had a more satisfying victory because there were so many things wrapped up in this one. I couldn't be happier. It's something special when it comes against the Cowboys—against a man I admire as much as I do Coach Landry. And yet, deep down inside I hurt a little bit. But I knew he was going to be out there trying to kick my teeth in. I certainly wanted to win, but I hurt because I know how competitive Coach Landry is."

An hour later, when the Dallas Cowboys were already en route to the airport and the television lights had been dimmed in the Broncos' locker room, the place almost empty now except for the reporters who still dogged John Elway, the bins of dirty, grass-stained uniforms, and the wads of adhesive tape that dotted the carpet, Reeves was still talking about what the day had meant, his grim game-face gone, the competitive set of his eyes replaced by signs of exhaustion. "Yeah, this has been an emotional day," he said in answer to a question. "And I'm an emotional person, even if I don't show it sometimes."

Did he aspire to a career in Denver similar to Landry's career in Dallas? someone wanted to know. "I hope I can do for Denver what Coach Landry has done for Dallas," he responded, his hoarse voice now growing reflective. "But I could win ten games a year for the next twenty years and still fall short. And yes. It'd be nice if in twenty years I had one of my students on the other side of the field."

Then at last Reeves left, climbing the concrete stadium steps that took him to a post-game party still in progress in the owner's suite, cradling a football in his forearm as he had done for years in Dallas.

October 12

This is getting a bit monotonous, the Broncos looking like a consummate football team, John Elway's heat-seeking missiles turning into a steady succession of touchdowns, a true running game returning after a long and rough hiatus, Denver's defense playing more aggressively than it ever has perhaps, six games now logged in the win column like so much mere formality.

Following today's game, a 31–14 rout of the Chargers in San Diego—a game so securely in the bag that scores of fans back home did the unthinkable, switching channels away from what was basically a boring football game to see the final innings of one of the best baseball games in history—the Broncos lead the league in scoring, they have a two-game edge over the Seattle Seahawks in the AFC West race, and they are one of only two undefeated teams in the NFL. To add to the excitement, a photograph of a scrambling John Elway, his tongue sticking out in trademark determination, graces the cover of *Sports Illustrated* this week, and a story inside by Paul Zimmerman once again raises the issue of the Super Bowl, for heaven's sake.

In the midst of the swelling euphoria, the only conceivable sore point, the only real problem at issue in the coaches' meetings and at the breakfast counters of myriad cafes, is Jack Weil's punting, which has gone from good in Greeley to mediocre against Dallas and San Diego. "The kind of punting we've had lately can get you beat," said Dan Reeves the day after the Dallas game. His words didn't prove prophetic against the Chargers, but if you stuck with the Broncos this afternoon, instead of switching to the brilliant Angels-Red Sox baseball play-off, you saw that Weil is a hometown boy in a bunch of trouble.

Although Jack Weil was the best collegiate punter in the nation in his senior year at the University of Wyoming two years ago, averaging 45.6 yards per kick, he hadn't been able to land a job with an NFL team until the Broncos swallowed hard and chose him over veteran punter Chris Norman as the season opened. The Broncos—the team he'd had his heart set on since his dad took him as a tyke to watch the legendary Floyd Little run the football in what was then called Bears Stadium—wanted *him* to be their punter. It seemed too wonderful to be true, and perhaps it was. After five games this season, Weil ranked twenty-second among the league's twenty-eight punters, averaging just 40 yards per kick and having little luck booting the ball out of bounds inside the 20-yard line. Somehow, it seemed, the demands of punting in pressure-cooker game situations were limiting Weil's ability to kick the ball.

Then Tuesday, the Broncos turned up the pressure a notch by inviting the recently released Norman and former Kansas City punter Jim Arnold to Denver for tryouts. The coaches presumably knew what Norman could do, but, for some reason, they wanted to see him one more time, and Arnold, also currently out of a football uniform, was the AFC Pro Bowl kicker in 1984. Yet, although both punters reportedly kicked well at the tryout—reporters were barred, as though it were a desert bomb test—Reeves announced at the end of the day that Norman and Arnold were already en route back home, and that Jack Weil remained the Broncos' punter. "He has too much talent not to get the job done," Reeves told the anxious reporters, who finally had a story with some grit to it in the midst of the Broncos' successes. "Maybe I'm to blame. I've mentioned a couple of times that I was disappointed and maybe that was putting too much pressure on him. He's the hometown boy whose dream came true. I think he's been trying too hard. Sometimes those dreams can be hard to live up to. But I think he'll get the job done, and now, he has a long time to prove he can get it done."

With word that their son had been reprieved, Weil's parents

went ahead with their plans to join the 5,000 or so Broncos fans who flew to sunny San Diego to see today's game in person. But Pat and Jack Weil, Sr., didn't enjoy the game much more than the 55,000 San Diego fans did. The young man who wears his lucky number 13 averaged only 34.1 yards on three punts, the shortest a 19-yard duck that sent Dan Reeves into silent agony.

It wasn't a *bad* football game; that adjective simply won't work when you win. And the Broncos continued to look like they may deserve their pre-season billing, falling behind by a touchdown early, then rebounding with 31 unanswered points before the Chargers got a second, face-saving touchdown with a little more than a minute to go in the game. The Broncos sacked the Chargers' geriatric quarterback Dan Fouts five times and intercepted two of his passes; John Elway threw for 242 yards and a touchdown; Sammy Winder ran for 74 yards and a touchdown of his own; and Mike Harden returned a punt for a late-game score. With the exception of Jack Weil's punting, the Broncos were remarkably well rounded, especially considering that they have a history of falling to piddling pieces on the opening kickoff in San Diego. If you follow the Broncos, you couldn't call it a bad game. Yet oh, how it paled in comparison to the ball-and-stick game they were playing in Anaheim Stadium, ninety miles up the coast.

The city of Denver has had its own baseball team for decades, but it has been the minor league Denver Bears. Other than an occasional exhibition game, major league baseball has never been played alongside the South Platte River. And that is a sore subject, not just among the region's baseball addicts, but also among a surprising coalition of politicians and business people who are convinced that Denver can't be a major league city without the secure presence of big-time baseball. Franchises that belong to the first tier of professional sports, they say—the NFL, the National Basketball Association, the National Hockey

League, and, of course, major league baseball—do far more than bring to a town a measure of prestige and a bit of idle entertainment. They are potent shots in the economic arms of their cities; they mean jobs and stadium leases and tax revenues, and they do a lot in the way of making out-of-town business people, conventioneers, and tourists aware of those cities and what they have to offer. If your football team makes the Super Bowl, or your baseball team the World Series, the rest of the country— at least for a week or so—simply can't ignore you.

In Denver's case, its football franchise seems firmly rooted, to say the least. The Denver Nuggets of the National Basketball Association, owned by Houston and Denver entrepreneur Sydney Shlenker and coached by the witty and mercurial Doug Moe, are one of that league's mid-level franchises, better than average on the court in recent years, better than bankruptcy-bound at the box office. The short-lived Colorado Rockies of the National Hockey League struggled here until they stole away to the Meadowlands a few seasons back. When the team's new owners decided that the New Jersey Rockies didn't sound quite right, they changed their name to the Devils.

But baseball. Baseball hasn't so much as given us a chance. In cities like Washington, D.C., currently bereft of baseball, they have at least had the opportunity to try a few teams before— failing financially—they have been transplanted like greenhouse seedlings to towns where they've grown and prospered. Then there are teams in towns like Cleveland and Pittsburgh, where ball clubs are gamely fielded each spring, as they have been for decades, but where nobody ever wins and nobody ever watches. And in Seattle, a western city not unlike Denver, they play baseball indoors during the only months of the year when the drizzle stops long enough to let people get out to see the light of day. So far, it's an experiment with sad results.

Yet in Denver, a city with lots of sunshine, with fans whose money is burning holes in their pockets, with civic leaders dying to prove that things here are up-to-date, where a whole generation of children is growing up without seeing George Brett or Mike Schmidt step up to the plate, without hearing the major league crack of the bat, there is no big-time baseball. It did almost arrive in the mid-1970s, when oil billionaire Marvin Davis—whose girth would have demanded some custom seating in the owner's box—came close to purchasing the Oakland As from fickle Charlie Finley. Money was no object—it never is with Davis—and the sale seemed so certain at one point that Davis's wife, Barbara, publicly discussed the color to which the As' yellow-and-green uniforms should be changed, but then Finley found trouble when he tried to get out of his Oakland Coliseum lease, and the deal and the move were off.

In the ensuing years, rumors have regularly circulated that Davis was about to buy the Chicago White Sox, the Pittsburgh Pirates, and most recently, the San Francisco Giants, but all such rumors have proved nothing more than expensive smoke. Beginning in the early 1980s, Denver's Dikeou brothers, cornerstones of a wealthy Greek-immigrant family, announced that they, too, would like to own the city's major league franchise. They started attending baseball owners' meetings around the country and they purchased the minor league Denver Bears to prove their interest in baseball. But when they renamed the team the Zephyrs—roughly equivalent in the minds of many old-time Denverites to switching from, say, "Yankees" to "Dipshits"—more than a few people wondered about their suitability.

Today, major league baseball in Denver remains a distant dream. The city government supports an official Denver Baseball Commission, whose job it is to capture a team by hook or by crook, but the commission, the Dikeou brothers, and Marvin Davis all seem to agree that there is little they can do but wait. Baseball commissioner Peter Ueberroth has said that baseball's National League is likely to expand by two teams someday down the road. Denver, Washington, Tampa, Indianapolis, Phoenix, Oakland, and New Orleans are all possible expansion cities, with Denver and Washington currently considered to have the inside track—Washington because of its political clout, Denver because of Marvin Davis. But baseball is nothing if not *delib-*

erate about making big decisions, and Denver's summer game fans seem certain to be watching the Zephyrs for a few more seasons.

Football, for now, is the only game in town, say a surprising number of people who forget or don't count the Denver Nuggets, and that, they go on, is the only reason in the world why the Broncos have become the phenomenon they have. If the city had a baseball team from the bigs, the goings-on in Greeley each summer would receive only a bare bit of the attention they do now, and at least until the baseball season ended in early October, the Broncos would have some stiff local competition. The sports consumers in this city would, with the larger selection of games and teams to watch, put the Broncos in a bit of perspective. Few would actually abandon them, but, so the thinking goes, those orange horses could no longer keep their emotional hold.

Nonsense, say those on the opposite side of the argument. Sure, a baseball team would do very well for a couple of seasons. Even a lousy expansion club could pack the house for a while. Then, fans would lose interest in this interloping loser of a baseball team, and that would be that. Oh, it would probably survive, and, likely as not, make a little money. But the Nuggets, a perennial play-off team (in a league where you have to be truly terrible *not* to make the play-offs), compete alongside the Broncos from mid-October until at least Christmas each year, and they steal little more from them than a bit of space in the sports pages. There really isn't any comparison between the city's successful basketball team and a team like the Broncos, in which literally millions of people have made such a strange and wonderful psychic investment. Why would a baseball team necessarily make more of an impact?

Because baseball is the national game, say the people on the other side. Then the discussion slides into bedlam.

126

October 15

___

The suburban city of Northglenn, its modest homes and middle-class cares and commitments anchored to a once grassy mesa north of Denver, can no longer boast that one of its own plays football in the NFL. Jack Weil, the Northglenn Bronco, was terminated today. He was "cut," in the football parlance, told by head coach Dan Reeves just prior to the team's noon classroom session that his services were no longer required. A week ago, Reeves had said that Weil would now have a long time to prove himself, to prove that his right leg could dependably whip a football into a high 40- to 50-yard arc, but the coach had also said there are no guarantees in this business. Although Reeves wouldn't contradict the latter statement, he surely wished today that he could erase the former one from the record. "I would have liked to have given Jack more of a chance than I did," Reeves told the reporters who crowded around him outside the coaches' building, "but I just felt like he was getting continuous pressure on him and wasn't handling it well. He was putting a lot of pressure on himself, and I didn't see him working his way out of it." Reeves was stony when he was asked why he hadn't given Weil the time to kick his way out of his slump that he had said he would. "When you've got forty-four people who are playing well and one guy who was struggling," he said, setting his jaw, "you need to make a change. You've got to try to get the forty-five best people you can, and I just felt Chris could make us better."

Chris Norman, the much-maligned punter who had spent two unspectacular seasons with the Broncos before being replaced by Weil at the start of the regular season, had been called at his home in Putney, Georgia, early this morning and offered a job. He was back in a Broncos uniform, sporting the new number 4, punting footballs at the end of the afternoon.

Jack Weil made a quick exit. He cleaned out his locker, had a brief departing physical, and stopped for a moment to talk with reporters as he left, his dreams ended for now. "I don't have any regrets," said the always soft-spoken young man, defeated but not vindictive, "not the way they handled me. They treated me fairly. You have to perform in the games, and I wasn't doing too well." Then he drove home to Northglenn, where he was still a high school hero, and where the Broncos had lost a few fans.

October 21

It would be misleading to say that the Broncos had those little town blues, but they were anxious to play in New York, New York, or nearby at least, to prove that they were A-number one, king of the hill, the top of the heap. And it did have all the appearances of a terrific matchup—the 6–0 Broncos against the impressive, 5–1 New York Jets at the Jets' home in a place called Giants Stadium, which is actually in New Jersey (things get complicated in Gotham), in front of a Monday night national television audience. The Broncos, a team made up almost exclusively (and presumably by accident) of small town and suburban boys from the West and the South, seldom play in the nation's media capital, and this was an opportunity to demonstrate that they build some good ballplayers out in the sage-brush. Besides, Reeves had reminded them of what Dallas coach Tom Landry had said back when Reeves was a player: Every great team eventually has to play in New York. Not that Reeves's own memories of playing the Giants in Yankee Stadium in the Bronx and the Jets in Shea Stadium in Queens were particularly sweet. If you grow up in Georgia, spend a four-year sojourn in South Carolina, then hightail it to Texas, you never really develop a particular enchantment with the city that never sleeps.

"I remember being with Walt," Reeves said, waxing nostalgic about his years as a player, when he, former rodeo cowboy Walt Garrison, and assorted hayseeds gave the Cowboys a decidedly rustic flavor, "back when Walt was a rookie. We got in a cab in New York one time and Garrison said to the guy, 'Hey, you know what I'd do if I lived here? I'd get me a job and work long and hard to save up enough money to buy me a gun and *blow my brains out.*' "

Reeves could be forgiven if Garrison's response to the plight of being in the big city came to mind again at about 12:30 this morning while he stood in a small supply room in the concrete bowels of Giants Stadium in the Meadowlands, surrounded by members of the tri-state sports media, all of them speaking in the strangest accents, all of them wanting to know how his Broncos could have been so thoroughly whipped, so successfully dominated by the Jets. "Well, if that's domination," said Reeves, the hair standing up on the scruff of his neck, the country boy not of a mind at the moment to back down like some sort of sissy, "then . . . then I'd like to meet them again on down the road sometime. I don't see it quite that way." When *Rocky Mountain News* reporter Steve Caulk asked him a few minutes later about Chris Norman's mediocre return engagement, Reeves was still angry and frankly not in a mood to talk to a bunch of damn bookworms who hadn't ever played the game. "I don't care to discuss the punting," he said, his demeanor like dry ice. "You guys do that yourselves. You do a good job of it." Then Reeves retired to the locker room, where his somber players

129

quickly showered and dressed (like Landry's Cowboys, the Broncos travel in coats and ties) for the long plane ride home to the backwoods West.

Perhaps the reason Reeves didn't think the Broncos were dominated by the Jets was that he had already forgotten the first half, played a few hours earlier, when the day was still Monday and the Broncos were still in some sort of bright lights trance. It was a half in which the lads from Denver managed only one first down and a total of only 24 yards of offense while the Jets bombed them from a low altitude, scoring two touchdowns, two field goals, and a safety, making the vaunted Denver defense look like little more than orange hicks from the sticks. At halftime, when the Broncos briefly escaped the pretzels and bagels that were being flung at them by the Jets' deranged but happy partisans, they trailed 22–0.

And although the Jets didn't score again in the game, they managed to keep control of the ball, keep Denver's heretofore high-scoring offense away from the end zone all but one time, and keep John Elway from causing aerial trouble by making him run for life. For the first time in fourteen consecutive games, Elway did not throw a touchdown pass.

The Jets' defensive end Bruce Bennett also tried to contain the Denver quarterback by thoroughly cleaning his clock. When he grabbed Elway in the end zone for the safety, he lifted him into the air, then slammed him onto the hard carpet, Bennett forgetting for an instant that this wasn't All-Star Wrestling. Bennett's outburst earned him a personal foul as well as the sudden angry attentions of Broncos guard Keith Bishop, Elway's close friend and on-field protector. But while Bishop and Bennett rolled on the AstroTurf, their fists flailing, Bishop suggesting to Bennett that he ought not try that again, one of Bennett's punches landed on Bishop's throat, splitting his larynx, causing him to spit up blood and leaving him nearly speechless. Bishop left the game, and the team doctors quickly assessed his injury as being relatively mild, despite the loss of his voice. Yet they cautioned him that he shouldn't even try to speak; a spasm of his damaged larnyx could shut off his airway.

And as if the game wasn't grim enough, Bishop's fellow guard Mark Cooper tore a ligament in his foot when the stadium's turf grabbed his shoe and didn't let go, linebacker Karl Mecklenburg suffered a deep thigh bruise that took him out of the game, and Elway a concussion that briefly took him out of the eastern time zone.

Following a 13-yard gain on a quarterback draw early in the fourth quarter, Elway was inadvertently sandwiched between Jets' tackler Harry Hamilton and his own teammate, Gerald Willhite, who was attempting to provide him a block. After the collision, Elway said later, "I remember sitting there on the field. I knew I was a little woozy, so I sat there for a minute. But then I got to the sideline, and I don't remember anything after that." He didn't return to the ball game, and it's probably just as well that he couldn't remember the rest of it—it wasn't the sort of football anyone would call memorable—but Elway's injury was potentially serious enough that the trainers and doctors monitored him closely on the sidelines, in the locker room after the game, and on the flight home. "I cleared up after the game," Elway said, "and I slept some on the way home. But I still don't remember parts of it."

The Jets' fans did little to endear themselves to the struggling Broncos when they cheered the announcement that Elway had suffered a concussion. It was not a moment that did New York and New Jersey proud, though it may well have been quintessential, and it wasn't very surprising, given the barrage of objects that pelted the players on the sidelines throughout the game. "They were throwing pretzels, Oreo cookies, tennis balls. Shit, it was a rough bunch," said linebacker Ricky Hunley. "But that's football. I'd never played in New York. I didn't know what to expect. But it was fun. I like being on that end of it, where you've got the crowd against you, throwing things at you. It gives you the incentive to fight back. I get pumped up for it."

But as the Broncos' charter lifted off the runway at Newark

International Airport at about 2:30 A.M., an exhausted Dan Reeves—another bad trip to the big city under his belt—wasn't about to use the word "fun" to describe the New York fans. "I've never heard so much foul language, so many four-letter words, coming from the stands," he said. "Everywhere you go, you hear people shouting things from the stands. That's all part of it. But these were organized cheers, people screaming four-letter words in unison, and making the hand signals to go along with them. It was amazing. That must be the reason they call the New York teams the Mets and the Jets. They're four-letter words. The people in the stands can spell them."

His Broncos, now sleeping like babies in the back of the plane, were no longer undefeated. They had played their worst football of the season; they had squandered the opportunity to make a lasting impression on sportswriters and teams around the country, to intimidate people a little, as Reeves liked to say; and they had lost a game that, come time for play-off pairings, could come back to haunt them. Four key players had been banged up, and they faced the tough Seattle Seahawks in just five short days. But their DC-8, cruising against the jet stream, was headed westward, and there probably wasn't much reason to get a job and buy a gun.

October 26

I declined the offer of champagne served in plastic stemware for the ride up the elevator to the penthouse suites; it was a workday even if it was Sunday, reason enough to be abstemious. But I did enjoy the duet performed by a harpist and flutist, both dressed in black evening gowns, while I waited in the entryway. Somehow, it just wasn't your everyday elevator music. And the people I joined for the express ride up weren't your usual celebrants in "Raider Hater" T-shirts and hats made out of beer cans. This was a more sedate crowd, everyone in a kind of carefully harnessed good humor, their orange apparel limited— if visible at all—to silk scarves pinned with brooches and baggy-sleeved golfing cardigans. There wasn't a cap on a single head, as best I could survey.

When the doors opened onto the foyer of the lower level of the penthouse suites, we were greeted by Pat Bowlen's Frederick Remington bronze sculptures, mounted on slim pedestals, and by servers in starched white shirts and orange bow ties who offered us more complimentary libations. Mustering still more resolve, I declined again and made my way down the long corridor to number 13, the Adolph Coors Company suite, past doors with bronze nameplates identifying lessees as diverse as Coast To Coast Hardware and First Interstate Bank; as competitive as the *Denver Post* and the *Rocky Mountain News*, as *fiercely* competitive as MCI and US West (a consortium of Bell system companies); past the cola wars waged by Coke and Pepsi.

Inside the Coors suite, where I was greeted by Coors' community affairs director John Fellows, who had kindly agreed to let me crash the company's party, the guests were donning name tags and milling in front of the cold cuts; many cradled soft drinks in their hands; surprisingly few were drinking the company's own refreshment.

Near the entrance to the suite were a secluded restroom and coat closet, and a small kitchen separated by a long bar from the carpeted lounge with its two cocktail tables and chairs. Against the bank of windows that formed the suite's eastern wall, twenty-four plush theater seats offered a panoramic view of the field—seemingly *straight* below us—the sunlit eastern arc of the stadium and, beyond and still higher, the towering buildings downtown. Three television monitors, one above the bar,

133

the others at the upper corners of the windowed wall, were dark now, but would soon show replays of game action, as well as show the game in its entirety to those who preferred the vantage of television. And it was a difficult choice to make, I discovered when the game began, the Broncos jumping out to a 10–0 first-quarter lead over the Seahawks. Should I choose the distant but straightforward eye-to-action view out the windows, or the distilled, crisp, and close-up images offered by the video screens? It would prove to be a luxurious game-long dilemma.

Today was "Orange Sunday," as officially proclaimed by Denver mayor Federico Peña—a day of civic note devoted to the football team, an occasion on which fans were implored to wear orange (as if they wore clothes of any other color on any other Sunday), and each was offered an orange pom-pom at the ticket gates, provided courtesy of the *Denver Post* and the Adolph Coors Company, two local businesses that are indebted to the Broncos for a not insignificant portion of their sales. At the base of the bowl of orange, the 5–2 Seahawks were battling the 6–1 Broncos for a share of the lead in the AFC West, and outside the stadium a few minutes before, on this last home-game day before the November general election, the state's senatorial and gubernatorial candidates had been battling for the partisans' votes. Shoot, there hadn't been a day this momentous since the Dallas game three weeks ago—the last time the Broncos were in town.

At 1:00 this afternoon, as people streamed toward the stadium from every direction, the politicians took their strategic places— Colorado Springs Congressman Ken Kramer, the Republican candidate for the U.S. Senate seat held by retiring Gary Hart, stood at the corner of Bryant and Seventeenth streets in a cheerleader's sweater that was a match to the one Dan Reeves is partial to, waving broadly at the cars that passed, shaking hands with Broncos-bound passersby, the signs held by supporters who stood beside him making it clear who the glad-hander was. His

134

Democratic opponent, Boulder Congressman Tim Wirth, an ally of Hart's and currently edging Kramer in the polls—the race far too close to call—was positioned farther up the hill near Seventeenth and Federal, alongside the stream of pedestrians who made their way from the westside Hispanic neighborhood to the stadium. Hart himself, a senator for two months more, and currently the front-runner for the Democratic nomination for president in 1988, strolled the crowded sidewalks in an orange sweater, sporting a blue Wirth placard mounted on a stick, shaking hands with the citizens who recognized him, signing autographs so often you'd guess he was an aging wide receiver. His near miss to Walter Mondale in the 1984 campaign had earned him a notoriety in his home state that he never seemed to have had before. Coloradans, like all Americans, seem to have this thing for losers.

State Treasurer Roy Romer, the Democratic gubernatorial candidate, seemed the model of practicality as he and his supporters passed out thousands of paper "Romer For Governor" visors on this sun-drenched day. Kathy Arnold, Republican candidate for lieutenant governor, campaigned in her running mate's stead, passing out Broncos-orange balloons that just happened to mention the Strickland and Arnold ticket. Single-engine airplanes chugged through the clear sky overhead, trailing bright banners that lauded the merits of one and all.

For the office seekers, this pre-game Broncos crowd provided the ultimate flesh-pressing opportunity—better than dozens of county fairs or fund-raising cocktail parties, better than hundreds of issues forums or shift-change hours at factory gates. Fully one-seventh of the population of the city of Denver was converging on this single spot before the game, about one-twentieth of the metropolitan population, more voters by far than these political hopefuls had encountered in all their months of campaigning. And although the crowd seemed far more interested in crushing the Seahawks than in making America strong again or getting us out of Nicaragua, they took the campaigning in festive stride, accepting the freebies without complaint, occa-

135

sionally telling a candidate they were with her all the way, rarely telling another he, by God, ought to be deported. After all, contests were contests, weren't they? Kramer versus Wirth just wasn't all that different from the Broncos versus the Seahawks. Each to his own kind of competition. You simply decided who to root for, then waved the appropriate pom-pom.

Mile High Stadium sits on a flat floodplain that was an asparagus field fifty years ago; the area was once spotted with the false-front shacks that supplied the gold rush a century in the past, and 150 years before, it was a small piece of the wild and unsettled piedmont country ranged by the Cheyenne and Arapaho.

There wasn't a particularly compelling geographic reason for a town to spring up at the spot where a prairie stream called Cherry Creek emptied into the small mountain-born river called the South Platte—no logical reason except that minuscule quantities of gold were found near the confluence of the two waterways. But the contiguous villages of Denver City, Auraria, and Cherry Creek, which sprang up on the heels of the gold fever, proved to be efficient supply stations for the true gold rush that soon was under way in the mountains thirty miles to the west. When the Denver Pacific Railroad was completed in 1870, connecting the now joined and incorporated towns, called Denver by mutual agreement, with rail lines in Kansas and Wyoming, the city's future as a natural resources supply and distribution center was forged for the subsequent century.

Gold boomed, then busted. Silver boomed, then suffered the same fate. Homesteaders, cowboys, and cattle barons made agriculture into a going concern at the turn of the century, then a world war spurred demand for lead, iron, and other hard minerals that ran in elusive veins through the mountain ranges. Mining busted again in the thirties, along with agriculture and everything else under the sun, then another world war brought them back again with a profiteering and patriotic flourish, and the end of the war saw a boom in a strange new mineral called

136

uranium. A kind of checkered prosperity continued in the hard metals and cattle markets in the 1950s; petroleum booms came and went in the early 1960s and middle 1970s. The nascent communications and data-processing era brought a boom of a white-collar kind in the early years of the current decade.

Through all the surges and disasters, the rises and falls of fortune during its first century and a quarter, Denver has served as the region's supply center and transportation hub, as well as its financial ballast. It has become the Rocky Mountain region's only real urban environment (though the denizens of Salt Lake City would argue against that strenuously), yet its metropolitan population of 1.8 million ranks it only twenty-second among American cities—smaller by half than Houston, a million people smaller than Miami, smaller than Seattle and Tampa, larger by a bit than twenty-third-place Cincinnati.

At the end of the 1980s, most of the city's residents have come from elsewhere (though a few sport NATIVE bumper stickers on their cars as badges of parochial honor) and are employed in the largest numbers by the federal government, communications and commodities companies, aerospace and defense firms, schools and universities, real estate development, construction, and the retail trades. Denver isn't now and never has been much of a manufacturing town, and its ties to the reeling agricultural industry grow more tenuous every year. It is a curious blend of red-brick midwestern rationality and lustrous West Coast experimentation, a city that appears stodgy and bold by turns, a place inhabited by preservationists as well as break-all-the-molds modernists, one where politics move on a steady pendulum from innovation to frightened reaction. Like all cities, it is a place of contrasts and stubborn conflicts.

The city itself is heavily Democratic—it has returned Congresswoman Pat Schroeder to Washington by huge margins for five, going on six consecutive terms—and its ring of suburbs is largely Republican. The state has had a Democratic governor for twelve years (and seems certain to elect another Democrat for at least four more in ten days' time), yet the legislature resembles a Republicans-only club. Denver mayor Federico Peña, the first Hispanic to hold the job, a boyish, mere button of a man, who runs marathons for relaxation and who exhorts his fellow citizens to "imagine a great city," was the underdog winner of the race in 1983 over a longtime city district attorney, and the incumbent mayor, William McNichols, a consummate, cigar-chomping old pol who held the post for fifteen years and who was never convinced of the rationale for doing business outside the confines of the back rooms. Peña's administration has been a popular one at times, but a swing back in the conservative direction already seems under way, and a handful of candidates are anxious to try to wrest the office from him in May 1987. Although none are campaigning with the words "imagine a great cow town," there is no question that his political foes see Peña's modestly liberal programs as the road to wreck and ruin.

And if Denver can boast a sound—if recently slumping— economy, relatively low unemployment and decent incomes, vibrant inner-city neighborhoods, good schools and medical services and museums, a lively arts community and a model, if underfunded, park system, the city also has to acknowledge some serious problems. Largely because of its altitude and its citizens' devotion to their cars, Denver's air often has the most harmful carbon dioxide levels of any city in the country; Los Angeles is the only metro region whose air quality is worse overall. Denver's per capita crime rate places it fifth in the nation; the city's outskirts are dotted with toxic waste dumps; its airport (the fifth busiest in the world) is in serious need of replacement; its transportation system lags years, decades some say, behind its needs; and the city's racial minorities—the 15 percent who are Hispanic and the 5 percent who are black— are chronically undereducated and underemployed.

Yet what you can fundamentally say about Denver is that, despite its problems, it is young and still becoming. It is a town that is only now defining itself. It isn't confronted with once integral industries that are now in terminal, dream-shattering decline, or with once stable populations now set adrift from security and opportunity. Its problems are still those of the frontier—people streaming full of aspirations into a place that is never ready for them when they arrive, that has to play a kind of constant civic catch-up, a place where the newcomers have no constraints, but little or nothing to offer security. Growth is both Denver's boon and its biggest problem, and because of that fundamental fact, the city makes a steady, sometimes maddening string of mistakes. Yet its appeal, and perhaps its ultimate hope, is its constant flux.

If you wanted to spend a Sunday afternoon with Denver's current corporate chic, its vanguard of movers and shakers, you wouldn't have joined the Coors family and guests for the Seattle game. They are old Denver, not new, and besides, Coors beer is actually the product of Golden, Colorado, for much of its history a town a distant twelve miles away, now a suburb that has to struggle to claim its own identity. And although the Coors brewery is one of the metro region's biggest private-sector employers, the company's state and local taxes more than merely substantial, the publicly owned but still family-controlled business eschews glitz and glamour in favor of promoting All-American values (which include drinking a little beer and watching a little football) and quietly influencing the direction of American politics.

As the frontier town of Denver was bustling with the prospector trade in 1868, a Prussian native named Adolph Herman Joseph Coors was arrested in New York for having stowed away on ship from Hamburg. Coors was able to make a deal that allowed him to remain in the United States if he worked off the cost of his passage. After his debt was paid he, like thousands of other immigrants, made his way west to the wild gold camps where, so the stories held, riches awaited everyone. But Coors didn't want to mine for gold. A brewer's apprentice in his homeland, he envisioned making his fortune by slaking the thirsts of the miners. He settled in Golden, a town on the stage route from Denver to the booming burgs of Blackhawk and Central City, a locale from which he could ship kegs of his pilsener beer to Colorado Territory's many settlements and where water from Clear Creek was plentiful.

When Coors produced his first beer in 1873, there were nearly two thousand breweries in operation in the United States; virtually every village of modest size could claim one; Colorado itself had dozens. But the beer business, like so many others, was destined for consolidation and for the free-market survival of only the fittest. A little more than a century after it began its operations, Coors, still governed by Adolph's great-grandsons, Joe and Bill (*their* children in charge of day-to-day management), is a survivor. The fifth-largest brewing company in the country, Coors is one of only a few dozen that remain.

Coors's success hasn't been by accident, nor have its brewing waters always been clear. A public company for little more than a decade now, the brewery has always been operated precisely to suit the instincts of its controlling family—instincts that, by and large, have been remarkably good. The beer achieved a kind of national cachet in the early 1970s precisely because the family refused to distribute it too widely. Since it was almost impossible to obtain in much of the country, it took on the renown of something special; it was a beer that was brewed with pure Rocky Mountain water and perhaps a bit of magic.

But at the same time that the Coors mystique flourished outside the West, charges mounted at home that members of the Coors family were racists; dissidents claiming the brewery's hiring practices proved that they were, and black and Hispanic activist groups organized vocal boycotts. When their boycotts were joined by the efforts of the AFL-CIO, long unhappy with the nonunion brewery, Coors's sales slipped markedly, and the company was forced to begin a massive marketing campaign designed both to praise the beer and to alter the image of the company that produced it. Before long, the beer was being advertised in Spanish, and newspaper ads featured personal profiles of minority employees.

Although the company never softened its nonunion stand, it did make a concerted effort to increase its minority and female employment, and it even went so far as to welcome CBS's "Sixty Minutes" for a snoop around its operations. Bill and Joe Coors took lessons on how to be interviewed; company employees devoted lunch-hour sessions to explaining what a great place to work Coors was, and Mike Wallace of "Sixty Minutes" came away shaking his head, confessing that he hadn't been able to uncover any dirt, saying it looked damn near like a model corporation.

The effects of the boycotts slowly ebbed, Coors's sales bounced back, and the beer is now marketed in forty-seven states. The company is about to open a bottling plant in Virginia, its first operation of any kind outside its mammoth gray plant in Golden. Yet Coors beer will never be everyone's political draught of pilsener. Although the company recently announced that it is ending its long-standing use of polygraph tests on prospective employees, it is considering replacing them with drug tests. And Joe Coors and his wife Holly continue to be very active in conservative Republican politics. They played a key role years ago in convincing an actor and former California governor that he was presidential timber, and have been part of an informal kitchen cabinet during the Reagan administration.

Specifically because of Coors family politics, it is easy to find people in Denver and the state of Colorado who won't consider drinking their right-wing swill. Not on your life, they won't. But you encounter many more who, out of a firm regional pride, purchase nothing else. There are those who drink Coors simply because they are partial to its taste, and there are those who drink it because Coors for so long has supported the Broncos. The company is the longtime sponsor of the Broncos' media guide, as well as the annual highlight film which is offered free of charge to schools and Kiwanis clubs around the region. Although a variety of beers are sold at Mile High Stadium, 75 percent of the beer that is consumed during three-quarters of play is Coors. (Sales are shut off at the beginning of the fourth

141

quarter in the hope that people will drive home without severe impairment.) At an average game, Coors dispenses 500 sixteen-gallon kegs of beer, and an almost equivalent amount is poured out of aluminum cans—12,000 gallons or so in total if the game is good and the weather warrants.

I was drinking a Coors beer myself at the start of the second quarter—more as a sort of research project than a political statement—and I was enjoying the hospitality of the Coors family; these people clearly were not the Draconian upper crust they sometimes were made out to be. Joe and Holly Coors, sons Joe, Jr., and Peter and their families, had come to witness the battle against Seattle, and, together with brewery employees who had won awards, distributors whose sales had earned them invitations, assorted business associates, and friends, they settled in for some serious watching. This decidedly was not a penthouse suite where the game was a kind of backdrop and the cocktail chatter carried the day. The lead in the AFC West was on the line, and the Broncos took precedence over less compelling topics.

Early in the second quarter, the horses up, ten-zip, disaster seemed to strike when Seattle's Eric Lane blocked a Chris Norman punt; Seahawk Paul Skansi recovered the ball and returned it 11 yards for a touchdown, but the score was nullified when the play was called back because of a pre-punt holding penalty—a ruling that Seattle coach Chuck Knox screamed was a hometown call.

Knox was again infuriated early in the third quarter when, Denver leading 13–0 now, Seattle quarterback Dave Krieg's 13-yard pass to Ray Butler was called back, this time for an illegal screen by Byron Franklin. But not only was his team getting jobbed, as far as Knox was concerned, neither could they muster much in the way of an offense, and he wasn't a happy man. The Hawks did get two Norm Johnson field goals before the Broncos opened the fourth quarter with two Elway passes to Steve Watson, each for 16 yards, followed by a 34-yard touchdown taken from their fat notebook of "gotcha" plays—Elway handing off to Sammy Winder, who pitched to Steve Sewell running a reverse to the left, who lateraled to Elway, who had dropped back deep, and who sent a cannon shot to Vance Johnson—back at work catching footballs following his knee injury—who leapt above the goal line, battling Seattle defender Patrick Hunter, and who somehow came down with the ball. Broncos 20, Seattle chagrined.

But the Broncos couldn't scrape up any more points, and, with 2:34 to go in the game, Seattle mounted a four-pass-completions-in-four-tries, 71-yard drive culminating in a touchdown that narrowed the score to 20–13. Reeves sent his onside kick-return team onto the field with instructions to treat the ball like a gold brick, but Seattle somehow recovered the ball—or so it seemed until the replay officials in the booth determined from the videotape that the ball had not traveled ten yards, as required, before a Seattle player touched it. When referee Gordon McCarter announced the ruling, the touchdown denied in Pittsburgh was formally forgiven and forgotten by every Broncos partisan in the place.

Seattle had to kick again, and this time safety Randy Robbins smothered the onside kick and the Broncos retained possession. With Seattle out of time-outs, John Elway then took three snaps from center, three times dropped to his knee, and the game was history.

The Broncos had escaped by just seven points, but they had thoroughly trounced the Seahawks in the statistical department—evidence, if you ever needed it, that statistics alone have a hard time winning football games. John Elway, completing eighteen passes for 321 yards and a touchdown, had his most productive day of the season; Steve Sewell rushed for 26 yards and caught four passes totaling 52; Steve Watson's four catches accounted for 61 yards; Rulon Jones had two sacks of his own and shared a third with Freddie Gilbert.

The only individual Bronco who had what you'd have to call a bad day was Chris Norman, whose punting average after two games back with the team is slightly poorer than Jack Weil's six-game average—despite some special tutoring: On Wednesday of this past week, the Broncos brought to town one Ray Pelfrey of Sparks, Nevada (not an NFL stronghold), a reputed "punting guru" who operates an off-season school called Professional Kicking Services. Pelfrey, a former punter with the Green Bay Packers, assessed Norman's kicking style, then suggested he adjust the way in which he releases the ball from his hands, as well as supplying him with the special lightweight punting shoe that Pelfrey markets.

And as far as Pelfrey was concerned, Norman came away from the Seattle game with a good performance, especially considering the fact he was trying a new technique. Dan Reeves, far from willing to entertain the notion that the switch in punters might have been a mistake, called Norman's performance a sound one as well. Reeves wasn't about to reopen that particular can of worms—at least not after a win on Orange Sunday that gave the Broncos a two-game lead in their division, that leaves them undefeated against division opponents and 7–1 overall at the halfway point in the season. No, life could be worse out West.

The lights in the Coors suite were off when I looked up from the field an hour after the game. Monday was a school day, an office day at the brewery, and the Sunday afternoon festivities were curtailed by 6:00. But there was plainly something to celebrate in more than a few of the sixty suites that sit atop the stadium like a long horizontal high rise. Music wafted through windows that were still open to this balmy night, and you could see groups of people—cocktails, Coors, and Coronas in their hands—engaged in animated post-game conversations, which by now probably had more to do with limited partnerships and tax deferrals than with the Denver Broncos.

Save for the sea of refuse the fans had left behind, the bleachers below the penthouse suites were empty now, dark and abandoned except for the few boys in sweatshirts who were collecting discarded pom-poms.

November 8

—

The Broncos were in Los Angeles last Sunday, preparing to play the Raiders for the second time this season, when the story broke back home. Careful to prevent the *Rocky Mountain News* from picking it up, the *Post* withheld the story from all but its final Sunday edition. And it went so far as to copyright the front-page account by Broncos-beat writer Joseph Sanchez that ran beneath a banner headline. BRONCOS WANT ELWAY FOR LIFE, it read, and beneath it was a subhead that proved to be problematical: WILL OFFER $17 MILLION-PLUS CONTRACT WHEN SEASON ENDS.

In an interview conducted on the Friday before the story appeared, Joe Sanchez had asked Broncos' owner Pat Bowlen whether the team planned to renegotiate Elway's contract a year before it expired, a practice that has been something of a policy during Bowlen's tenure. Bowlen said yes, the club planned to meet with Elway's agent, Marvin Demoff, at the end of the current season. "As far as I'm concerned," he told Sanchez, "John's going to be around here for the duration of his career, and maybe after that as well. I have no intention of having him go elsewhere."

At the opening of training camp in Greeley, Bowlen had told a group of reporters that he hoped to come to terms with Elway

145

and his agent on a new contract well in advance of the expiration of his current one, but his comments to Sanchez about what is known in the sports world as a "lifetime" contract were new, and they were the heart of Sanchez's story. In speculating about what Elway might earn from a career-long contract, Sanchez did a little simple arithmetic. Elway currently earns $1 million a year. If he were to sign a ten-year contract (a good guess as to how many more years he might play), the minimum his salary could appreciate each year would be 10 percent, according to the NFL Players Association's current agreement with the league, making such a hypothetical contract "worth well over $17 million, not counting interest on deferred money, or any bonus money," Sanchez wrote. He didn't discuss dollar amounts with Bowlen, but he did quote the team's owner as saying that "signing him is just a function of John wanting to be here and a function of us paying him what he's worth. I think I've proven that I'm the kind of owner who's going to pay a guy what's fair."

Yet somehow, perhaps because he wished he was doing something else on a Saturday night, the *Post*'s headline writer decided Sanchez had written that the Broncos "will offer $17 million-plus," which he clearly hadn't. Sanchez was convinced the salary story was a good one, a legitimate one, but the headline rankled, he said, because it was wrong.

The Sunday *Post* story would initiate a storm of discussion in Denver during the coming week. Competing reporters would say it was old news; the Broncos' general manager would strangely say that you can't negotiate lifetime contracts; the *Rocky Mountain News* would first ignore the story, then take pains to say that the story its readers presumably didn't know about wasn't true; and columnists and radio talk show hosts would have several heydays, debating just how good Elway was, comparing him with the league's other outstanding quarterbacks, and speculating about just how much he really was worth. But first their attentions were distracted by a meeting in Los Angeles's Me-

Quarterback John Elway

Head Coach Dan Reeves

Veteran linebacker Tom Jackson in his last season

Reeves and Elway confer on the sidelines at Mile High Stadium

Club owner Pat Bowlen

All-Pro linebacker Karl Mecklenburg in the second Raiders game

Defensive end Rulon Jones battles Cincinnati Bengal Rodney Holman

Elway prepares to pass in the home game against Seattle

morial Coliseum, a negotiation of another sort attended by John Elway.

It was a Broncos-Raiders game, all right, but somehow it didn't live up to its billing. In the last six meetings between these two AFC West rivals, the team leading at half-time had lost the game; the final point differential had been three points or fewer; four times the games ended in sudden-death overtimes. Every Broncos-Raiders game had become a guaranteed rip-snorter. It was academic, as Lester "The Molester" Hayes would say.

This one, however, just didn't have the stuff. Neither team was at its best on Sunday, November 2, in front of a rare capacity crowd in the Coliseum, but the Broncos were a damn sight better. The Raiders—who had won five games in a row after starting the season 0–3—playing with a hobbled Marcus Allen and without defensive end Howie Long, squandered four opportunities to score from inside the Denver 30, lost two fumbles, suffered 69 yards in penalties, and quarterback Marc Wilson was sacked four times and was intercepted four times as well, once for a touchdown by Broncos cornerback Mike Harden. Apart from that, they did enjoy the warm 81-degree weather.

But the Broncos weren't merely lucky. For every Raiders' turnover, you could credit a Denver defense that played "with its ears pinned back," to quote Rulon Jones, who was sidelined with a sprained knee. The Denver defense gave up a whopping 407 yards in total offense, yet it surrendered only ten points— a first-quarter field goal and a fourth-quarter touchdown pass from Wilson to tight end Todd Christensen.

And although the Broncos' offense didn't necessarily look like a steamroller itself, its 80-yard touchdown drive in the second quarter, coupled with a 72-yard touchdown drive in the third, would have been enough to give Denver the win even without Mike Harden's fourth quarter heroics, which brought the game-end score to 21–10. Eleven points—an absolute blowout by one of these two teams over the other.

147

And what of John Elway, who back in Colorado was being called "the $17 million man"? Well, his first pass of the day was incomplete. But then he completed eleven in a row—every single pass he threw for the rest of the afternoon—including a 53-yard cannon shot to rookie Mark Jackson that set up the first touchdown.

"Elway's unstoppable," said Lester Hayes—the defender whom Jackson beat to make the catch—in the Raiders' locker room after the game. "He does things I've never seen before, and I've got lots of film. Without Elway, they wouldn't be 8–1. That thought's null and void. As long as he stays healthy, that team has the possibility of going 15–1. He's a step beyond stupendous. I think he's euphoric, even at sea level." You got the impression that the Raiders' quotable cornerback rather respected Denver's number 7.

In the Broncos' locker room, Gerald Willhite was in agreement. "In years to come, John will be the best that ever was," said the running back who had somehow held on to four of Elway's frozen ropes, "if he isn't that already."

On Tuesday, *Rocky Mountain News* beat reporter Steve Caulk, without mentioning the *Post* or Joe Sanchez, said that Broncos' general manager John Beake, interviewed the day before, had "discredited a report about an impending 'lifetime' contract for quarterback John Elway." According to Beake, by way of Caulk, "in the world of football, there's no such thing as a lifetime contract. There are a lot of ramifications about how contracts can be structured. They have to be limited to a [specific] length." But Beake did make it clear that he and Bowlen had been discussing how Elway's services could be retained for the rest of his career. The distinction seemed rather fuzzy.

Come Wednesday, as if to bolster Joe Sanchez from the battering he was getting, *Post* columnist Buddy Martin reported: "Despite Beake's rantings and ravings about the Sanchez story being 'out of context,' I have it on good authority that the

Broncos intend to do just as Sanchez wrote: make it possible for Elway to finish out his career in Broncos orange and blue." Martin, who was miffed enough at Beake for claiming his newspaper was out of line, went on to note that it was Bowlen, not Beake, who owned and operated the Broncos, and Bowlen had made it clear he wanted to keep John Elway in Colorado and was willing to spend big money to do so. The general manager, snipped Martin, shouldn't get some "notion of grandeur about who actually runs the team."

It was *Rocky Mountain News* columnist Teri Thompson's turn on Thursday, but she toned things down a bit, quoting Bowlen as saying he'd like to sign Dan Reeves to a lifetime contract as well, then getting Reeves's reaction: "A lifetime contract? I've got one. As soon as you start losing, you lose your life."

Except for the occasional spoil-sport who would call one of Denver's sports-talk shows and argue that it was obscene to pay a football player millions of dollars a year when schoolteachers receive little more than poverty wages, everyone in the city seemed to agree that Elway deserved big bucks, and no one seemed to mind that the money would be coming from Pat Bowlen instead of a mill-levy increase. Elway was one of only twenty-eight people in the United States currently deemed capable of doing a specific job—the suicide job of an NFL starting quarterback—and he was, by Denver consensus at least, the best of that small lot.

Although Elway's salary is the highest among the Broncos players, the rest are hardly unrewarded. According to NFL Players Association figures for the 1986 season, the fifty-three current Denver players (the forty-five who are active and the eight on injured reserve) will receive an average salary of $145,100—a total that includes base pay, signing bonuses, bonuses paid for showing up (it's true!), plus salaries from previous years that were deferred until 1986—and that is far below the league average of $201,900. Yet when 1986 salary deferrals are included in the total—deferrals that, in some cases, are not payable for as long as fifteen years—the Broncos average "base salary" (to use the strange and confusing terminology of the NFLPA) becomes $196,300, a good bit above the league base-salary average of $179,600. In other words, the bucks the Broncos will put in their pockets this year are below the NFL average, but the money they will ultimately receive for their services this year is above the leaguewide mark. According to Bowlen, deferrals make sense because they benefit players after their careers have ended. "We have to fund the annuities, so it doesn't save the club any money. I encourage them because I think the younger players ought to think about their lives after football."

In John Elway's case, no money was deferred in his current five-year contract, but we can assume that the economics major has taken steps to ensure his family's security. He received a $1 million bonus when he signed his contract in 1983, and a salary that year of $600,000. His salary has increased by $100,000 each year since; it will total $900,000 this year, a million in 1987. Nine games into the 1986 season, Elway has received roughly $3,550,000 from the Denver Broncos. During that period, he has been the starting quarterback in forty-three games, the Broncos winning thirty-three of them—a .767 percentage, which is indeed impressive. Just for fun, you can figure that he's been paid $82,558 a game, or, if you don't want to pay him anything for a loss, call it $107,575 per victory, more money than you and I make, yes, but then neither of us possesses his arm, nor do our jobs entail suffering the full-speed assaults of indignant defensive ends.

John Albert Elway was born in Port Angeles, Washington, on June 28, 1960, a few minutes before his twin sister, Jana. Their father was a football coach, which, some people would say, was cheating. "What was apparent early," remembers his father, Jack, "from the time I can remember, he was interested in any kind of ball. He had the ability to concentrate."

Jack Elway's profession took his family—his wife, Jan, and

eldest daughter, Leann, as well as the twins—to a succession of college campuses. A move from Port Angeles to Missoula, Montana, was followed by one to Washington State in Pullman, then on to the head coaching job at Cal State/Northridge in southern California, to the top job at San Jose State back up the coast, and finally, at least for now, to the head coaching post at Stanford. In a departure from the usual course of things, Jack Elway went to Stanford because it was his son's alma mater.

It was while his dad was at Cal State/Northridge that a teenaged John Elway began to look as if he had more than average athletic ability. During his senior year at Granada Hills High School, he completed 129 of 200 passes for 1,837 yards and 19 touchdowns as the football team's quarterback, and batted .491, with a pitching record of 4–2, for the baseball team. The Kansas City Royals drafted him to play baseball, and virtually every major college in the country tried to entice him to come play football for them. He selected Stanford because he was a good student and he liked the idea of attending a school that was known for something more than its gridiron glories, plus he was aware that Stanford had a history of producing impressive NFL quarterbacks.

Although the Stanford Cardinals were never world beaters during Elway's collegiate years, he was, well, spectacular. He concluded his Stanford career as the holder of five NCAA Division 1-A records and nine Pac-10 conference records. He was a three-year All-American and, in the 1983 Heisman trophy balloting, he finished second to Georgia's Herschel Walker. Still a baseball buff, he spent the summer between his junior and senior years playing for the New York Yankees' Oneonta farm club, and the Yankees tried to lure him away from football following graduation.

They almost got him. As the most sought-after college football player since Joe Namath, Elway was certain to be picked first in the NFL's 1983 draft, and the Baltimore Colts had the coveted initial selection. Yet Elway did not like what he knew of Baltimore owner Robert Irsay, and he was sure he didn't

151

want anything to do with head coach Frank Kush, who ran his football club like a boot camp. Elway said repeatedly that if the Colts drafted him, he would simply abandon football and become a New York Yankee. He was roundly criticized from many quarters for being a spoiled, prima donna surfer boy, but he held his ground. And the Colts ultimately took him seriously. They did draft him, but immediately sent him to Denver in an elaborate trade (which had Elway's tacit approval) that brought the Broncos' first-round choice, tackle Chris Hinton, plus backup quarterback Mark Hermann, and an eventual 1984 first-round pick, to Baltimore. Fans in Baltimore cried that Elway had been given away; jubilant fans in Denver could hardly believe that such a steal wasn't illegal.

Although he knew he was headed to a football-mad metropolis, there wasn't any way that Elway could have prepared himself for the attention his arrival generated in Denver. The Broncos had always made do with an over-the-hill gang of grizzled quarterbacks; never in the history of the franchise had a top-prospect collegiate signal-caller come to town. But the unbelievable had somehow happened. Not only was there a good-looking rookie quarterback in camp in Greeley in the summer of 1983, there was a kid up there who'd have the position named after him by the time he was finished. "My God," exclaimed Mike Haffner, cohost of KNUS's sports-talk show, after he had had a look at Elway, "he's Namath with knees, Bradshaw with brains!"

The national and regional media attention that avalanched on Elway was nothing short of astonishing. His every move was observed, recorded, and analyzed ("Elway spent some time Wednesday examining the earring Larry Evans wears under his helmet," reported the *Denver Post*), and fans treated him like a messiah wearing the number 7. Back in Denver at the end of August, he couldn't go out in public without being certain that he'd be mobbed. He once had to arrange a police escort at 11:00 at night to go have his hair cut.

Elway started at quarterback in the first regular-season game of his rookie year, Dan Reeves giving him the nod over veteran Steve DeBerg. But in that game, against the Steelers in Pittsburgh, Elway completed just one of eight passes and was sacked four times before Reeves pulled him. Then it looked as though Reeves was getting really sadistic when he started Elway the following week . . . in *Baltimore*. The Colts fans had a field day, and they took out all their lousy-team frustrations on the smart-aleck Californian who had shunned them. "It was horrible," remembers Reeves.

Elway and his head coach had more than a few confrontations that year, if only because both so badly wanted to be successful. "The big thing John and I have in common, we're both impatient," avers Reeves. "We both wanted it and we both wanted it yesterday. But it was my fault. I was too inexperienced. There was no way I could prepare John for all the things they threw at him that year."

Elway survived that year, but barely. In 1984, with the gawking attention subsiding a bit, and with a year of Reeves's Machiavellian offense under his belt, he led the Broncos to a 13–3 regular-season record. In 1985, the 11–5 Broncos led the league in total offense; Elway threw four touchdown passes in one game, three in three games; he threw two touchdowns twice, and one touchdown five times. He rushed for 253 yards over the course of the season, leading the league's quarterbacks.

During his three and a half professional seasons, Elway has always had his detractors, those who say he's been slow to mature, who say he doesn't put any touch on the ball, who contend that his willingness to run with the ball will earn him a serious injury one of these days. Elway isn't perfect, if you want to get picayune about it, and the stats aren't in for 1986 yet, but a *Sport* magazine–assembled panel of former NFL players and coaches recently rated Elway number two, behind Chicago's Jim McMahon, among all NFL quarterbacks. When each of the five panelists was asked which quarterback he would choose to build a franchise around, they were unanimous in their choices: Elway.

Says Craig Morton, who formerly held the job that is now John Elway's, and who has been his friend and mentor since his arrival in Denver, "He is simply the best quarterback I have ever seen."

By the end of the week, the Democrats had won the big races for governor and the U.S. Senate, the Republicans had retained their hammerlock on the legislature, the Elway salary story was dying of natural causes, and the weather had grown wintry. At the end of the Broncos' first practice of the season inside the bubble, Elway was, as usual, chatting with reporters. When Joe Sanchez walked by him, Elway stopped in midsentence and called out to him, "You know how much grief you've caused me this week?" Sanchez nodded and smiled; it hadn't been the easiest week in the world for him either. Then Elway offered him his broad, toothy, what-the-hell grin, saying without saying so that he knew they both had jobs to do.

At midmorning today, the wind was howling out of the north, the temperature was falling with a certain icy drama, and the new houses scattered on the treeless hills near the town of Parker seemed somehow set adrift in the storm. Janet Elway invited me into a large but less than palatial house with a circular drive, a sloping lawn, and a satellite dish standing at its flank—the sort of home where the formal living room and dining room seldom see human habitation, where the country kitchen and the brick-fireplaced family room with a video center the size of NASA's mission control are the places people congregate. She offered me coffee and explained that she wouldn't join me since she was newly pregnant, her second child due late next spring. Daughter Jessica, just over a year old now, was with a sitter, husband John was at work, and she joined me at the kitchen table to talk about life as the wife of someone whose stature in

Colorado makes the early-sixties attention to the Beatles seem like the briefest sort of celebrity.

Tall, blonde, her face an angular counterpoint to her husband's doughboy features, Janet Elway is a native of Tacoma, Washington, a former NCAA record-holding swimmer, who met John when they were both freshmen at Stanford. "Swimming was the only sport I really knew anything about," she said with a smile. "Before we met I remember going to a football game with some friends. The crowd was chanting 'Elway, Elway,' and I asked, 'What's an Elway?' Well, now I know what an Elway is.

"John was well known at Stanford, but it wasn't a big deal, probably because it seems like everybody at Stanford is a star. My roommate's father was an astronaut—you know, things like that. So being the star of the football team doesn't really set you apart."

The couple became close during their college years, but Janet, who graduated with a degree in sociology, moved to Seattle to work in the summer of 1983 when John came to Colorado to enter life in a football fishbowl. "What he went through that first year was incredible. He would call and tell me things that amazed me. Everyone just expected so much of him, and they wanted to know every little thing about him. He's just a normal person, and he's kind of shy in a way, and it was really hard for him. I knew how depressed he was about it, but maybe somehow it helped him to have to go through it. There was even one point when John got so down that he talked about quitting football and going back out to Stanford to coach with his dad. I'm sure one of the reasons we decided to get married when both of us were still so young was because of what his life here was like."

John and Janet were married in March 1984, and Janet moved to the rolling Colorado plains, which seemed a world away from the lush forests at the edge of Puget Sound. "It really has taken me a while to get used to it here. It's such a different sort of place from the one I grew up in." I told her I was surprised they hadn't moved into the fir- and pine-covered foothills west of Denver. "Well, that's what probably would have appealed to me," she said, "but it was important for John at first to be near other players. They and their families were really the only people he was close to. Lots of guys on the team live out in this part of town. Now, I don't think it would be that important, but it was when he was first here. When John bought this house— the year before we were married—a reporter for the *Rocky Mountain News* found out what it cost and published it. John was so furious. He couldn't figure out why on earth it was anybody's business what the house cost. I don't think he's ever really forgiven that reporter."

What had the salary furor of the past week been like, I wanted to know. "I hadn't seen the paper on Sunday, so I didn't know anything about it," she said. "Then I got together with some other players' wives to watch the Raiders game. We were in the car, and they started kidding me, saying 'Oh, so John's getting seventeen million dollars?' And I didn't know what they were talking about. Things like that do kind of bother me. I mean, I don't know what *their* husbands make. Their salaries aren't printed in the papers. But . . . I guess it just comes with the territory. We have lots of advantages, and there are a few things we have to put up with."

When I asked her what it was like for them to go out in public, she laughed. "Well, for one thing, we don't go out that much because it's just too much trouble. It's a lot easier just to get together with people at home. There are a couple of restaurants where we can go in a back door and sit in a kind of private room. And when we go to a movie—which we don't much— we sit in the car in the parking lot until it's started. Then we sit way in the back and rush out just as it's ending. Otherwise. . . . When I'm by myself, shopping or doing things, nobody has any idea who I am, so it's easy. I help coach a swim team, and most people don't make the connection unless they know my last name. But with John, everyone always whispers and points and wants autographs. What's funny, though, is that people are often too uncomfortable to talk. They don't know what to say. With Jessica, it's made that easier. I guess it's always easy for people to talk about kids."

"What's it like for you at the stadium?" I asked. "Surely you occasionally hear people say nasty things about him, don't you?"

"Oh, sure. But I've gotten pretty used to it. There was a game last year, against Kansas City. John had lots of interceptions; it was a bad day, and the fans were really getting on him. There was this guy sitting right behind me who just wouldn't let up. Finally he yelled, 'Hey Elway. You can get your g.d. wife pregnant, but you can't complete a so-and-so pass.' I turned around and slapped him across the face. He was pretty shocked, and I wasn't very proud of myself for doing it, but. . . . When the friend I was with told him who I was, the guy was very apologetic and felt bad, but . . . they forget that the players and their families are real people."

Janet told me her closest friends in Denver are other players' wives; perhaps it isn't surprising that they tend to have a lot in common. They sponsor a variety of social and charitable functions throughout the year—such as the Broncos Wives' Food Drive on the Sunday of the Seattle game, which netted 2,100 cases of canned goods and $31,000 in cash contributions for needy families—and most wives take part. "There are a few who don't want to be involved in group activities, and that's fine, but most of us really are pretty close. There are a few who prefer their mink coats and who think they're a little too good for that sort of thing, though. I've got my mink coat, too—so I don't really mean that—but I'm afraid this is the more normal me." She pulled at the ribbing of her sweatshirt. She was telling me she was learning how to ski when John came in the door.

Rufus, a black Labrador, rushed into the house ahead of him, spinning with ecstasy on the occasion of his return, startling Leroy, a small and shaggy poodle who was napping under the table. "God, it's getting cold out there," he announced. I asked him what was forecast for the game. "Cold, but no snow, I guess. I'd a lot rather play in cold weather than wet weather, though." He asked Janet if she knew where the tool was that they used to drain the lawn's sprinkling system. She did know, and he excused himself to go attend to the chore. I drank a second cup of coffee, and Janet and I discussed the pleasures of skiing and the tolerability of the state of Colorado before I thanked her for her hospitality and got up to go.

His domestic duties finished, John by then was sprawled on the family room sofa, his cap still on his head, intent on a Stanford-UCLA game that was about to begin, the pre-game hoopla filling the giant screen. I stopped on my way to the door and asked him if he had seen that morning's column by the *Rocky Mountain News*'s Dick Connor, a piece in which the writer praised Elway's amiability. "There is still," Connor wrote, "even now, even after all the exaggeration that has surrounded him on both the positive and negative side, an engaging naïveté to this emerging superstar, a quality that distinguishes him from some of his more surly contemporaries."

"Yeah, I did see it," he said. "That was real nice of him." He confessed that he hadn't been thrilled about the salary stories, but that it hadn't really troubled him. "I know there are people who've never met me who have the image of me as a spoiled brat who makes too much money. It used to bother me a lot more. But basically, I've just got to try to make the guys on the team and the people in the organization happy, and let everyone else have their opinion. To me, seventy percent of what you get paid for is what you have to deal with off the field. It's nothing I'm ever going to be really comfortable with. Sometimes I wonder what it'd be like to be somebody who wasn't noticed, who wasn't in the newspapers. I don't like to stick out."

But I was distracting him. The Stanford team was about to kick off, and when the camera scanned the sidelines, he looked to see if he could spot his father, the man, he said, "who's still my hero." I wished his alma mater good luck and him good luck tomorrow against the Chargers, then left him alone—a man with a high-pressure job eager to enjoy his Saturday afternoon, a kid on a couch in front of a football game.

November 10

On the evening before the Chargers game, I joined Jim Saccomano for a drink in the lobby lounge of the Westin Hotel Tabor
Center, each of us—significantly smaller than your average Denver Bronco—nearly disappearing inside our plush, overstuffed
chairs. Rick Smith, the Chargers' director of public relations,
was, at that moment, nineteen floors above us in a production
meeting with the NBC crew that would work tomorrow's game.
When producer Steve Danz, director Dick Cline, and announcers
Charlie Jones and Jimmy Cefalo completed their inquiries of
him, it would be Saccomano's turn. It was a Saturday evening
ritual for him. Prior to virtually every Broncos game, at home
or away, he met with the people who would be televising it to
update them on injuries and player performances in previous
games, to try to answer every question that crossed their collective minds.

"Oh, there's no question that television has changed football," he told me while we waited. "Beginning with the so-called
greatest game ever played—the 1958 Giants-Colts championship—pro football began to attract television viewers who had
never gone out to see a game before. And via television, interest
in pro football spread to areas of the country where it didn't
exist before. We're sitting in one of them. TV has made the fans
more knowledgeable, made the game more accessible and understandable, and it's obviously made the franchises a lot of
money."

As the Broncos' director of media relations, it is Jim Saccomano's job to facilitate coverage of the team by all manner of
television, radio, and print media. When *Sports Illustrated* calls

saying it wants to do a piece on John Elway or Karl Mecklenburg, it is Saccomano who contacts the player and makes the necessary arrangements. When John Madden wants to tape a pre-game interview with Dan Reeves, he approaches Saccomano, who in turn diplomatically tries to arrange the interruption. When a reporter for the Casper, Wyoming, *Star Tribune* wants a seat in the press box for a big Broncos game, it is Saccomano's lamentable job to try to find him one, then, likely as not, to tell him he didn't succeed.

"I always say this," he told me, "it is often perceived by more than a few members of our organization that I work for the press. They sometimes think I look out for the press's interests more than I do the team's, which I don't believe is true. I am solely an employee of this football club, and my job is to get for us the maximum amount of publicity, and the best publicity, nationally and locally, as I possibly can. But there's the constant question of what constitutes good PR. There are people, obviously, who hate to see stories in the paper that are speculation about finance and so forth. But are they necessarily bad publicity? I don't think they are."

Saccomano, a native Denverite whose Italian-immigrant family farmed land that is now covered by a housing development, came to the Broncos in 1979 from the Denver Bears (now Zephyrs) organization. Although hopelessly charmed by the game of baseball, he has been a Broncos fan since their humble beginnings. And despite the fact he now knows more minutiae about the Denver Broncos than he ever could have imagined, he has yet to become jaded about the sport or the people who play it. Game days drive him crazy, not because of their long hours and endless demands, but because he still gets amazingly wrapped up in the emotional issue of winning and losing. Close games that have a lot riding on their outcomes can drive him to stomach-twisting anxiety, and he has been known to rush away from his desk in the press box, his fingers stuffed into his ears, in the seconds before the Broncos try a crucial, game-tying kick. Small, gregarious, relentlessly cheerful, he is the sort of person who

160

experiences a minor pleasure each time he checks an item off his must-do list, neatly recorded in a pigskin-covered notebook.

"PR guys in football are often caught between the devil and the deep blue sea. Coaches and players often see the media as a huge pain—which they can be. And the media, on the other hand, sometimes decide they have some inherent *right* to know absolutely everything that pertains to this organization. You sometimes have to remind people that we are a privately owned corporation. When, let's say, Steve Caulk comes to me and says, 'I need to know this,' I have to say, 'No. You *want* to know it. It doesn't necessarily mean you are somehow morally entitled to know it.'

"What I try to do is to be as honest as I can be. It's a cheap way out to answer a reporter's question by saying 'I don't know anything about it.' What I try to say is, 'Yes. I'm aware of who's been cut, but I'm not at liberty to say.' But on the other hand, the media live with us in a very literal way, and we benefit greatly from them. Outside of the teams in the New York and Los Angeles areas, I'm sure the Broncos get more coverage, more inches of print, and more TV minutes, than any *two* other teams combined. The media play a role in our success, there's no question about it. And that's what I try to remind the coaches and players of. You've got to remember that what we ultimately do is sell tickets to the fans and sell programming to the television networks. And the day we sell no more tickets is a very bad day for all of us."

Ten minutes later, Saccomano sat in the CEO's chair in a board room in the lofty heights of the hotel and gave the NBC producer, director, announcers, statisticians, graphics and camera people a quick rundown on his team. On the injury list, Mark Jackson, Rulon Jones, and Keith Bishop, all with knee injuries, were listed as questionable; Dave Studdard had a thigh bruise and was listed as probable. Except for the injured players, there would be no changes in the starting lineup. By way of promoting his team, he pointed out that Denver running backs had rushed

161

for a hundred yards or more in six of the last seven games; the Broncos continued to lead the league in sacks and in total points; there had been fewer than three hundred unused seats at Mile High Stadium in the four home games to date; the forty-six no-shows for the Dallas game set a franchise record. Before the questions began, Saccomano added an observation: "Dan has been stressing all week that you can't take any 1-8 team too lightly, especially not the San Diego Chargers."

Then the questions ensued. Director Dick Cline wanted to know about the remainder of the Broncos' schedule. "Based on opponents' records so far this season, our seven remaining games are the most difficult schedule in the NFL." Charlie Jones, the play-by-play man, wanted to know how many different positions Karl Mecklenburg plays. "Seven." Which is the most common? asked color commentator Jimmy Cefalo. "They like to line him up next to Rulon Jones to counter the double blocks." What about this rookie Mark Jackson? He's having quite a season, isn't he? "He has the three longest receptions on the team." And what about Keith Bishop's wife, what's her name? "Mary." Yes, Mary. Her baby's due any day now, right? "As far as I know, it's a few days overdue." Would she be at the game? "I was told that she'd be in a loge-level box." Did he know *which* box? "No, but let me make a note. I'll try to find out for you." Steve Danz, the producer, wanted to know about Dan Reeves's relations with his assistant coaches. "Dan's delegated a lot more authority this year, in meetings and so forth, than he used to. And he gives Mike Shanahan, the receivers and quarterbacks coach, a lot of credit for the innovations in the play calling." What about your defensive backs? Are you still going into the nickel? Cefalo wanted to know. "Yes," said Saccomano. How do you pronounce Darren Comeaux's name? "Co-mo. As in Perry." Who's been your best offensive lineman, in case I want to do an isolate on him? asked Cline. "The traditional answer is Billy Bryan." Are you guys enjoying yourselves, someone asked when the questions began to wane. "Well,

I think everyone certainly feels that they're glad to take the 8–1, all right," said a smiling Saccomano.

"Appreciate it, Jimmy," Steve Danz said when there was nothing else to ask. "Have a good game tomorrow."

Charlie Jones, silver-haired and silver-throated, has been working football games for twenty-seven years, twenty-two of them spent at NBC Sports. As NBC's press information packet puts it, he "holds the distinction of broadcasting professional football longer than anyone in the history of sports television." Jones provided the play-by-play for the first televised game of the fledgling American Football League in 1960, and he joined NBC in 1965 when that network purchased the five-year rights to televise AFL games. He was part of the NBC crew that broadcast the game that will go down in history as Super Bowl I, but which was known on January 15, 1967, as the NFL-AFL Championship. Charlie Jones has seen a few touchdowns in his time.

"When I get on the plane on a Sunday night," he joked, sitting in the broadcast booth at Mile High Stadium on Sunday, he and his partner, Jimmy Cefalo, wearing matching NBC parkas to ward off the arctic cold, "there's a good chance I'll be able to tell you who won the game, but no way will I know the score. You focus on the game all week long, preparing with tapes of the teams' previous games, tear sheets from the papers, with the teams' media guides and promo material. That one upcoming game is all you pay any attention to, then the second it's over, by God, it's over. I kiss Jimmy good-bye at the airport; he gets on a plane headed east; I get on a plane headed west. He does his 'NBC Sunrise' thing in New York; I'm smart enough that I take a couple of days off at home in La Jolla. Then we meet up again in some new city at the end of the week and start all over again. It's wonderful," he said, adding his robust laughter.

"Basically, I just don't sleep," said Cefalo, Jones's color counterpart—his "analyst" to use the network's terminology—a second-year broadcaster for NBC who was a wide receiver for the Miami Dolphins in his first life. "With 'Sunrise' and the weekend games and the other assignments I have with 'NBC Sports-World,' I stay pretty busy. But I love it. I haven't had a day off since the season started, but this is an exciting time for me. It's a great opportunity."

"He's young. He's crazy," was Jones's simple assessment.

Looking out at the field, its grass kept green and lush despite the advancing winter by heating coils cross-hatched beneath its surface, I asked them which stadiums were the best from which to broadcast. "Well, the stadium itself can't ever make the game. You can have a great stadium, but if the game's a dog, the broadcast is going to be tough. But I like Arrowhead in Kansas City, just because it's such a great facility, and this place right here. The way this place is constructed, you're right on top of the field, and the crowd's such a part of what's going on. It's hard to translate the crowd's involvement to television, but it's a lot easier here than in most of the stadiums we work."

Was today's game's potential for being lopsided posing special problems for them? The two broadcasters looked at each other and grinned knowingly before Jones answered. "Oh, Jesus," he said, "it could be disastrous if you weren't ready for it. But we've got a whole contingency package ready. If we have a blowout, we're going to lose most of our San Diego audience. They're just not going to stay with us to watch their guys get hammered. So we'll be playing to a Broncos audience, and what we've got ready is a Broncos Super Bowl report card. We'll look at this team compared to the '77 team; we'll compare them by position with the other AFC contenders; we'll look at their remaining schedule. Hey, if we need to, we can go twenty, thirty minutes on nothing but their Super Bowl bid. The Denver fans will love it."

"And if it's a blowout, they're obviously going to be looking like a Super Bowl caliber team," Cefalo added, "so in the course of the game itself, we can focus on what they're doing right, where their strengths are. It ought to be fun."

Why was it, I wondered, that football seemed to work so well on television? Why did many people prefer watching a game on television to seeing it from the stands? "I'm pretty new at this," said Cefalo, "but what I'm discovering is that these guys do a heck of a creative job in broadcasting these games. There's a lot more to it than just pointing a few cameras at the field. So I think one of the reasons it seems to work so well is that it's done right; the coverage adds to the game."

"But they're made for each other to begin with," said Jones, the broadcasting sage. "I mean, look at it. You've got a sport that's about controlled violence, and that's what people love. You can watch TV any night of the week and figure that out. The action in football is focused; even with the passing game, it's not all spread out in every direction like baseball. You've got built-in drama every four plays. You either advance the ball ten yards or you fail and you have to give it to the other guys. Then they have a go at it. It's perfect. I'm serious, if football hadn't existed already, television would have invented it."

The amazing futuristic invention called television was used experimentally in 1939 to telecast, of all things, a football game, yet it wasn't until the early 1950s that football telecasts became commonplace. And one of the first lessons learned from the regularly scheduled broadcasting of NFL games was that, without some careful restrictions, the tube might bankrupt the teams who permitted its use. In 1950, when for the first time the Los Angeles Rams telecast each of the club's home games, stadium attendance dropped to a total of only 110,162 for the season, down from 205,109 the previous year. In 1951, the worried Rams blacked out their home games and attendance bounced back to the 1949 level.

Convinced that the league's owners had to act in unison in the face of television's potential drain of gate revenue, NFL commissioner Bert Bell hammered changes into the league's by-laws that mandated the local blackout of all home games and other teams' games when the home team was playing at home, and which required member franchises to negotiate television contracts in unison. A federal court decision in 1953 upheld the blackouts under the terms of the Sherman Antitrust Act but denied the NFL the power to control the television negotiations of its member franchises. Eight years later, however, spurred by the astute lobbying of Alvin "Pete" Rozelle, the league's new commissioner, Congress intervened and passed the Sports Broadcasting Act of 1961. Rozelle argued that package contracts were essential if revenues were to remain relatively equal among franchises and if the teams that met on the field were to remain competitive. The members of the United States Congress were chastened by his message, and their resulting legislation allowed the professional leagues of all sports to negotiate package broadcast rights. It was that specific bill, signed into law by a football fan named John F. Kennedy, that began an era of skyrocketing television contracts and of ever-proliferating sports broadcasting which continues today. "What Rozelle did with television receipts probably saved football," commented Vince Lombardi, the legendary Green Bay coach, who wasn't necessarily given to hyperbole.

CBS paid the NFL $4.5 million for the rights to broadcast the league's 1962 games, but just two years later the figure had jumped to $14 million annually. In 1964 as well, NBC, which had lost the bidding war for the NFL's games, gambled on the struggling AFL and agreed to a five-year, $42 million contract—the first of the multiyear contracts which then became the norm. By 1970, even though the two rival leagues had merged, professional football was becoming popular enough, its commercial minutes easy enough to sell, that the league was earning $50 million annually from the three networks' broadcasts—CBS's NFC contests, NBC's AFC games, and ABC's "Monday Night Football," which, in itself, became a national phenomenon of astonishing popularity.

Seven years later, "Pete the Shark" was able to twist a four-year, $656 million agreement from the three networks—a package that guaranteed each NFL franchise roughly $6 million annually in television revenue. For the first time in 1977, each NFL team earned more money from the sale of broadcast rights than it did from selling tickets to fans who watched the games in person. Yet the networks weren't throwing their money away. Football's television ratings continued to climb, the cost of commercial minutes seemed to go up exponentially, and at the end of the 1977 season, 102 million people watched the Broncos lose Super Bowl XII to the damnable Dallas Cowboys—more people than had watched any other single event in the history of television.

The league's current contract with the networks, which will expire at the end of this season, was negotiated in 1981 for a five-year, $2.1 billion total—almost $14 million dollars annually for each NFL franchise, well over half of each team's annual revenue—a whale of a lot of money spread evenly around the league. "We're twenty-eight Republicans who vote socialist," quipped Cleveland Browns' owner Art Modell.

The Cincinnati–San Francisco Super Bowl which capped the 1981 season attracted 110 million viewers, and last year's Chicago–New England Super Bowl blowout set yet another single-game record, with 127 million viewers. Yet the ratings for regular season games have fallen sharply in recent years, and the networks are losing money. They say they cannot match the 1981 contract figure; ABC is even making noises about dropping "Monday Night Football" (though no one really expects the network to go that far—at least not yet) and Pete Rozelle seems to see the handwriting on the wall. He is courting cable television in hopes of bringing a little leverage to bear against the networks, and he has gone so far as to state publicly that he'll be happy if the league's new television contract simply retains the status quo. As of now, it appears that Rozelle will be an unhappy man come the off-season.

No one is predicting the end of television's football era, however. Football remains by far the most widely watched sport on television, and the networks' production staffs and equipment which are devoted to football broadcasts are nothing short of awesome. The NFL itself contends that the ratings drops merely represent the inevitable peaking of the football audience, and the networks will be tempted to agree if they succeed in reducing their annual ante to the league.

If football has had a huge impact on the fare available on American television over the past two decades, television has had its own, not-so-subtle influence on the game. Under the terms of the current television contract, *every* NFL game is televised. Even a yawner in which the Indianapolis Colts play host to the Tampa Bay Bucs is beamed back to Tampa, if not to anyplace else. It's a requirement which the networks aren't thrilled with, one the league forced them to agree to back when the ratings were shooting through the roof, and it means that, for now at least, there is no such thing as a professional football game free of television's time constraints. At each and every NFL game, the most powerful person on the field isn't the referee, nor is it the hometown team's head coach nor the $10 million rookie with a complexion problem. The person on whom *everything* hinges is the nondescript man on the sidelines with the huge headphones stuck to his ears and the Day-Glo orange gloves rising up to his armpits. It is he who signals when the game can commence (normally at precisely 1:02 or 4:02 P.M., eastern time, each Sunday), when the game must stop for commercial messages (and it must, for at least twenty-four spots each game), when it can begin again (either after a one- or two-minute break, depending on the status of the game), and when it's time to play ball again following the fifteen-minute half-time (down from twenty, at television's request). Football games telecast in the 1950s and early 1960s were normally allotted two and a half hours of air time. But by the mid-1970s, the schedule had to be lengthened to three hours, in part because the trend toward more passing resulted in more incompletions and hence more onfield time-outs, and in part because a rule change meant overtime games were now a regular possibility, but in large measure because the networks had increased their commercial commitments. This year, NFL games are averaging three hours and twelve minutes in length, meaning that virtually every game runs long and post-game programming is interrupted.

The people who still watch football in the flesh have had to become inured to the strange pace of televised football games. Unless they pack pocket TVs to the stadium with them, they can observe no logical reason why, following a punt or an intercepted pass, the two teams on the field suddenly take what appears to be a coffee break, some players going so far as to lounge on the grass during the not-so-brief intermission. It's boring and it makes the game seem awfully lethargic from the stands, but, as everyone now knows, it's easy to explain: TV time-out, an interlude for selling beer and cars and the joys of the American armed forces.

Yet the fans in this stadium, all of whom watch at least the Broncos' away-games on television and likely a few more games besides, seem to understand that television lends an air of importance to football games which they otherwise wouldn't have. The fact that John Madden and Pat Summerall come to town to broadcast a Broncos game to the nation gives it a stature that the mere 75,000 fans can't match. The broadcasting of a given game transforms it from a strictly local event to one that has consequence across the country. It is television that makes celebrities of twenty-two-year-old men who can run like the wind, and it is television that lauds their team and their town to the nation.

The banners that fans hang from upper-deck railings and that line the fence that skirts the field aren't there for the people across the way to read. They're hung for the panning television cameras and in the hope they'll catch a director's eye: LIMON, CO. LOVES RULON JONES. AN OLD COWBOY AND HIS BRONCOS GALLOP TO THE SUPER BOWL. YOU GO YOUR WAY, WE'LL GO ELWAY. HI CINDY AND BRUCE IN SAUDI ARABIA-GO BRONCOS-WELCOME DICK AND MERLIN.

The people who spend hours—sometimes days, to judge by the elaborate lettering—making signs seem intuitively to understand that television has the magic to take a game and turn it into a pageant, into an event that is at once literal and fantastic, as real and palpable as a torn piece of turf, as mythical as the images beamed onto an electronic screen. They know the game's the thing, but the medium's the messenger of how much it finally matters.

A few minutes before the start of the game, I squeezed my way into the NBC production truck tucked under the stadium girders, joining seven men who were fitted into the dark, six-by-five-foot space like Mercury astronauts into their capsules. Each of them faced a wall filled with two large color monitors that displayed the broadcast and the local "feed" (the signal that would actually be sent from the stadium), plus eight small black-and-white screens, each one showing graphics displays, instant replays, or what was currently being seen by the six cameras aimed at the field. Three men—producer Danz, director Cline, and an engineer who executed their commands—had front-row seats, their legs jammed underneath the sound- and camera-board that was a maze of dials and switches.

At seven minutes before 2:00, mountain time, the men in the truck were working with a graphic they would use early in the game, which listed the five head coaches in the history of the NFL who had been born in foreign countries, one of whom was Al Saunders, a native of Britain and, following the resignation two weeks ago of Don Coryell, the Chargers' new head coach. And in the announcing booth up in the stadium press box—you could see via the right-hand color monitor—Jones and Cefalo were rehearsing their opening remarks.

"Five minutes to air, gentlemen. Five minutes to air," called Danz.

"Guys, aren't there any good banners out there?" Cline called to his camera operators through the microphone on his headset. "Can't you do some banner shopping for me?" Two cameras immediately began to pan the fence line, and, watching the monitors, Cline found a few he liked. "Have a good game, everyone," he added. "May your camera position be in the sun."

At 1:58 came a crisis. "They're running behind," called the timekeeper from the second row. "Anthem's late."

"Oh, shit," said Cline. "Watch it. We might get caught with the anthem."

"Hey, I hate to talk over the anthem," said a relaxed-sounding Charlie Jones, his resonant voice filling the tiny truck. "We'll get nothing but letters. Let's don't do it."

"Okay, Charlie," said Danz. "Don't voice-over the anthem. We'll just go to it and try to get it miked. Here we go, everybody. Ten-nine-eight-seven-six-five. Roll X. Sound on X. We're on the air."

The NBC logo filled the color monitors, followed by the NFL and AFC logos, presented with stylish computer graphics and accompanied by the network's own melodramatic football music. Then came a cut to an aerial shot of the stadium and the voice of a studio announcer in New York. "Today, from Mile High Stadium, it's the Denver Broncos versus the San Diego Chargers." Cline cut away to a camera focused on a flag wafting above the high south scoreboard, held that shot for a moment, then cut to the band on the field. "Ten to Charlie," Danz called, as the anthem reached its climax. "Cue Charlie."

"Good afternoon, everybody. I'm Charlie Jones along with Jimmy Cefalo welcoming you to a cold Mile High Stadium in Denver, Colorado, where the AFC West–leading Denver Broncos play host to the San Diego Chargers." The two announcers spoke into the camera in their booth while they outlined the game, doing their best to make the contest sound like it would be worth watching, and the men in the truck were momentarily calm. Then the Chargers won the coin toss, the Broncos kicked off to them, and the truck assumed a kind of controlled frenzy, the feed appearing impossibly smooth and coordinated in the midst of the shouting and the sudden, seemingly desperate demands.

"Cue it up Y. I got him all the way. Got him isolated. Graph. *Graph!* White 89. Goddamnit! Get it on there."

"Good, good. Should be good on Z. Cue Z. Freeze it right there. Freeze it. Good. No replay."

"Flags! Flags!"

"It's against Denver."

"Get me that flag. Find it!"

"No running backs. Give me far-side receivers, anybody. Get me a receiver. Quick. Quick."

"I need two for live action. Two. Two."

"Freeze Z. Go to X."

"On X."

"Oh, shit. I liked that shot better."

"Jesus, who was that?"

"Anderson."

"Get him on X. Now. *Now!*"

"Isolate on Benirscke. The ball. The ball. Stay with the ball."

"Commercial cues."

"Five-four-three-two-one. We're away."

"Very good, gentlemen."

The Chargers, a team with a new head coach, playing in freezing weather with its third-string quarterback, Tom Flick, had just marched 78 yards in seventeen plays, their drive culminating in a 24-yard field goal. The nine minutes and thirty-eight seconds consumed meant that two-thirds of the first quarter had been played before the network got its first commercial break. Michael Weisman, the executive producer of NBC Sports, who was monitoring all the games his network was broadcasting at that moment, wasn't pleased, and he made his feelings known on his direct line into the truck. But the men who heard him weren't particularly bothered—at least not for now. They were pleased with their performance during the Chargers' first possession, and so far the contingency package, the Super Bowl report card, was idle.

At the end of the break, they were back to frantic work, the Broncos beginning their offensive series on their own 20-yard line, the first play from scrimmage an incomplete pass from Elway to receiver Steve Watson.

"Breaks the string, Jimmy. Breaks the string," Danz said into his microphone, followed a second later by Cefalo's announcement: "And that also breaks John Elway's string of consecutive pass completions at ten."

But the Broncos, too, were able to move the ball, advancing on a mix of running plays, flare passes, penalties, and a spectacular 51-yard pass from Elway to rookie Mark Jackson, the drive impressing Jones and Cefalo, but its length earning Weisman's ire in New York.

"Steve. Weisman's going crazy," called the man in the second row who received the New York line in his headset. "He wants you to call the field. We're already four spots behind. Gotta have a break."

Danz obliged and rang his contact on the field but was frustrated when he came away from the call. "They won't give us one. Not till we get a score or the quarter break." The man in the second row relayed the message.

"Steve. He says we've got to have one." The man tried to be solicitous.

"They won't give us one, goddamnit."

"Try again. Weisman's going ape-shit."

But before the crew could plead its case with the field judge, perhaps reminding him that commercials paid his salary as well as everyone else's, the first quarter expired with the Broncos' ball on the Chargers' 18. Weisman got the commercials he was desperate for during the two-minute quarter break, then two more, five plays later, following Rich Karlis's field goal, which tied the score. The men in the truck were off the hook, the game was even, and the contingency package still sat on the shelf. Jones and Cefalo ignored the Super Bowl bid and concentrated on the action—the Chargers marching right back in eleven plays to score their second field goal—and the frenzied men in the truck made it unfold like magic.

We never saw the Super Bowl report card, nor were Jones and Cefalo ever forced to wing it. The audience in San Diego surely

173

grew throughout the game as word spread that their 1–8 Chargers, who hadn't been victorious since their season opener, were not only staying abreast, but staying ahead of the heretofore flashy Broncos. The Chargers—a far cry from the offensive machine they were during their "Air Coryell" heyday and playing without Dan Fouts, their own superstar quarterback—nonetheless played smart possession football, tacking three field goals on the scoreboard and snatching *five* turnovers from the hapless horses.

Never before in the history of the Denver franchise had the Broncos lost a game at home in which it held its opponent without a touchdown, but the Chargers' thin nine points turned out to be five more than they needed. The Broncos' offense, which had averaged 23.3 points a game so far this season, managed merely three, and John Elway had his worst game of the season, his worst since the game a year before when his wife assaulted the insulting fan. Elway lost a fumble on the Chargers' 9-yard line, and he threw two interceptions to Chargers defensive back Jeffrey Dale, one at the Chargers' 12-yard line, the other in their end zone. Had he and the Broncos been able to hold on to the ball on just one of those three possessions and score a touchdown—something they'd done with alacrity to date—the game would have been theirs.

Elway's hat-trick interception came with just twenty-four seconds to go in the game. The Broncos had moved quickly from their own 27, 48 yards in seven plays. They had time for at least two more plays that might move them the 25 yards for a touchdown, but, under pressure from the Chargers' rush, Elway launched a floater to Clint Sampson in the end zone. Sampson, however, was able to do little more than watch Chargers' safety Vencie Glenn steal the ball and ruin his day. It wasn't the worst play of the game for the Denver offense, but it was the last. Chargers 9, Broncos 3, in front of 75,012 cold and disbelieving fans, in front of a television audience in the Rocky Mountain region who guessed that the game somehow had been preempted by "Amazing Stories," in front of a San Diego audience in awe.

His sallow expression lit by the local television cameras in the stadium conference room, Dan Reeves said, "Well, seems like we just can't stand prosperity. I felt like we had good practices all week. I didn't have any indication that we were taking them too lightly or that we weren't ready to play. But our intensity obviously wasn't there. The Chargers had a good game plan, but we helped them every way we could."

Rocky Mountain News reporter Butch Brooks asked him if he agreed that the Broncos offense was slumping. "You don't put but three points on the board, I'd say slumping is a brilliant understatement," said the head coach, three parts disappointed and one part whopping mad.

The *Denver Post*'s Joe Sanchez wanted to know what happened on the interception in the end zone at the end of the game. Reeves explained that there was a miscommunication on the play he called from the sideline, and running back Gerald Willhite stayed back to block instead of running an intended pass route.

"What was the route?" asked Sanchez.

"It was just a route, Joe," said a momentarily surly coach. "You wouldn't understand it anyway." And how could Sanchez have expected to understand? This was *football,* after all. A question or two later, Reeves seemed to apologize for the nearly rude rejoinder by laying the blame for the game on himself. "Anytime you play as poorly as we did, it's just bad coaching." It was game of him to claim responsibility, and the reporters scribbled the comment down, but not one among them believed it.

In the locker room next door, the camera lights came on to witness John Elway putting on his clothes, a large, ugly abrasion obvious on his left thigh. "I made some bad mistakes," he said, willing, as always, to take the media heat following a poor performance. "I'm not at all happy with my performance. I know I'm not going to sleep much tonight, that's for sure." A pinch of snuff was cradled in his lower lip, and the lip moved little as he spoke. "New York brought us back into the stratosphere a few weeks ago. This one brought us back to earth."

As Elway continued to talk, repeatedly remembering his mistakes, Cefalo and Jones, their broadcast long since completed, were waiting at Stapleton International Airport, one with a ticket to New York's La Guardia, the other headed to San Diego International in advance of the victorious Chargers. They were in good humor at the end of the long day. Their Nielsen rating and audience share would be much higher than they had expected; they were pleased with their broadcast, and upsets were always enjoyable. Both of them still knew well who had won, and for once—since the numbers were small—each one still remembered the score.

November 11
—

The luncheon at the downtown Denver Athletic Club was hosted by the city's Emmy chapter (the association of people in the television industry whose awards grace Malibu's mantles); the fare was blue-tinted roast beef, peas, and mashed potatoes served in pretty swirls; and the issue at the postmeal panel discussion was whether Denver's television sportscasters were journalists or cheerleaders or something in between. Seated at the table on the dais were Mike Nolan, Channel 9, back at work after Jim Celania's demise; Ron Zappolo, Channel 4 ("the Broncos Station"), the city's longest-tenured and highest-profile sportscaster; Gary Cruz, Channel 7, sports anchor for the number three station in the network ratings wars; Jim Conrad, Channel 2, counterpart of the others at an independent station that goes heavy on sitcom reruns and light on local news; and Stefan Brodsky, sports producer at Channel 6, the city's PBS affiliate, today's moderator because public television is always presumed to be above the fray.

And although Brodsky assumed that the topic of discussion was a legitimate one, the men seated to either side of him tended to take it rather lightly, Nolan in particular, the sober-sided sportscaster in front of the camera now quite a comedian when at last he had a live audience—joking about the Celania shuffle, his own exile spent in Hawaii during Celania's reign, and his rather public marital trials and errors. But between quips, Nolan was surprisingly willing to come clean. "I'm a fan of the teams in this town," he said. "You can't help but be a fan. Our sports reflect what people are interested in, and, of course, that means the Broncos. I mean, in the middle of the winter you can do a Broncos story. You just can't go wrong with a Broncos story." So he was a cheerleader, was that right? "No, absolutely not. All of us here take our jobs very seriously. We're professionals."

Zappolo wanted nothing to do with the cheerleader label either, but he steered clear of calling himself a fan. "My job is to provide information to the fans—the audience. And it's crazy to talk about cheerleading. I've had everybody mad at me from one time to another. There have been times, for instance, when both Dan Reeves and John Elway refused to talk to me because of stories I've done." When he was asked about his role as host of the "Dan Reeves Show," Zappolo saw a clear distinction. "That's Dan's show. He's paid to appear on it. When I talk to him on his show, I'm involved in a very different line of questioning, which isn't as tough as during a regular interview." Nonetheless, Zappolo said, there are occasions when Reeves objects to questions he poses. "At the end of the show, he'll say to me, 'Why did you have to ask that?' With [Denver Nuggets' coach] Doug Moe it's very different. During a commercial, Doug'll say, 'Hey, why don't you find something we can argue about?' Part of the difference between the two of them is personality; Doug loves to go around with anybody about just about anything. Dan's not like that, and he's under a lot more national and local media pressure than Doug is."

Channel 2's Conrad was straightforward: "We only have about two minutes of sports coverage every night. We report on what's happening. We don't have time to cheerlead." Channel 7's Cruz was analytical: "People misinterpret my enthusiasm for cheerleading. I don't mind the cheerleading label, but I don't think it's accurate." Then he compared television coverage of the Broncos with that provided by the daily newspapers. "We can't have beat people follow the team twenty-four hours a day like they do. We only have a limited amount of time for the sports on each newscast—about four or five minutes. They've got how many pages every day? And I'll tell you something else. In the press conferences I attend, I never hear the newspaper guys asking the tough questions either."

Gary Cruz had a point, I suppose. In the weeks I had watched the newspaper beat reporters interview players and coaches, none of them had ever come on like Sam Donaldson having a shot at a forgetful president. I had yet to hear Michael Knisley ask, "With all due respect, Dan, you don't expect anybody to take this team seriously until you dump that accent, do you?" Steve Caulk had never inquired of the quarterback, "Aren't you ashamed to throw interceptions with your financial portfolio?"

Yet the beat reporters had a problem. The team was 8–2 and leading its division. Until the San Diego debacle, at least, there simply wasn't much to get investigative about. Sure, there was the question of whether the Broncos were playing musical punters, and, to Dan Reeves's clear dismay, the print reporters were asking plenty of questions about that issue. The team's once potent offense hadn't become truly impotent of late, but, as they used to say in polite company, it had certainly suffered a diminution of the marital impulse—and the papers were taking pains to point that out as well.

One of the inherent problems with sports journalism is that

you aren't covering elected officials or government employees who simply must be watched with the wariest of eyes. The teams you cover are private businesses that ultimately do nothing more than provide some seasonal hours of entertainment; none of them makes napalm or asbestos ceiling tiles; none pours toxic sludge into the nation's waterways. Sports reporting does offer some terrific opportunities to write with style and creativity, but—other than when an occasional twenty-two-year-old superstar kills himself with coke—there is seldom an opportunity to write about issues that are critically important.

Yet it seemed to me that both of Denver's newspapers did an impressive—if often obsessive—job of informing their readers about the Denver Broncos, the team's stumbles and shortcomings as well as its heady successes. I had no reason to suspect otherwise of the team's television coverage, but the truth was I didn't see each station's sportscasts often enough to know. Perhaps the Monday shows that followed the San Diego nosedive would offer some telling clues.

Ilene Lehmann at Video Monitoring Services kindly had the four videotapes cued and ready at her office this afternoon—the evening sportscasts of Denver's four commercial stations on November 10, 1986. All I had to do was to insert each tape and depress the PLAY button. I felt certain I could handle it.

Channel 4 was at the top of the stack. As its sports segment began, news anchor Bob Palmer turned to Ron Zappolo and said, "Well, it happened. What everyone feared actually happened." Zappolo, facing him, responded, "I still find it almost impossible to believe. As I was driving to the stadium yesterday, I could not concoct a scenario in which Denver could lose this game." Then he turned toward the camera. "Let's be honest," he continued, "the Broncos were flat and the Broncos were overconfident. All the factors were there to go into the game fat and happy and overconfident—and that's exactly what happened." His words introduced a piece by reporter Steve Alvarez that cited San Diego's ball-control offense and John Elway's poor performance for the outcome. "Holding their opponents to just nine points should have been enough for the Broncos to win, but it wasn't," Alvarez said.

The segment went on to include clips from interviews with Elway and with San Diego players Tom Flick and Charlie Joiner, an advance report on next Sunday's game with the Kansas City Chiefs, and a look at the University of Colorado's upcoming football showdown with hated Oklahoma. The Denver Nuggets weren't mentioned.

Channel 7's Gary Cruz opened his report with these words: "As a fan yesterday, I said, 'What's wrong with these guys?' And then I had to be a sportscaster again, and now I'll tell you what's wrong with them." Yet the promised assessment never seemed to materialize. Reporter John Keating did a taped piece on the game that included quick comments from players on both teams, Cruz called the loss "one of the toughest of the season for the Broncos" (yes, one of two), took a look at the AFC West standings, mentioned the CU-Oklahoma game and the Nuggets game the following night, but much of his segment focused on the shoulder injury to running back Steve Sewell, one that would probably keep him sidelined for four weeks, an injury Channel 4 hadn't mentioned. "It's one thing to lose a game," Cruz concluded, "but it's worse when you lose one of your best players."

Channel 2 opened its sports segment with clips from the "Monday Night Football" game which was in progress, then Jim Conrad segued into the Broncos' loss. "It was one of those games that looked like a fire drill," said Conrad before showing a bit of tape from an interview with linebacker Ken Woodard, who wasn't happy. Conrad mentioned the injury to Sewell, then—from out of the blue—he introduced a piece by reporter Greg Mills on the market price of an NFL franchise, which pegged the Broncos as the fourteenth most valuable club in the league. If you had $70 million burning a hole in your pocket, as well as Pat Bowlen's home phone number, it might have been critical information at that moment, and it *was* moderately interesting, but boy, did it suffer for lack of context. Were the Broncos for sale? No. Channel 2 just needed a feature.

At Channel 9, paternal Mike Nolan put it all into perspective. "They're professionals," he said, chatting with news anchor Mike Landess. "They can shake it off, put it behind them." Landess wanted to know how the players felt after the defeat, and Nolan said they had bucked up rather well. "You know, 8–2 is nothing to sneeze at," he reminded us. Channel 9's tape included clips from interviews with Elway and safety Dennis Smith and from Dan Reeves's press conference earlier Monday afternoon, in which he observed that "it's a real short journey from the penthouse to the outhouse." Nolan continued with a piece on the several NFL quarterbacks who were injured on Sunday, an advance on tomorrow's Nuggets game, and a report on an afternoon press conference at which Coors had announced the publication of its complimentary "Parents' Guide to Girls' Sports"—an exclusive the other stations simply missed.

I can't pretend that one evening's worth of sportscasts was enough to assess adequately the city's television sports coverage or to compare the several stations' broadcasts. Yet in the context of their comments at the Emmy luncheon, it was intriguing to take a look at how the four sports anchors addressed the issue of the Broncos' second defeat of the season. Only Zappolo offered any unvarnished criticism. Conrad's "fire drill" reference went nowhere. Did it mean that the team was lackadaisical? Cruz's decision to focus on Steve Sewell's injury made sense, but his early promise to tell us what was wrong with the Broncos was nothing but a tease. Nolan seemed to see his role as a kind of commiserator, reminding his audience that, by gosh, the Broncos were still pretty darn good.

What *is* the proper role of television in reporting on the hometown team? Should it simply be supportive? Should it use its ubiquitous presence to find fault when there's fault to be found? Or should it avoid any attempt at reflection and simply show the highlights and announce the myriad scores? As Jim

Saccomano had observed while we waited for the NBC production meeting on Saturday, television's greatest asset is its ability to provide a sense of immediacy to sport, the illusion that the viewer is part of the event. At that task, television is simply unmatched by any other form of communication. Live television sometimes can be terrific. And television can also provide valuable insight into any issue—nothing about the medium makes this by any means impossible—but to do so it requires a little time, lots of time when the subject warrants it. Four minutes just isn't enough to do more than set a simple stage, whether for a discussion on welfare reform or one on the Denver Broncos. The nightly television news—nationally as well as locally—currently provides little more than headline services, and that seems to be the principal distinction between the nature of television reportage and the coverage provided by daily newspapers. It isn't that one medium asks the tough questions and the other necessarily shies away from them, but rather that, while both begin with headlines, the newspapers follow them with stories.

And, at least in this city, when you compare the reporters themselves—the people who work with cameras and microphones and those who work with little Radio Shack lap-top word processors (today's equivalent of the symbolic fedora with the press card inserted into the band)—you find that while some of the TV sports journalists proudly acknowledge that they're fans, the print journalists, to a person, tell you they stopped being fans sometime roughly centuries ago.

Mike Spence, Broncos-beat reporter for the Colorado Springs *Gazette-Telegraph,* was born in the sugar beet farming community of Brush, Colorado, then moved with his family to Pueblo, Colorado's only true industrial city. Brush is eighty miles from Denver, Pueblo 110, right in the Queen City's backyard by western standards, and, of course, Spence grew up an avid Broncos fan. "My dad was a high school football coach, and he and I never missed a Broncos game on TV. But it would be hard for me to call myself a fan these days. It's not that you end up disliking the team in general—although there are a few assholes around—but the day-in and day-out familiarity makes it impossible to see these guys as heroes or something anymore. You find out that they're just normal people, and that definitely changes your perspective."

David Hutchinson is a Denver native and a reporter and columnist for the Boulder *Daily Camera,* a once maniacal fan who is planning at the end of this season to abandon sportswriting for law school, which does bring the issue of his judgment into question. Nonetheless, Hutchinson is convinced that it's about time to move on to new endeavors. "You get to the point where it's such a total routine. You watch the game; you go get quotes from Reeves and the players. You go back up and write your game story, the sidebars, notes, your column. I always write them in exactly the same order. During the week, you hang out for hours hoping to get people to talk to you for a minute or two. If they don't have anything to say, or if they won't talk, then you're stuck and you've somehow got to come up with a story idea. You finally figure something out and get it written, then the next day you're back in the same position.

"I used to be one of those guys that screams at the television set. Really. I was definitely into it. But not now. I've enjoyed doing this, it's been a great experience, but I don't want to do it for the rest of my life. I could move to bigger or more prestigious papers, but the work I'd be doing wouldn't be different at all. I don't want to end up doing this same thing when I'm fifty."

There are a lot of fifty-year-old writers in the sports world. By happenstance, there are few of them in Denver, but visits to press boxes in cities around the NFL convince you that writing about the games young men play isn't just a young man's racket. And sports reporting simply isn't ever going to make a list of the world's worst jobs. For one thing, there *is* such a thing as a free lunch in this business. (Broncos-beat reporters, assuming their appetites are up to it, can consume as many as five free meals a week, all in the line of duty—three lunches at the team's practice facility, a Saturday night dinner prior to Sunday road games paid for by a very generous Jim Saccomano, and the ubiquitous press box buffets which are spread out before the kickoff of every game.)

But I don't disagree with David Hutchinson. Frankly, I can't even imagine being a forty-year-old sportswriter, if for no other reason than that before I reached that milestone birthday, I'm sure I'd succumb from a terminal bout of boredom. Not that the games themselves are sleep-inducing, or that the writing is too pedestrian to hold your attention; no, newspapers' very best writers often work in their sports departments. It's just that during the course of a given week, for every hour you spend observing a game and writing about it, you certainly spend three more waiting to talk to players and coaches who don't really want to talk to you. Patience, in this particular branch of the typing trade, isn't merely a virtue, it's an absolute prerequisite, akin to demanding decent eyesight of the nation's fighter pilots. It's only now, after having spent much of the season watching the reporters watch the team, that I realize that the long hours they spent standing in the sun at the Broncos' training camp in Greeley were a kind of training for them as well. They were getting their patience in shape, honing it for the rigors of the long season, readying themselves for the really vicious waits they knew would await them down the road.

In order to ward off ennui, the reporters who spend their days at the Broncos' facility have assumed a several-pronged strategy. They have formed a fan club devoted to a Channel 4 weekend newscaster named Madeline McFadden. (They say they are truly impressed by their television colleague's journalistic acumen and claim that reports that her dark eyes and sensuous lips have influenced their attention are entirely mistaken.) They keep a "stiff list" of players who, for whatever reasons—anger or inability—currently refuse to talk. They maintain a small-stakes betting pool on the outcomes of each weekend's games—the one who picks the most games correctly collecting a dollar from each of the others—and they shoot endless baskets with a miniature foam-rubber basketball, some of them becoming athletes in their own right, launching long jump shots that skid across the trailer's low, acoustic-tiled ceiling, then swish through the tiny net for two points and a brief flirtation with glory.

But mostly they just wait.

The players are officially accessible to reporters and television crews following their morning meetings and their afternoon practices, and the media people strategically position themselves near the paths between buildings, waiting like highwaymen for a brief ambush of questions. As they approach each other, you can watch the reporters steel themselves for the inevitable ignominy that accompanies having to implore someone to talk. And you can see the players brace for the distasteful interchange as well, their hands on the bands of their sweatpants, their eyes trained on their running shoes unless the presence of a camera requires them to meet their questioner's gaze.

The relationships between players and reporters are symbiotic at best; more than occasionally they're adversarial. The reporters depend on the players' occasional comments to put meat on the bones of their stories, and the players, whether they acknowledge it or not, depend on the reporters to publicize their talents, to transform them from mere athletes into big-money media stars. And although the beat reporters and players by and large are cordial to each other, there are few true friendships among them.

Players contend they are too often "burned" by a gross misquote or by a story that magnifies a minor and meaningless slump to trust any reporter implicitly. They are wary because a vestige of privacy is so crucial in their profession, wary also because too much loose talk can destroy a team's fragile solidarity. The sports media, they say, is ultimately a necessary evil, a pain-in-the-ass kind of parasite you have to learn how to live with. You have to learn how not to let the pieces that appear in the papers and the stories on the evening news get under your skin. You have to learn how to answer long strings of sometimes stupid questions without saying too much, without giving too much away.

The print and television reporters, on the other hand, claim that the players quickly become little more than cliché artists, deliverers of lines that have to do with giving it 110 percent, with taking it a game at a time, while truly *saying* nothing at all. Rookies, they say, are refreshingly open about themselves and the game they play, but it isn't long before they, too, clam up and begin to begrudge the questions. The reporters can't resist pointing out the leaden irony in the groups of players who sit in the sun on Monday mornings reading the sports sections with the attention of tax accountants who then, moments later, tell the reporters who wrote the stories they've just read that they can't talk now, that they have to go work out, that maybe the reporters can catch them tomorrow.

Dan Reeves's relationship with the sports media is more straightforward, if for no other reason than that a head coach inevitably becomes his team's official spokesman. If a team mysteriously benches a star player, if it is plagued by internal feuds, or—as is now the case with the Broncos—if it begins to falter for no apparent reason, it is the head coach who has to answer the flood of media inquiries. And despite Reeves's own inherent suspicions when it comes to reporters' intentions, despite his conviction that the sports media too often digs for dirt that doesn't exist, he is remarkably willing to talk. By club policy, he is basically available to speak to reporters anytime they can catch him for a moment; he almost always seeks them out at the end of the day's practice to answer a quick flurry of questions; he arrives in the press trailer every Monday afternoon promptly at 1:30 to discuss informally the game just played; he dons a jacket and tie each Wednesday at 11:30 to hold a formal press conference in the large players' meeting room; and his third official act at the conclusion of every game (after shaking hands with the owner and leading his team in a post-game prayer) is to address a sea of reporters. By way of putting his accessibility into perspective, in the four months since training camp began the President of the United States has answered reporters' questions on only a single occasion, the outgoing governor of the state of Colorado has been busy traveling and has had very little to say, but the head coach of the Denver Broncos has held more than sixty-five press conferences and has been briefly buttonholed literally hundreds of times. It is a virtual certainty that to date this season he has answered more questions about his team than any other coach in the NFL, and it's equally certain that he'll have a little more to say before the season is finished.

Yet Dan Reeves's accessibility doesn't necessarily guarantee candor or cordiality. He has become a master at turning away questions he doesn't care to address, and, when pressed, his casual charm quickly boils down to a broth of venom. He doesn't suffer fools or reporters lightly, and lately—ten weeks into the season—he seems to have grown tired of all the talking.

November 17

—

The Broncos had just thumped the Kansas City Chiefs 38–17 yesterday when Dan Reeves had to face another onslaught of questions. His team had rebounded strongly from its defeat by the San Diego Chargers, it had led the Chiefs 31–0 before the first half had ended, and it had held on to beat them convincingly, but there he stood at the podium near the Broncos' Mile High Stadium locker room, defending his team's performance

187

against a pack of media jackals. "We won the game substantially," Reeves stonewalled in response to a slew of questions about what had happened to the Broncos' offense, "and I'm not complaining about any part of our football team." But the reporters continued to press him—if for no other reason than that they suddenly weren't sure whether they and Reeves had seen the same game.

It was a game in which John Elway was uninvolved in three of the Broncos' four first-half touchdowns, and his offense was only required to move the ball a single yard for the fourth, following a fumble recovery near the Chiefs' goal line. The Broncos got their first touchdown from punt formation when Chris Norman saw wideout Steve Wilson go unblocked, then Norman threw him a perfect pass; they got two more following bonehead fumbles by Kansas City quarterback Bill Kenney, and a fourth touchdown when Gerald Willhite made a spectacular 70-yard punt return. The Broncos' big offensive spurt of the first half was a seven-play, 37-yard drive that resulted in a Rich Karlis field goal.

In the second half, the Chiefs outscored the Broncos 17–7, and by the time the three-hour, forty-nine-minute affair finally drew to a merciful close, the Chiefs had gained more first downs than the Broncos, more yards rushing, more yards passing—more of everything except the requisite points you need for a win. And that was the only statistic that mattered, Reeves contended as he tangled with the press. He wasn't interested in the fact that the Broncos had gained only 67 yards rushing, or that the offense managed only one sustained drive all day, or that (despite his touchdown-pass heroics) Chris Norman had had a punt blocked, or that his punting average was a mere 37.5 yards, including an uninspiring 11-yarder—Norman's worst day since his return to the team. Reeves just didn't want to talk about poor performances. "Our offense was banged up and beat up," he said by way of a rejoinder, referring to Keith Bishop's nagging knee injury and Steve Sewell's absence because of a shoulder separation. "To make that many big plays early was tremendous. I'm not making any excuses. I'm not griping about any phase of our game. This was a great win for us."

When *Denver Post* columnist Buddy Martin piped up, unabashedly asking once again about the sputtering offense, Reeves sized him up for a moment, then snarled, "For about the *fifth* time, the game went the way it did because of the score." He cited, as he had already, the Broncos' need to protect their early lead, and the Chiefs' willingness, once they were far behind, to gamble on defense as the reasons for the Denver offense's modest production. Reeves glared again for good measure, and Buddy Martin decided to forgo a follow-up question. The television lights went dim, and Dan Reeves made a disgusted exit.

November 25

The waitresses at Barry's Coffee Shop, who wear Broncos pins on the lapels of their uniforms, have been worried about their "boys." The shoe shiners at Stapleton Airport have been perplexed for several weeks. The construction crews who meet each morning at El Noa Noa for conversation over steaming bowls of menudo have been discussing little else. Yes, the Broncos still lead the AFC West and are still odds-on favorites to win the division; their offense still plays with sporadic brilliance, and their defense is still very stingy about surrendering points. Yet somehow, the Broncos' bubble has burst. This just isn't the same team that led the league in offense for the first half of the season, the club that played seven games before it suffered a loss, the bunch who seemed invincible just three weeks ago when they routed the Raiders in balmy L.A. No one seems to be able to pinpoint precisely what's happened, but something has, and theories are in ample supply.

It's the injuries to key players like Keith Bishop and Steve Sewell that have done it, goes one popular assumption. The team's lack of an explosive running back is commonly claimed as the culprit. John Elway's arm is exhausted, say some; Dan Reeves's conservative play-calling has caught up with him, aver others.

Reeves himself lately has suggested an explanation, and it has to do with a creeping lack of concentration. As a case in point, Reeves confessed that on the day before the loss to San Diego, he filmed two television commercials—something he greatly regrets in retrospect. He didn't need that kind of distraction. On the day of the Chargers game, the *Rocky Mountain News* ran a splashy two-page feature comparing the current Broncos to the 1977 Super Bowl team, and his players plainly weren't helped by that heady preoccupation. The distraction of the $17 million contract story doubtlessly did not do his quarterback a bit of good. And then there was the potentially disastrous lure of the Christmas video the team had planned to produce. It was going to be a mighty impressive show, complete with cameo performances by Reeves and team owner Pat Bowlen, a special rendition of "The Twelve Days of Christmas" sung by a chorus of linebackers, and an inspirational tune composed especially for the Broncos entitled "Taking It to the Top." It really would have been something, but it would have been one hell of a distraction, and Reeves and Bowlen came to their senses in time to cancel it—just five hours before the cameras were scheduled to roll.

If you presume that Reeves's distraction theory of football is correct, then you have to assume it was the cancellation of the video that salvaged the victory over the Chiefs. And in the week following the Kansas City game, the distractions almost seemed to disappear. Not a single commercial was made; not a Super

190

Bowl story appeared. The talk show callers cooled down their crazy histrionics, and the columnists put away their poison pens. Everybody in town seemed to toe the line and concentrate on the terrible trouble that loomed ahead. The 9–2 Broncos had to return to the New Jersey Meadowlands to face the 9–2 New York Giants. Unlike the Broncos, the Giants hadn't hit the mid-season skids, and if the Broncos were going to beat them, well, we would all have to pay very serious attention.

Nobody in the state of Colorado was messing around come Sunday; the morning papers caused no undue distractions, and the radio call-in lines were mercifully closed. In New Jersey, the Broncos' players and coaches were safely and quietly sequestered in the Sheraton Meadowlands Hotel; there had been no late-night field trips across the Hudson to the seductive distractions of East Side singles bars. All seemed well; attentions were focused like lasers on the team known as the "New York Football Giants" (to distinguish it, I suppose, from the New York *Baseball* Giants—a team that's been playing nothing but road games for the last thirty years or so), and the Broncos were determined to prove to the Big Apple and environs that they were better than the team that was blown out five weeks ago by the Jets.

And all the concentration very nearly paid off. The Broncos' offense, AWOL in recent weeks, returned to active duty, logging 405 yards of total offense (their second-highest production of the season), John Elway completing a career-high 29 passes for a season-high 336 yards. And if the Denver offense played well, the defense played little short of spectacularly—at least until the final fifty-three seconds of the game.

Trailing 16–9 late in the fourth quarter, the Broncos drove 73 yards in nine plays to tie the score, Elway throwing five strikes—one of them to Steve Watson for 27 yards—Sammy Winder completing the textbook march with a 4-yard run for the touchdown. The Giants had a minute and fifty seconds to try to break the 16–16 deadlock. Starting from their own 28-yard line and quickly getting nowhere, they faced a third down needing 21 yards to retain possession of the ball. The Broncos called a time-out, defensive coordinator Joe Collier telling his troops that quarterback Phil Simms almost certainly would look for wide receiver Bobby Johnson up the middle. Sure enough, Simms fired a shot to Johnson, but the forewarned Denver secondary simply wasn't up to its task, and the Giants, too, were marching. Three plays later, against a Broncos' three-deep zone defense designed to prevent such calamities, Simms found receiver Phil McConkey astonishingly, unbelievably open deep in Broncos' territory for a 46-yard pass completion that effectively finished the Broncos off. Simms dropped to his knee on the two successive plays, then, with six seconds remaining on the clock, Giants' kicker Raul Allegre hit a field goal from the Broncos' 16, his fourth of the day—and that, friends, was that. For the second time in three weeks the Broncos had lost to a team it had prevented from scoring an offensive touchdown; the Giants' lone six-pointer had come near the end of the first half when, with the Broncos threatening on the New York 13, Giants' defensive end George Martin made a spectacular stab at an Elway pass, hung onto it, and lumbered 78 yards for the score. For the second time in six outings, the boys from the back country had journeyed to a reclaimed swamp in Bergen County, New Jersey—very nearly to New York, New York, itself—and had come away with nothing but heartache. They weren't pelted with pretzels and bagels this time, and the Giants fans were too worried for much of the game to shower them even with epithets, but that was little consolation.

Yet it was a wonderful football game. Not since the opener against the Raiders had the Broncos been involved in a game as close and well played and downright glorious as this one was. They could have won it; they *should* have won it, the players reported to the press, but they let it slip away. The offensive players, knowing they played better than they had in a month or more, were buoyant despite the loss, their confidence rekindled there on the Meadowlands carpet. But the players on defense—the undistracted, dependable, ass-kicking, name-taking Denver defense—were crushed. It was their momentary lapse that allowed the game-winning score. Seldom did a defeat depend on them; that kind of guilt was a new sensation for most of them, and they, at least, endured another ugly airplane ride to Colorado.

This time I had decided not to travel to the big city. I stayed in Denver and watched the game in an apartment on Capitol Hill, joining Ann Lacy, a friend from my college days, and two of her friends for their ritual Sunday gathering, a group of them—all teachers, all female, all black—having gotten together to watch every Broncos game for the past half-dozen years or so, no one daring to miss a Sunday unless something serious—nuclear war or something—happened to get in the way.

Although there were no reports of incoming ICBMs by noon on Sunday, the group was smaller than usual, perhaps because word had gotten out that some strange character was being allowed to crash their club. But after a tentative first quarter, Ann and her friends, Barbara Ingram and Diana Browner, seemed to decide that I was more of a curiosity than a nuisance, and Diana, at least, began literally to throw herself into her spectating—bounding in agony from the couch to the Persian carpet when Mark Jackson surrendered a fumble to the Giants, then discovering the will to live again on the subsequent play when Giants' wide receiver Stacy Robinson coughed up the ball to Ricky Hunley. The polite commentaries of the first quarter gave way to shrieks and cries and the sorts of oaths that would have caught Dan Reeves's delicate attention when George Martin slapped Elway's pass out of the air and headed hell-bent for the end zone. These three were fans who saw no worldly reason to watch a football game *passively*. Where was the pleasure in that? They shouted rude suggestions to John Elway, implored Gerald Willhite to stay on his feet for once, reminded Dennis Smith how handsome he was, then reviled him for letting a Giants' receiver beat him on an out and up. They, to be sure, couldn't be accused of succumbing to distractions, and by halftime they were already a little hoarse.

193

Ann Lacy is a special-education teacher at Denver's North High School, a Seattle native who lauds the wet Northwest but who somehow stays in arid Colorado. After a decade in Denver, and despite her stubborn efforts not to, she has become a Broncos fan. "You just can't help it after so long," she said, serving the enchiladas that were the day's half-time repast. "It's infectious. God, you can go into the teacher's lounge on Monday mornings and there won't be a person in there talking about anything else. And I have to admit that the games are a lot more fun if you're into it. We do seem to have a good time," she said, smiling at the understatement. Who does she root for nowadays when Denver plays Seattle? I asked. "The Broncos," she said, sounding just a little ashamed of herself.

Diana Browner came to Denver from Iowa City, Iowa, and had little trouble falling into the Broncos mania. But she claimed, rather facetiously, that now she's trying to quit. "I just can't watch these things anymore," she told me, "they're too depressing. They are way too hard on me. I mean it, I'm through." Diana teaches special education as well, but at crosstown rival South High, where she is also the cheerleaders' sponsor, which, after knowing her for half a Broncos game, seemed to make perfect sense.

Barbara Ingram, a Denver resident since she was a child, is an English teacher at North High who watches Broncos games with her friends while her husband—who can't be bothered—plays golf. "It's strange," she said. "I'm what I'd call a very 'feminish' woman, and yet I absolutely love to watch these football players get out there and smash each other up. It's the most macho thing in the world, but I'm crazy about the Broncos. You know, if we were going to pick a team to root for, it ought to be the Raiders. They're the only team in the NFL that has a head coach who's a minority. Tom Flores is Hispanic. But I *hate* the Raiders. I think the Raiders are scum. I can't help it. It really is ridiculous."

We talked while we ate about what it is that keeps them in Denver, about what the city has to offer, about schools, the arts, and race relations. None of them went so far as to say Denver is something special, a place somehow unmatched, yet they agreed that it is, perhaps most of all, comfortable. "Denver's midwestern," Ann explained. "Compared with Seattle, it seems so conservative, it *looks* conservative—all the brick houses side by side. Coastal cities, I think, are inevitably more open-minded, more tolerant, because they attract so many kinds of people. I love Seattle, but this is home now. My friends are here, my work is here, Colorado's beautiful. And I think Denver does seem to get more interesting, little by little."

Barbara lives in Park Hill, a large neighborhood near Stapleton Airport which is a model of integration, a pocket of the city in which the American Dream seems to work remarkably well. "There are people who take a quick look at Park Hill and decide that race relations in this town must be perfect," she said. "And it is a good neighborhood. Kids can grow up in contact with all different kinds of people. But no, this place ain't perfect by a long way. The racism here is subtle. You don't see it on buses or in restaurants, but it's there. There are certain neighborhoods that we just wouldn't try to move to if we wanted to. If you're Tom Jackson or some famous Bronco, maybe, but folks like us . . . no thank you."

"When I first came to Denver," Diana said, "I was interviewing for a job, and this one principal, turning me down, said, 'Well, I'm sorry, but I hired a black girl last week.' *Black girl.* Can you believe it? That's exactly what he said, like he had to have one, but *two*, why God forbid. And last week, a couple of white cheerleaders I sponsor came up to me to complain that this other white girl was 'acting black,' that's what was bothering them—she was 'acting black.' I guess meaning she was saying things the way her black friends said them or something, I don't know. I said, 'You're telling *me* this?' Sometimes you just can't believe things like that."

"The funny thing," Ann added, "is that the student body at North is almost totally Hispanic, and those kids are culturally very different from me. Just because you're both minorities doesn't

195

mean you have a lot in common. It's a real challenge sometimes."

I asked them if the Broncos play a role in providing some
common ground. "Oh, sure they do," said Barbara. "Football,
the Broncos, are the one thing you can be sure you can talk to
anybody about. Anglos, Hispanics, blacks. They sort of belong
to everybody, that's the way everybody feels about them. That
part of it is great, really. You can't talk to everyone about what's
at the museum, or a concert or something, or the situation in
your own neighborhood, but everybody knows how the Broncos
are doing."

The Broncos didn't seem to be doing too well early in the
second half when Raul Allegre's field goal put the Giants ahead
by seven points. They seemed to be doing worse—and Diana
began to despair—when tight end Orson Mobley fumbled away
the football after the Broncos had quickly rebounded into scoring position. Pandemonium descended on Ann's apartment when
the Broncos tied the score with little time left to play, but the
Giants' winning drive was nothing short of tragic. Barbara silently prepared to leave; Ann silently cleared dishes from a
serving table; Diana, her emotions spent, lay on the carpet and
swore she'd had enough. "I mean it," she said, "this girl has
had all she can take of this football team." But before she left,
she inquired—simply for information's sake—where they would
watch the Cincinnati game next Sunday.

Gully Stanford, director of public affairs for the Denver Center
for the Performing Arts, didn't disagree that Denver is a football
town when we met on Monday morning. "Of course, it is," he
said over eggs and sausage, "but my crusade is to demonstrate
that it is far more than simply that. It's true that our cultural
amenities are relatively young compared to some cities—but we
are a young city, after all—and our major news media do sub-
scribe to a sort of regional inferiority complex. Yet I can tell
you that we have attracted some of the finest creative minds in
the country. People like Richard Teitz at the Denver Art Mu-

seum, Donovan Marley at the Denver Center Theatre Company, or Nat Merrill at Opera Colorado are people that *any* city would be thrilled and proud to have. Our challenge is to convince the people who live here that the arts community is as talented and as successful as the Broncos are. It's perhaps more of a public relations challenge than anything else. Within the arts community around the country, Denver commands a lot of respect. Yet ironically, many people here, who live here and who don't investigate, have an image of us as a cultural backwater."

An ebullient Briton who has lived in Atlanta, Minneapolis, and New York as well as Denver, Stanford can be forgiven if he doesn't personally possess 50-yard-line season tickets to Mile High Stadium, yet he was careful during our breakfast conversation not to denigrate the city's sports mentality or to begrudge the Broncos their perceived preeminence. "Vitality" is a word he seemed partial to, and a vital city, he said, is one in which sports, arts, and recreation all share in enriching its citizens' lives.

And he presented me with some interesting statistics. Average annual attendance at the home games of the Broncos, Nuggets, and Zephyrs, combined with attendance at local dog tracks and at the two-weeklong National Western Stock Show, totals about 2.5 million people. Average annual attendance at the institutions and events that fall under the loose rubric of cultural activities—the Museum of Natural History, the Denver Art Museum, the Denver Symphony Orchestra, the Denver Center for the Performing Arts, Opera Colorado, the Colorado Ballet, the Arvada Center for the Arts and Humanities, the Children's Museum, the Denver Zoo, and the Denver Botanic Gardens—totals 4.3 million. Almost twice as many people attend museums and performances as attend sporting events, he pointed out, borrowing an accountant's kind of proof that Denver is more than just a football town. And although his figures—compiled by the Colorado Council on the Arts and Humanities—fail to consider that attendance at Broncos games would be double, perhaps triple the 750,000 annual average if the stadium were large enough, or that "television attendance" figures would bring the Broncos' annual total to roughly ten million, they do make a valuable point: The Broncos are not the only diversion in otherwise bucolic Denver, Colorado.

"There is very definitely a *there* here," Stanford said enthusiastically. "Of course, there's a residue of the old cow town image that remains. But I don't mind the cow town image, in fact, I rather like it. Why not strive to become a vital city artistically and economically and still retain some of the wonderful flavor of the West? It would be a shame to lose it, it seems to me. We're about to spend $31 million to renovate the Arts Complex into what in four years will be the finest performing arts center in the country, so you see there's certainly no lack of vision here. And I really believe that with our combined efforts, and with the proper leadership, Denver can someday blossom into an American cultural capital. It really can."

Yet if cultural Denver's future is bright, Stanford is willing to acknowledge that its present is one of financial complexities. Four institutions—the art museum, museum of natural history, botanic gardens, and zoo—share $4 million in tax revenues annually, in addition to each's endowment, grants, gifts, and admissions fees. The economic footing for the four is solid, if unspectacular, and their contributions to the community seem certain to continue unchecked.

But the city's other artistic amenities rest on far shakier foundations. The Denver Arts Complex, for example—which houses the symphony hall, a cinema, and the performing arts center's theaters—currently suffers an income shortfall of about $300,000 annually, a figure that will increase after the renovation is completed, according to a city-sponsored study. The Denver Symphony Orchestra came perilously close to bankruptcy this fall when the orchestra's musicians balked at, but finally accepted, a 20-percent wage cut to help offset a debt of $1.5 million. Unlike some other major American cities, Denver lacks a strong tradition of major corporate support of the arts, and there is a telling absence of government commitment in the fact that Colorado ranks forty-seventh in the nation in per capita arts expenditures.

Yet despite the economic hardships, the arts industry in Denver is growing, Stanford assured me. Total attendance increased by 32 percent between 1982 and 1985; income was up 20 percent in the same period, and employment in the arts citywide now totals 3,000 people. "This community obviously has the appetite," he said. "It doesn't necessarily understand why it does, but I'm sure it will somehow stay committed to the arts. And I would venture to suggest that there may well be the day when, for instance, Philippe Entremont and the Denver Symphony draw as much attention to Denver as John Elway and the Broncos do."

November 26

Perhaps because of the long flight home from the Newark airport, and surely in part because he was at work by seven that morning to look at a tape of the Giants game, Dan Reeves looked more than a little sleepy as he sat in front of the Pepsi machine in the press trailer on Monday afternoon, facing fifteen reporters and three television Minicams. He was pleased with his team's overall effort, he said, the players' attitudes and their aggressiveness. "The other games we've lost have been because we made more mistakes than the other team. This one, well, we lost it basically because one or the other of us had to. I thought it was a heck of a football game."

By the time the inevitable question about the punting game

was asked, Reeves had grown a little testy. "I don't know if that's something I really want to talk about. I've talked about it enough. We'll do what we think is right for our football team and go from there." Chris Norman had had another bad day against the Giants, averaging only 34.3 yards on three punts, his six-game average slipping to 38.9 yards, poorer than Jack Weil's had been when he was dropped from the squad. Was Reeves saying that he might make another change in punters? "I'm saying I don't want to talk about it. You guys write what you want to," he said, sarcastically. "I'm sick and tired of talking about our punting." When *might* the coach be ready to talk again about the punting? asked an intrepid reporter. "What punting?" said Reeves, trying to warm the suddenly icy room with a smile.

On Tuesday, the players' day off, Reeves and a cadre of assistant coaches snuck downtown to Mile High Stadium under a cover of light snowfall—careful not to alert the pain-in-the-ass reporters to the fact they were once again taking a look at replacement punters, this time four of them, each a former NFL punter who currently found himself sidelined and otherwise employed, if employed at all. The coaches liked what they saw on several counts, but they were particularly impressed with the directional punting of an ex–Philadelphia Eagle named Mike Horan, a left-footer who had kicked well for two seasons before he got caught in coach Buddy Ryan's shotgun purge prior to the start of this season. Horan had returned to his job as a mechanical engineer at Hughes Aircraft in his hometown of Fullerton, California, but had remained ready for another NFL opportunity by kicking balls to his wife on his lunch hour. When the Broncos contacted him, he took the day off from his job and flew to Denver to demonstrate what he could do. When the team offered him a job late on Tuesday afternoon, he called his boss to see if he could stretch it to a leave of absence.

The reporters, of course, got wind of the covert kicking tryout and were on hand by the time Reeves was ready to make a decision. "I just feel like he'll make us better," Reeves commented, echoing his words from six weeks before. "The thing that was most impressive today was his ability to kick it out of bounds. He had more consistent hang time than the others, and he got it off most consistently." Reeves explained that Norman had been informed of the decision to replace him, then added, "I think Chris, as well as Jack before him, both have tremendous talent. But . . . talent'll get you fired if it doesn't come through for you."

December 2

The action had been quiet because of the Thanksgiving holiday, but by Friday it had picked up again. The Cincinnati Bengals were 8–4, tied with the Cleveland Browns for the lead in the AFC Central; they had an explosive offense led by a left-handed mirror image of John Elway; their mobile defense made pass protection more than problematical, and yet the line favored Denver by eight points. *Eight.* Sure, the Broncos were playing at home, they were coming off a loss, and they hadn't lost two in a row all season, but those eight points seemed awfully seductive, and Richard Armenta's phone had really begun to ring.

I had spoken with the man I'll call Armenta several times before, hoping he would agree to meet with me to tell me a bit about sports betting, Broncos betting in particular. When we first talked, he told me he didn't think a meeting would be possible; then, when a friend of mine who was a betting client of his interceded, he decided that perhaps it would be okay, sometime when he wasn't so busy. After a series of regular phone calls, Armenta finally agreed to meet for lunch on Friday at a little place he knew near his office. After I had waited for him for an hour, I knew, of course, that he wasn't coming. An hour and a half after we were scheduled to meet, I called him at his office and he apologized for standing me up, telling me how he had become ill at midmorning, but how by now he felt good enough to return to work. "You just aren't comfortable with this, are you?" I asked.

"Listen," he said, "you sound like an okay guy, but honestly, there's just no good reason for me to talk to somebody about this sidelight of mine. I can't see what it'd do for me except maybe cause me trouble."

Richard Armenta is an accountant for an oil-field services company, a fellow whose facility with numbers suits his illegal sidelight, one which earns him an extra and unreported $30–$40,000 annually, depending on the action. He is one of dozens, hundreds perhaps, of bookies in Denver who blatantly break the law, but whose odds of being apprehended are so small as not to make much of a bet. His bettors are bankers, lawyers, salespeople, and construction workers; some of them sink little more than $50 into their weekly bets, others deal exclusively in four figures. Armenta earns 10 percent of every losing wager, and it is his handling fee that makes his and his bettors' enterprise a crime. "Social betting" between individuals, in which there is no third-party bookmaking involved, is legal in Colorado. You can privately bet with a friend on anything, for any amount you choose. But when you pay Richard Armenta a hundred dollars to take Cincinnati and the eight points on Sunday, you and he and the guy he hopes will take the Broncos and give the points are all entangled in a criminal football betting racket that is estimated to attract as much as $50 billion nationally each season.

"Well, how about if I just ask you a few questions over the phone? Do you have a minute?" I asked him.

"You swear you won't use my name?"

"I swear."

"What do you want to know?"

"Well, for one thing, are most of your bettors Broncos fans?"

Armenta laughed. "The smart ones aren't. But I make a lot of money off the ones who are. A guy who's sophisticated about his football betting is never much of a fan. He's not interested in football because he needs something to root for. He's interested in it because it can make him some money, and because of the basic thrill of gambling. But if you're a Broncos fan, and you bet on the Broncos, you can't tell whether you've made a bet because you hope they'll cover the spread or whether you *know* it, if you see what I mean. Besides, the name of this game isn't winning or losing, it's covering the spread. That's all you ask of any team. Win, lose, I don't care."

I asked him how the Broncos were at covering the spread.

"Pretty good this year so far. The last couple years, with all their close and overtime games, just so-so. Karlis is a problem. You can't depend on his foot. If the line is Broncos by two or three points, it's risky because that means a field goal's the difference, and your money's in his hands. That's why you hear of people getting on Karlis's case so bad. It's not because they care about the game that much. It's because if they give three points on a big bet, sure enough Karlis will miss a field goal and the Broncos will win it by only one and there goes the rent money."

"What happens when the Broncos or some team are favored by three and they end up winning by three?"

"That's a push. No bet. Everybody gets his money back. Too many pushes and the bookie goes broke."

"Do many of your bettors here in Denver regularly go against the Broncos?"

"Sure they do. The smart ones do, anyway. Look at this week. They're favored by eight over Cincinnati. That spread looks pretty tempting. Lots of my people are going crazy for this one. The Broncos'll have to win by nine for them to get hurt."

"So who's betting the Broncos and giving the points?"

"All those fans you asked me about."

Twenty years ago, roughly 80 percent of all illegal bookmaking was made on horse racing, despite the fact that playing the horses was legal at tracks in every part of the country. Today, team sports make up 80 percent or more of the nation's illegal bookmaking action, with football far and away the preferred betting sport. That shift seems in large part attributable to television's role in exposing, perhaps overexposing, football and other sports to the American public, but it's attributable, too, to a betting innovation devised by a Chicago gambler and bookmaker named Charles K. McNeil. Prior to McNeil, people bet on football using a standard system of odds—2 to 1, or 10 to 1, or what have you—that one team would beat another. But McNeil's system did away with the issue of winning and losing, replacing it with a betting scheme concerned only with the point differential between the two teams. McNeil's system was suitable to any team sport, but particularly so to football, a sport in which points were not scored strictly in single- or double-point progression. Any fool could figure the system out, and virtually every fool had a television set at home.

As the television networks aggressively began to market the professional football games they had spent so much money for during the sixties and seventies, they added a novelty to their coverage which has now become a staple—the betting shill, a kind of colorful and folksy commentator, epitomized by CBS's Jimmy "The Greek" Snyder, who discusses point spreads as openly as if they were cookie recipes. Network officials have always strenuously denied that their broadcasts in any way promote gambling, but it's virtually impossible to watch the antics on any pre-game show and come away thinking they are doing anything but lying through their teeth.

Yet television isn't alone in its encouragement. An Associated Press survey of 125 newspapers around the country recently found that 77 percent of them run betting lines for each weekend's games. And many of them—including the *Rocky Mountain News*'s weekly column by Teri Thompson—offer regular betting tips and advice. No, they're not encouraging anything *illegal,* say the newspapers' editors. Nothing illegal about writing about who's an underdog, and by how much, and which games are absolute locks, is there?

The National Football League takes a similar laissez-faire attitude toward the enormous amount of gambling that is done on its games. Its stance is that it doesn't presume to tell the fans how to enjoy its games, yet it does pay lip service, at least, to making sure that illegal bookmakers don't become too closely associated with teams' players and management. NFL commissioner Pete Rozelle suspended Baltimore quarterback Art Schlichter for heavy gambling back in 1983, and league officials say that they issue ten or so warnings a year to players who appear to be running with the wrong crowd, but most observers say the league is fundamentally more interested in keeping the gambling issue quiet and contained than it is in ferreting it out into the open. No one suggests that point-shaving is widespread in the NFL—it isn't—but it is easy to see how a key player with large and looming gambling debts and a knee-breaking bookie could conceivably face some very troubling temptations.

Yet as long as the games themselves stay unspoiled, is sports betting—even illegal bookmaking—all that detrimental? Wouldn't the attempt truly to prevent gambling be as foolhardy as Prohibition was? People are gamblers, risk takers by nature, are they not? Unless it becomes pathological, surely gambling can be a simple source of suspense and excitement. Or it can consume you. "For my money," professional poker player Jack Straus told *Sports Illustrated* last summer, "there is no thrill in life more exhilarating than listening to a ball game with half your bankroll bet on it."

"I don't know anything about point spreads. I don't know what that means," Dan Reeves always replies when he is asked if he is surprised that his team is an underdog by two points, or is favored by eight. Although you could safely bet that he knows a bit more than he claims to, his is a very smart way to answer that kind of question.

"Hey, it's all just part of football," said Richard Armenta

before he had to go, encouraging me as he hung up to get in touch again if I ever wanted to make a little wager.

On Sunday morning, the snow spit and sputtered and finally stopped, but not before it had blanketed the city with a foot of wet, early-season cement, an incapacitating kind of storm even in a place where a measure of snow is common. By noon, the parking lots at the stadium were still nearly empty; only the most intrepid RVs had arrived for their pre-game encampment. Brooklyn's was quiet, almost deserted, except for a few Chicago Bears fans who had braved the elements to catch the early game. It seemed strange that there were no vendors on the streets; no one was hawking caps and orange pennants; not a soul was scalping tickets. Inside the stadium, plows scraped the snow from the prophylactic tarps that had been laid down over the field the day before, and crews made a token effort to scrape the snow from the bleacher seats.

It was the first snow game of the season, and the gamblers were either encouraged or concerned, depending on their outlooks and the nature of their bets. Snow tended to make for sloppy games, some of them supposed. Neither team would be able to accomplish much and the score would stay low, too low for comfort if you'd bet on the Broncos and had given away eight points. And what if the rumor circulating was true, for heaven's sake?—the one that claimed John Elway had broken his arm on Saturday. One Las Vegas casino was sure enough that *something* had befallen Elway that it took the Broncos-Bengals game off its betting board. Without Elway, Denver wouldn't have a chance to cover the spread. But on the other hand—and assuming Elway was as healthy as the Broncos swore he was on Saturday night—weren't blowouts prone to occur in cold and wet weather, and wouldn't the Broncos, playing at home, be the likely beneficiaries of the breaks? You had to wonder, if you'd taken Cincinnati and eight fragile little points.

Only 58,705 fans were in their seats when the sun came out and the tarps came off the field and the game got underway.

(The 17,444 who stayed home and shoveled snow and watched the game on television were the largest number of no-shows in the team's seventeen-year string of sellouts.) But the people who braved the elements—all bundled and wrapped and booted—seemed somehow more festive than usual because of the snow and the sense of adventure it lent to the afternoon. And the two teams, at work on the field below them, as dry as a lawn in July, quickly diverted the fans' attention from the snow that lay at their feet. No, this one would not be a fumble fest, and, given the two teams' quarterbacks, we could expect to see a pass or two.

On the first play of the game, Cincinnati's Boomer Esiason, his nickname presaging trouble, nailed a 36-yard pass to running back James Brooks. Eight plays later, the Bengals were at the Broncos' 21, but they got no farther before they had to settle for a shot at a field goal—one that sailed wide to the right and left the scoreboard empty. When the Broncos got the ball, Elway proved both arms were operable, beginning an eleven-play drive with a flare pass to Gerald Willhite, a drive that ended with a 49-yard field goal by Rich Karlis, gravity getting the better of the ball as it cleared the crossbar by inches.

Then the two teams traded touchdowns, the Bengals getting a long kickoff return and needing only four quick plays to find the end zone, the Broncos requiting in seven plays, including a 33-yard pass from Elway to Mark Jackson and a 4-yard toss to Vance Johnson for the score. The Bengals bounced right back with an 80-yard drive and a touchdown, giving them a 14–10 lead, then they virtually announced from the loudspeakers that they were finished scoring for a while. Before the half-time break, Denver added two touchdowns, one that culminated an 80-yard drive, the other the result of a Cincinnati fumble at the Bengals' seventeen. Denver 24–Cincinnati 14. So far, so good—if your bet was on the Broncos.

The Bengals did nothing in the third quarter but fumble once and throw one interception, while the Broncos found ten more points—Sammy Winder's 11-yard run for a touchdown and

Karlis's second field goal of the day. It was the fourth quarter and the Bengals trailed 34–14 before Boomer Esiason got serious, before the money invested on Cincinnati began to look like it might earn a good return. First it was a mannerly 89-yard drive for a touchdown, Esiason completing six of seven passes on the eleven-play trek down the field. Then, after the Broncos had quickly punted the ball back, Cincinnati tried again and Esiason ignited—four plays, four passes, eighty yards, seven points. It was brilliant, and the Bengals were only behind by six.

The Broncos had to punt again—newcomer Mike Horan's fifth punt of the day—and Cincinnati had an opportunity to take the lead with six minutes left in the game. Bengals bettors were already lighting up cigars, their money looking very smart at the moment, but Bengals fans were in excited suspense; as hot as Esiason was, a victory seemed well in hand. And Broncos fans had the sinking feeling they were right when it took just one Esiason pass and two runs by Stanley Wilson for Cincinnati to move from its own 20-yard line to the Broncos' 37. All of a sudden, there just wasn't any stopping these guys. But then Esiason was off the mark on two successive throws, and the Bengals faced a third and ten to keep their drive alive. Esiason stepped back into a shotgun formation, the Denver fans shouted "DEFENSE!" as loud as 58,000 could, and Bengals center Dave Rimington, unable to hear Esiason's count, simply launched the snap when he guessed his quarterback was ready for it. The ball went scooting past Esiason and rolled 23 yards before it was recovered. Cincinnati had blown its scoring opportunity, and now had no choice but to punt the ball.

The Broncos had a little more than four minutes to chew up, and with the help of an Elway quarterback draw on a third and fourteen, they chewed them, getting three first downs and reaching the Bengals' 28-yard line. With only seconds remaining now, Elway took two snaps and dropped to his knee to protect the ball and protect the victory. The fans began to celebrate, but the bettors who needed eight points were aghast. My God, the

Broncos didn't even try to score a final touchdown; those suckers didn't even attempt to cover the spread. Somehow, they were content with just winning the ball game.

The Broncos had gained 401 yards of offense, Cincinnati had a total of 426; Elway threw three touchdown passes, Esiason had a couple. And before they were through, the two teams put a total of sixty-two points on the board. "It looked like a track meet out there," said a jubilant Dan Reeves. "I'll tell you, it was mighty exciting from where I was watching it."

A hundred and thirty yards away, across the length of the stadium, Cincinnati coach Sam Wyche also had a date with an impatient press corps. He was distraught about the loss; he was incensed about the officiating (convinced that his team should have had a touchdown on a fumble recovery that was overruled in the fourth quarter); and he made his entrance into the dim, concrete-walled conference area by kicking open a metal door, then toppling a folding chair as he walked toward the podium. He surveyed the circle of reporters standing in front of him, his anger about to erupt, then he saw something he didn't like. "Wipe that smile off your face," he commanded of a reporter who had the audacity to be grinning at a colleague's comment. "There's nothing funny going on here." The reporter did his best to obey, then there was a protracted period of silence before Wyche turned to KHOW radio reporter Lee Frank and barked, "You ask the first question."

Frank hadn't been ready with a question, but one suddenly came to mind. "Why did you kick the door?" he asked.

"You — you get out of here," Wyche screamed, stepping off the podium and lunging at Frank. "This guy is out of here. I want him out of here," he yelled, shoving the reporter, trying to tear his microphone out of his hand. "Who is that? What kind of question was that? Get him out of here. Get him out. This interview is over unless you get him out. He's a fucking piece of sponge." Wyche was finally restrained, and Frank re-

209

treated, and suddenly nothing Wyche said thereafter mattered in the least. Suddenly there was a better story, a story about an out-of-control coach who couldn't contain his frustration and who thought roughing up a small, bearded reporter might just atone for a terrible call, one of those stories that would write itself about a Cincinnati team that had played a valiant football game despite the coach who had proven himself a chump.

Under the south stands, unaware of Sam Wyche's sore-loser hysteria, Dan Reeves was changing clothes and watching a football game on television—the Los Angeles Raiders and the Philadelphia Eagles in overtime. With the score tied at 27, the Raiders seemed poised to win it with the ball on the Eagles' 15 and dependable Marcus Allen in the backfield. Chris Bahr had already kicked two field goals in the game, but the Raiders weren't going to take any chances; they were going to hand the ball to Allen as many times as it took for him to carry it safely across the goal line. But somehow Allen let the ball slip out of his hands. Philadelphia's Andre Waters scooped it off the grass and raced 81 yards before he was tackled on the Raiders' 4-yard line. Two plays later, Eagles quarterback Randall Cunningham scored on a one-yard sneak, and the Raiders' play-off hopes were all but history. Dan Reeves's war whoop seemed to shake the south-stand girders, and he poked his head out into the locker room where a few players were still getting dressed and a few reporters were still drumming up questions. "Guess who won?" Reeves gloated.

For the first time in several weeks, the season seemed to be looking up. The Raiders had slipped to 8–5, and now all the 10–3 Broncos had to do was win *one* of their three remaining games and they would win the AFC West, regardless of how the Raiders or the division's other three teams finished their schedules. In the last two weeks, the Broncos had played with a phoenix offense, they had finally hired a guy who had a knack for punting the football, they were getting healthy again, and in a week they would travel to Kansas City to face the reeling

Chiefs. It was a setup. They could ice the division title in chilly Kansas City, then try to get two final regular-season victories to secure the home-field advantage throughout the play-offs. Shoot, there wasn't anything to this business.

Sam Wyche had already called KHOW radio in Denver to apologize publicly to Lee Frank on Monday when Dan Reeves sat in front of the Pepsi machine in the press trailer and fielded yet another set of questions. Was he aware of the Wyche incident? Not until he read it in the morning papers. What were his thoughts about the Bengals' coach's outburst? "Well, I guess I can't really imagine anybody ever losing their temper with the press," he deadpanned. "I don't think a reporter's ever asked me anything that made me mad." The reporters seated in front of him laughed heartily at that one, but the head coach played it straight.

December 7

—

You knew you were in the heart of the heartland when all the fans arriving at the stadium seemed to be wearing insulated coveralls and gimme caps from tractor companies. You knew you were there when the Northwest Missouri State University Marching Band moved in formation to music from *Man of La Mancha*. But you knew it in particular and without any kind of question when the national anthem was followed by an invocation, the voice of the Baptist minister booming throughout the stadium, ". . . and we pray, Our Heavenly Father, that these football fans assembled here today come to understand that Your love is like money in the bank, waiting to be cashed in. Amen." He said it. I heard him. I was there.

Kansas City still seemed asleep when we drove to the stadium this morning in a cold and relentless rain—Bob McDowell, Steve McDowell, and I—our stomachs full from a breakfast of eggs and grits and gravy, our thirsts already slaked by a beer or two to celebrate old friendship. The McDowell brothers, born and bred in Topeka, Kansas, and friends of mine since God was a boy (as they say in that part of the plains), had sojourned in previous years in such strange outposts as Quebrada Aseca, Peru, and Albuquerque, New Mexico. But each of them by now had returned to their wheat-swept homeland—Bob to Kansas City proper, Steve to a spread in rural Tecumseh, Kansas, he calls "Anomaly Acres."

It was going to be a brutal day for a football game, but we had already prescribed alcohol as an anesthetic, and en route to Arrowhead Stadium we had had the surprising foresight to stop at a K mart to buy five-dollar rain suits, fashioned from plastic about as thick as the stuff the dry cleaners use. We and 47,000 other fools were ready to tough it out. But just about the time "Ninja Nick" Lowery kicked a field goal to give Kansas City an early lead, the rain abated and my friends, the Chiefs fans, began to opine that life sometimes was perfect.

Perhaps because anyone who was out in that weather obviously wasn't burdened by the demands of reason, or perhaps because rooting for a perennial also-ran requires a hale and sanguine character, but whatever the reason, Bob and Steve McDowell and the fans we sat in the midst of seemed far more capable of enjoying the game, of enjoying each other and the simple Sunday recreation than the frenzied Broncos fans I'd become familiar with in Denver. If the Broncos fans, saddled with a Super Bowl contender, envisioned tragedy on every interception and screamed injustice with every penalty for illegal procedure, the Chiefs fans, in contrast, seemed to consider steady and comic banter as their highest calling. Although the 7–6

212

Chiefs were not yet mathematically eliminated from the play-offs, few of these corn-fed folks were making plans for Pasadena, and—strangely enough to my Broncos-drowned sensibility—they were treating the game on the field like little more than a *game*. Go figure, I thought, till their good cheer and good beer and the mercifully clearing weather turned me into a kind of convert.

The Broncos got a field goal of their own before the first quarter was out, and, in the second period, the two teams traded touchdowns. The required hot dogs had been consumed, and the empty Busch beer cups embossed with the red Chiefs logo were stacking up impressively by the time the Broncos went bust early in the third quarter. And by the time Rich Karlis's field-goal attempt hit the left upright and bounced back onto the field as a symbol of the futility of the fourth, the Chiefs led 27–10. John Elway threw his fourth interception of the day, then took to the bench; backup quarterback Gary Kubiak—always one to commiserate—threw an interception of his own; the Chiefs tacked on ten more points for good measure, and their fans were entirely tickled by the time the gun sounded to end the game. Kansas City 37, Broncos 10 and badly embarrassed.

Sure, the Broncos had gone into the game tied for the best record in the AFC, and yes, they did look worse today than the team New Orleans had humbled in the pre-season four months before. But hey, the McDowell brothers reminded me, the division championship was still like money in the bank—still waiting to be cashed in. And besides, it didn't snow, and nobody died, and a whole bunch of flatlanders had had a hell of a time. Somebody had to win, after all, and if the Broncos weren't willing to, then damnit, the Chiefs didn't have any choice. Their logic seemed impeccable, and I sure hated to say good-bye.

Trainer Steve Antonopulos administered Taiwan flu shots to the players and coaches in the locker room after the game—in case the bug that just had bitten them was contagious—then the erratic Broncos headed for the high country, the plane ride quiet, if not quite comatose. "We made too many mistakes to win it. We just didn't deserve it," said a pensive Rulon Jones. "You got me," John Elway confessed, "I don't know why this team can't seem to get over the hump." "It's a game of psychology," Tom Jackson said, "losing is losing, but we beat ourselves." The huge crowd that was expected to be awaiting them in Denver, had they clinched the division title, was composed of precisely three—sisters Patti, Sheri, and Linda Griffin, black teenagers who stood outside the security fence at the United Airlines hangar holding a sign that read, WHY THE LONG FACE? WE STILL LOVE YOU. But their gesture was hard to appreciate. Although a few players did wave and offer the girls wan smiles, most of them just scraped the ice and snow from their cars' windshields, then drove the devil on home.

December 14

Sunday had been a bad day, but the week that followed was worse. The Kansas City game didn't look a bit better when the coaches and players reviewed it on videotape on Monday afternoon. On Monday night, the Seattle Seahawks beat the Raiders—giving the Broncos the division title in the process—their fourth divisional title of the past decade. But Reeves and his team spent much of Tuesday denying that they had "backed into" the AFC West crown. "We damn sure didn't back into anything," Dan Reeves insisted. "We fought our tail off for fourteen weeks. We played as tough a schedule as anybody. We didn't play any pigeons." On Wednesday, a snowstorm forced the Broncos into their practice bubble, hampering their short-week preparations for Saturday's home game against the Washington Redskins. Then on Thursday, Clarence Kay drove his Datsun 300 ZX into a Chevrolet.

Trouble had been gaining on tight end Clarence Kay all season. He was arrested in Greeley at 2:00 A.M. one morning in August for speeding and driving while his license was under suspension. A legendary bon vivant and a determined free spirit, Kay was chronically late for morning meetings at the Broncos' practice facility, and one midseason weekend he only avoided missing the team plane by seconds. Late again on the morning of November 15, the day before the game against Kansas City in Denver, Kay snapped his head coach's final straw and suffered a one-game suspension—which he used as an opportunity to take a short vacation to see friends in Texas and Georgia. He returned to the team four days later, but said the suspension was "nothing I feel upset about." He was worn out, he told the Denver reporters, but assured them he wasn't in any kind of serious trouble. "People think I was tied up with drugs or in some kind of legal hassle. That's not true. After a while, you get burned out on a situation, that's all, burned out on an environment."

Kay returned to the starting lineup—where he was sorely needed. Reeves has long referred to Kay as the best blocking tight end in the NFL—playing against the Giants and Cincinnati before he was benched during the calamity in Kansas City. Kay's absence again Sunday, coupled with guard Paul Howard's hamstring injury, seriously depleted an offensive line that has been battered all season, and no doubt played a role in the debacle. On Monday, Reeves said Kay would start again as soon as he proved he was ready, and Kay told the curious reporters he was well aware he was walking a very tight rope. "That's the line that's been drawn. Either I do what I'm told or I may be out of here."

On Thursday morning, Kay—tardy yet again—was rushing

215

to get to work when his car skidded through an icy intersection and hit a parked Chevrolet sedan, sending the second car crashing into a metal pole, virtually demolishing Kay's sports car, and bruising his left hip and thigh. Absent a driver's license, Kay used a credit card for identification at the accident scene. He called Reeves to explain the accident, then was examined by the Broncos' team doctor, agreeing to a urinalysis, and arrived at the Broncos' headquarters in the afternoon. "If I didn't have bad luck, I wouldn't have any luck," Kay told the reporters. "These last thirty or forty days have gotten kind of rough on me. I think the car's totaled, but I'm going to see if I can fix it before I throw it away. That's one of my favorite cars."

On Friday, Kay's concerns had broadened beyond his car. Reeves announced that Kay had tested positive for an illegal drug—which drug, he wouldn't say—and that the three-year veteran had been suspended for four weeks under the terms of an NFL player classification called "Reserved—non-football illness." Reeves acknowledged that Kay had tested positive for the same drug four weeks before—at the time his tardiness first became chronic—then said that Kay could return to the team and would be welcome to if he successfully completed a drug treatment program at an NFL-approved drug rehabilitation clinic.

Following a meeting with Reeves on Friday afternoon, Kay agreed to talk with reporters for the *Denver Post* and the *Rocky Mountain News*. He was shaken and soft-spoken, confessing he was very confused and felt terrible for his family. "This is the lowest I've been," he told Steve Caulk and Joe Sanchez, the two reporters who questioned him, their own voices subdued, wanting to hear Kay's story but reluctant to badger him. Kay told them he wasn't sure whether he would enter the clinic, then suggested that perhaps it was what he needed. "But Clarence Kay is not a drug addict," he wanted them to know. "He does not wake up and go to sleep on cocaine." Despite that denial, he wanted to offer this bit of advice: "People think it's a recreation. There's no such thing, because it catches up to you."

Asked if he had informed his family of his suspension, Kay whispered. "I just talked to my sister on the phone, and I haven't cried like that in ten years, since my mother died." When Caulk asked him how he felt about eventually returning to the Broncos, Kay considered before he spoke. "I don't know if I can ever come back to Denver. I let a lot of people down."

You could make the case that Clarence Kay is lucky he's a football player, lucky he belongs to an organization that keeps close enough track of its employees to be occasionally aware of bad habits before they become ruinous. Or you could argue that if Clarence Kay weren't a professional football player, if he weren't a twenty-five-year-old man making roughly $200,000 a year and looking for ways to spend it, he would have been much less likely to fall into cocaine's clutches—if indeed that is the drug responsible for his suspension. You'd probably be right on both counts.

Drug use pervades American society, of course. Most of us use so-called recreational drugs on a daily basis. Even Ronald and Nancy Reagan, who "just say no" to street drugs, are regular users of alcohol. Our parents were drug users, and our children will be as well, if they aren't already.

A Michigan State University study recently reported that 82 percent of the students at that campus had used alcohol at least once in the past year; 27 percent had used marijuana; 12 percent, cocaine; 11 percent had tried prescription narcotics; and 3 percent had experimented with psychedelics. Those figures didn't surprise many people. What *was* intriguing about the study was that among the group of student athletes surveyed, an average of 5 percent fewer had experience with the several drug groups than did the student population as a whole. That statistic certainly didn't imply that the kids on the full-ride football scholarships were virtual Pollyannas, yet it did provide a counterpoint to the current crisis-center attention that is being given to the role of drugs in collegiate and professional sports. Drug use and abuse is an issue that spans our whole society, and drugs are a

217

part of the current sports scene simply because they are everywhere.

You would be burying your head in the Gatorade bucket, however, if you failed to recognize that sportswriters have been forced to write a lot about substance abuse in recent years. Between 1983 and 1985, fifteen famous professional athletes—football, baseball, or basketball players all—very publicly went to prison or to rehab programs because of drug abuse. So far this year, Michael Ray Richardson of the New Jersey Nets has been banned from the National Basketball Association; John Lucas was fired by the Houston Rockets; Len Bias, drafted the day before by the Boston Celtics, died of a cocaine overdose; Cleveland Browns defensive back Don Rogers died of a cocaine overdose; Cleveland draft choice Willie Smith was arrested on cocaine and weapons charges; and now Clarence Kay will miss the rest of the Broncos' regular season. Even the deaths of Bias and Rogers would have gone largely unreported if the two had not been stellar athletes. Young Americans O.D. every day, yet somehow it is shocking news when athletes are among their number. We expect athletes, especially those who earn enormous salaries, to be nearly perfect at their craft, and we profess disbelief when they sometimes prove to be as fallible and vulnerable as the rest of us.

Yet Clarence Kay and his athlete colleagues *are* inarguably different from everyone else in ways that work to their detriment. They are athletic wunderkinds whose talents have been impressed upon them since they were just pubescent, who are thrust to the pinnacle of their profession at an age when their contemporaries are still washing dishes, who are paid salaries that seem like all the money in the world, and who, to top it all off, are suffocated by the strange adulation that comes from tittering autograph seekers and the glare of the TV Minicams. Is it any surprise that some of them seek refuge in double scotches, that a few of them sniff reassurance into their nostrils? If anything, it's surprising to me that more of them aren't unable to decline the lure. "Cocaine is God's way of telling you that you make too much money," Barbara Ingram had said the day I watched the Broncos-Giants game with her and her friends while we were discussing Giants' linebacker Lawrence Taylor's widely publicized rehabilitation from substance abuse. I laughed, but she was very serious, and I began to see her point.

NFL Commissioner Pete Rozelle's response to the issue of player drug abuse had been to try to get tough. In 1982, the last time the league and the players association had to hammer out a bargaining agreement, Rozelle was able to push through a drug-testing policy that called for mandatory pre-season testing of every player on every club, as well as selective testing whenever a team physician suspected a player of drug dependency. Many players strenuously objected to the agreement on civil rights grounds, but their union representatives ultimately acquiesced. Then this year, faced with mounting public attention to drugs in sports and with increasing numbers of his players making headlines for the wrong reasons, Rozelle tried to expand the policy to include rigorous random testing across the board. The players union balked without budging this time, and, just over a month ago, a federal arbitrator ruled that the new plan violated the terms of the 1982 agreement. When a new collective bargaining agreement is laid on the table next summer, it seems certain the league will push for more clout than it presently has, but players' representatives maintain that, while they understand the importance of keeping the sport free from the taint of addiction, they will not summarily surrender their civil rights. And there is the curious indication that the league is more than a little selective in the drugs it is choosing to do battle against. Team physicians and former players are almost unanimous in their agreement that anabolic steroids are the most widely abused drugs in the NFL, followed by prescription narcotics, amphetamines, alcohol, and cocaine, in that order. Yet although the league says it is studying the problems posed by legally available drugs and makes public assurances it is concerned about their abuse, it appears that, for the foreseeable future, only a positive test for street drugs such as marijuana, cocaine, or heroin will result in a player's suspension.

Like several other teams, the Denver Broncos have chosen to try to avoid drug problems by doing their best to see that players who join the club via trades or the draft are thoroughly investigated for, and appear free from, chronic drug use—sometimes paying as much attention to a player's nocturnal habits as to his speed in the 40-yard dash.

Yet interestingly, two of the nine players drafted by the Broncos prior to this season tested positive for illegal drug use at a scouting combine—a kind of NFL merchandise show at which teams can shop for prospective players—held in New Orleans last January. Of the 350 players who attended the combine, three tested positive for cocaine, and fifty-seven showed evidence of marijuana use. When he was queried about why the team had chosen to break its unofficial policy of avoiding problem players by drafting the two, Reeves assured reporters that his scouting staff had thoroughly investigated both players once a decision was made to try to draft them. "I'm not convinced," Reeves said, responding to a question about whether the two were drug free. "Nobody can guarantee me that, as far as each one of them is concerned, the kid doesn't have a problem, but in every shape or form of checking that our staff did, he doesn't."

Reeves had said prior to the draft that he "wasn't going to mess with anyone who showed on that test," yet after the two players had been acquired, he amended his position. "I'm not condoning marijuana, but I can't throw a blanket over fifty-seven guys and say they're guilty before being proven innocent." He remained adamant, however, in his determination to steer clear of cocaine users.

Then seven months later, suspected cocaine dependency cost him his best tight end.

By beating the Raiders Monday night, the Seattle Seahawks presented the Broncos with a coveted gift, one they'll undoubtedly enjoy when they take a short Christmas holiday next week. Following their final regular-season games against the Redskins at home and the Seahawks on the road on December 20, the Broncos will have a two-week break before, as division champions, they begin a one-, two-, or three-game sudden-death play-off series. Yet whether any or all of their play-off games will be played in Denver remains to be decided by the way they and four other teams finish their schedules. Even if the Broncos were to finish the season 12–4, they might still have to travel throughout the play-offs, better win-loss records and tie-breaking procedures possibly sending them back to the dreaded Meadowlands to play the Jets, or to Cleveland to battle the Browns. Yet given the proper set of circumstances—and a couple of wins of their own—the Broncos could indeed play the first two play-off games at home in Mile High Stadium. The third game, if they were to get that far, would definitely send them to Pasadena—a trip they'd willingly make.

But the road to Pasadena is littered with bad-tempered linebackers and with explosive offenses capable of giving the Denver team fits. Although the horses rebounded from their pitiful performance in Kansas City and from the disclosure of the personal travail of Clarence Kay by playing back up to par on Saturday, they faced an excellent Redskins team which they ultimately beat by just a breath.

With first-year player Joey Hackett starting in Kay's position and Mark Cooper playing in place of the injured Paul Howard, and with Steve Sewell's shoulder still on the mend, the Broncos' offense sputtered through the first two quarters, John Elway running a quarterback draw into the end zone a minute before the half-time whistle for Denver's only score. On the arm of quarterback Jay Schroeder and the legs of running back George Rogers, Washington got two touchdowns in the half, but only managed thirteen points because of kicker Max Zendejas's missed extra point—a blunder that would come back to haunt him and his teammates.

The Redskins slept through the third quarter while the Broncos recorded two more touchdowns—the first finishing a 72-yard drive, the second the result of a Mike Harden interception. Early in the fourth quarter, Washington got a 48-yard field goal (this one from kicker Steve Cox) before the Broncos galloped 80 yards for another touchdown. With eight minutes to go in the game, Denver had a comfortable 28–16 lead, but by then, the Redskins were finally warmed up. On a two-play, two-pass drive, Schroeder took his team into the end zone, 77 yards in fifty-nine seconds. Denver responded with a field goal. Then, with three minutes to go, the Redskins roared right back, but this time needing all of seven plays to traverse the length of the field. Following a successful extra point, Washington trailed 31–30.

The Broncos' task, with a minute and a half remaining, was nothing more than to hang on to the ball. With the fans—who weren't sure whether they were seeing the last football of the season in that stadium—screaming for joy, shouting thanks to a gracious God, the Broncos ran for a first down, ran out the clock, then ran delightedly off the field, Elway saluting the south stands as he disappeared beneath them.

"Wasn't even close, was it?" quipped a jubilant Dan Reeves as he stepped in front of the press. "It was a great win for us, and it puts us in a position to have a chance for the home field in the play-offs."

"Dan, what are your feelings with this win coming after a chaotic week?" the *Post*'s Buddy Martin wanted to know.

"Well," Reeves replied, "I think our team knew they couldn't be distracted by anything. And the fact that we bounced back after Kansas City means a lot. It was a great ball game. It's a shame a game like this had to be decided by a missed extra point, but it's nice to see somebody besides us miss it."

Then Reeves was asked about Clarence Kay. Becoming un-characteristically loquacious, he acknowledged that he would "welcome him back with open arms" if he solved his problem, saying he could forgive the big tight end's mistakes because "I've

222

made so many myself that I can sure feel compassion for him." When an out-of-town reporter suggested that Kay was already on the trading block, Reeves responded strongly. "That's not true. This team is like a family. When you have a person in your family that has a problem, you don't kick them out."

In the adjacent locker room, the players were in the process of saying a collective *"So there"* to the reporters and fans who had accused them five days before of backing into the division title. "I think everybody just realized what had to be done," observed linebacker Ricky Hunley. "This game will do wonders for us," added Hunley's friend and roommate and fellow linebacker, Tom Jackson. "If the second half of this game was play-off tempo, you can bet that the whole thing in Seattle will be."

December 22
—

Despite Tom Jackson's confidence, the Broncos were snakebitten by statistics. They had not won two games in a row since November 2, and they kept their dubious string intact by going indoors in Seattle and playing their worst single game of the season—much worse than the collapse against Kansas City, far lousier than the sleepwalk against San Diego or that long-ago, bagel-and-pretzel bombardment by the Jets. Although you had to admit the Seahawks played superbly, there was no denying that the new AFC West Champions soiled the Kingdome carpet. Seattle Seahawks 41, Denver Donkeys 16.

On the Wednesday before the game, five Broncos' players were named to the American Conference squad that will play in the Pro Bowl—the NFL's all-star game—in Honolulu the weekend after the Super Bowl. Defensive players Rulon Jones, Karl Mecklenburg, and Dennis Smith, all of whom were Pro Bowl players last year, were again voted to the team by their fellow players from around the conference. In addition, Keith Bishop became the first Broncos' offensive lineman ever to make the team, and John Elway was the first Broncos' quarterback to receive the honor. Conspicuous by his absence was cornerback Mike Harden, who, by general consensus, has had nothing short of a spectacular season—at least through fifteen games.

Harden joined the teammates going to the islands and those who will stay on the mainland in playing a game in Seattle that was nothing short of dismal. According to the head coach, it was the worst single-game effort he had seen since coming to Denver in 1981. According to Tom Jackson, whose hopes had been so high, he hadn't been part of a more pitiful performance since he became a Bronco in 1973. If you saw it, you no doubt share their sentiments. If you didn't, consider your fortunes cresting.

"I can't believe our team would play like that," said a seething Dan Reeves, doing a decidedly rapid burn on a podium outside the Broncos' Seattle locker room. "To me, when you're champions, you play like it, damn it. I don't give a dadgum what's at stake. It's embarrassing to play like that. I don't like it worth a damn, and I don't expect us to play like that. It's ridiculous. We didn't play worth a damn, period."

At long last, the regular season was over, ending in a defeat so hollow few players had words to describe it. The six weeks of grueling summer camp, followed by the relentless punishment of sixteen games on as many weekends, had ended with a whimper that was all but inaudible inside the cacophonous Kingdome. Five months had passed since the players reported to camp and the football pundits began to predict that this bunch was bound for the Super Bowl. Facing one of the league's toughest schedules, the Broncos had made their guesses look good, turning the first half of the season into a stellar 7–1 performance. But then they somehow fell out of orbit, finishing the season at a decidedly earthy 4–4. "I think a lot of the guys have to take a look inside and decide what they're going to do," Jackson said, standing in a towel, looking very defeated and, for the first time, a little old. "This is a time when we really should be coming together," said Rulon Jones as he sat staring at the floor, "but we're not. We just aren't. I don't know."

For eighteen of the NFL's twenty-eight teams, the season ended this weekend—that's that; it's finished—sixteen battles and the long war was finally over. But the embarrassed and bedraggled Broncos will be among the ten teams who'll play again before the long winter recess—at least there's that. There will be one more game, and maybe more, to add to this perplexing season; Christmas will come as always, then a new year will be ushered in, and in Denver, despite the trouble, they'll still be playing football.

December 23

—

With just two shopping days until Christmas, business is booming in the souvenir sections at J.C. Penney's, it's wild at the Sport Shop in the Tabor Center, but things are an absolute storm of chaos at Mr. K's, an out-pass away from the players' building at the Broncos' practice facility.

Wally Kenney was right in his hunch that people somehow might believe that officially licensed Broncos T-shirts, caps, boxer shorts, and windshield scrapers were a trifle *more* official if they were purchased within eyeshot of the Broncos' hallowed home.

225

East Fifty-seventh Avenue isn't exactly one of the city's retail meccas, you understand, but here is where the Denver branch of Mr. K's Broncos Souvenirs—a division of the same enterprise established in suburban Brighton in 1978—is located, hard by Randy's VW Stuff, around the corner from Colorado Remnant King. And today the place is abuzz. Never mind that the ink is still wet on the newspaper accounts of the Broncos' biggest humiliation since the Super Bowl drubbing by Dallas, which refuses to fade from memory. Never mind that the call-in lines are packed on this afternoon's sports-talk shows, fans demanding a cold accounting of what the hell has gone wrong. Those issues are just so much misdirected hysteria as far as these shoppers are concerned, what with stockings to stuff and a play-off game kicking off in just twelve short days. You don't hear *them* whining, do you? There's simply no time for that, not with the official Broncos dog dishes and the orange, diamond-shaped BRONCOS FAN ON BOARD signs being yanked from the dwindling supplies on the shelves.

Red-haired and ruddy Wally Kenney—a sort of Broncos orange himself—began his entrepreneurial odyssey with his wife nine seasons ago, the two of them purchasing twenty-four dozen orange cowboy hats and selling them from card tables set up outside the stadium. Although the hats weren't quite the hit Kenney expected them to be—he still has a few on hand, if you're interested—he quickly realized that the Broncos souvenir vein was a rich one waiting to be mined. "We took in just $2,500 that first year," says Kenney, standing out of the way of the frenzied shoppers. "By the second year, sometimes we'd sell $400 or so out of our house in just one night." By the third year, Kenney had given up his truck-driving job, the retail shop in Brighton was open, and he was selling caps and T-shirts out of a van in the hours before each Broncos home game. "The NFL strike in '82 damn near killed me," he confesses. "I lost my house and had to refinance the business, but we hung in because I knew the fans would be back after the strike. It took me two years to pay some of my companies off, but I did. I periodically have to remind some of them that they've never lost a penny on me."

Kenney says that he now sells ninety-five different souvenir items wholesale and over four hundred retail. "We average a new item about every week, and I think I'm currently buying from seventy-six different companies. We have people coming in the doors from South Dakota and farther away, saying they heard about us from friends. We send stuff mail-order to Europe, Asia, everywhere." Although he doesn't want to discuss what his own business grosses, he says that the Broncos accessories business throughout metro Denver amounts to $5 million a year, maybe more.

The National Football League, via its NFL Properties subsidiary, is very careful to control the distribution of merchandise incorporating the names and logos of its twenty-eight teams. Back in 1978, Kenney could sell his orange cowboy hats without earning the wrath of NFL Properties only because the hats made no mention of the Broncos. If they had, he would have been in a heap of trouble, he says. In order to protect its merchandising rights, Kenney explains, NFL Properties acts as a kind of patent office, examining prototype souvenirs, clothing, and accessories submitted to it by companies around the country, deciding with its own complex criteria whether a product is worthy of its official license. Team-logo toilet seats and hundreds of other dubious proposals are turned down annually. And those relative few deemed acceptable are licensed under an agreement that earns the league and its member teams a royalty of 7.25 percent. In addition, just in case, say, a new football-helmet snack bowl proves to be a bomb, NFL Properties demands a nonrefundable $10,000 advance against the royalty before the product hits the shelves. It's a bit of a risky business, and items appear and disappear with lightning speed. I inquire of Kenney which of his four hundred products are currently the hottest sellers, and he leads me on a tour.

"This Cliff Engle sweater is something I can't keep in stock, mostly just because Dan Reeves wore it at a few games this season. If you'd have asked me about it before the season, I'd have probably said it'd do all right, but that it was too big-ticket to really take off. You just never know what to expect—except that T-shirts are always going to be the biggest sellers, caps second, then jackets. But you never know about the specific styles, or the player numbers that'll be popular. For some reason right now, Tony Lilly's all the rage."

"What about something that's bombed?" I ask, and we walk to the "Mach 7" poster display—a photograph of John Elway standing near the nose of a jet fighter on the tarmac at Lowry Air Force Base, the quarterback wearing cowboy boots, jeans, and a pilot's leather jacket, cradling a football in his arm, his signature etched by an auto-pen.

"I thought this was going to be dynamite," Kenney confides. "I did. I expected really big things from an Elway poster. I don't know what the problem is. My hunch is that there isn't anything in it that means Broncos to anybody."

Then there is "Broncomania," a thirty-minute videotape pro-duced by NFL Films and marketed for the Christmas season, containing highlights of game action from the 1977 season till now and comments by players, coaches, and the most truly unstable fans—all of it set to epic music which sounds as if it were originally scored for a low-budget knights-of-the-round-table movie, and narrated by John Doremus, the familiar voice of NFL Films, his portentous baritone intoning, "It's called Broncomania, and the telltale orange fever has reached epic proportions in the Rocky Mountains." It's yours for just $19.95, available in VHS or Beta. "Oh, these are gone as soon as we get them," Kenney tells me. "This is incredible. Everybody's got a VCR these days, for one thing. But part of the reason this is big is that it's about the fans as well as the team. I mean, it's about the people who buy it, which makes it fun."

Kenney admits that not every Broncos fan is a souvenir and sweatshirt buyer, however. There *are* self-respecting Broncos fans who do not own a Broncos-helmet telephone, for instance, who do not fly Broncos flags from their television antennas, who would be hard-pressed to produce a simple Broncos key chain, or so much as a cigarette lighter. "I say there are two types of fans, basically," Kenney says, waxing sociological. "I call them the People Who Wear Orange, and the People Who Don't Wear Orange. The People Who Wear Orange come to the stadium real early; they come out to the Saturday practices; they go to the stores when players make personal appearances; they really get into it. The People Who Don't Wear Orange are more laid-back; they're only interested in the games, which is fine, but they aren't my market. It's the People Who Wear Orange who *buy* orange."

January 5

It was the day after Christmas, and at the Broncos' training facility, not a cornerback, or a groundskeeper, or an assistant coach was stirring. The place hadn't been this deserted since the organization's annual June vacations seven months before. Despite their spoiling his holiday with the surrender in Seattle, Dan Reeves had given his players three days off to rest and recuperate and rekindle the fire that somehow had dampened to coals. It was a generous gesture, but it left the ever on-duty beat reporters with dozens of pre–play-off game stories to write and paltry raw material.

The Rocky Mountain News responded to the challenge, surely in the spirit of the season, by selecting its own "All-Time Denver Broncos Roster," the best players from the excellent and the merely mediocre teams that had been fielded during the team's twenty-seven seasons. Of the twenty-five players selected, ten were current Broncos players, John Elway and Karl Mecklenburg making the list after just four seasons of play. Dan Reeves got the nod as the all-time head coach (he's already held the job longer than anyone else), but Pat Bowlen was beaten out by Gerald Phipps for the rather unusual title of "all-time owner."

The *Post*, on the other hand, chose the investigative route to fill up space, asking area football experts to explain "What's wrong with the Denver Broncos?" Fred Tesone, football coach at perennial powerhouse Cherry Creek High School, opined that it was basically a lack of a superstar running back and a decline in defensive intensity. Bill McCartney, head of the University of Colorado's struggling football program, said it was a simple matter of a very long season, the Broncos having to play some tough teams at a time when they were running down. Former Broncos safety Billy Thompson thought it was a combination of fatigue and overconfidence. Former Broncos guard Tom Glassic thought it was simply nothing to worry about. "How can anybody complain about an 11–5 record?" he asked.

Although Dan Reeves wasn't part of the poll, it was his opinion that there was nothing wrong with the Broncos that a little scratching and clawing couldn't cure. The assessment of Reeves and his assistant coaches was that their decision to lighten up late-season practices—often opting for half-speed run-throughs instead of full contact with pads in the hope of offsetting the inevitable grind of the season—had backfired, resulting in poor habits and sloppy performance. So, once their Christmas break was over, the coach let it be known, the Broncos' practices would seem like training camp—replete with blocking and tackling and righteous indignation.

The Los Angeles Raiders finished with an 8–8 record, a break-even season that was disastrous by Raiders standards. The inconsistent Seattle Seahawks closed out their schedule by playing better football than perhaps any other team in the league; yet they had lost too many games, early on, and their 10–6 record

230

left them at home for the holidays. The inconsistent Kansas City Chiefs, however, landed one of the two American Conference "wild card" play-off berths with a similar 10–6 record, but by virtue of having a better record in games played against AFC opponents than the Seahawks or the 10–6 Cincinnati Bengals.

It was the first time in fifteen years that the Chiefs had survived into the post-season, but their longevity didn't amount to much. On December 28, they had the dubious honor of traveling to the New Jersey Meadowlands to do battle against a Jets team that had followed an initial 10–1 record with five straight losses to end its regular season. The Jets were reeling—they had been riddled with injuries—but the Chiefs choked, and the Jets finally won one, 35–15. Their first-round victory sent them to Cleveland on January 3, the day before the AFC East champions, the New England Patriots, sauntered into Mile High Stadium to meet the Broncos.

Denver and New England both finished the regular season with 11–5 records, and their play-off game was slated for Denver rather than Foxboro, Massachusetts, because the Broncos' September victory over the Patriots gave them the better record in head-to-head competition. It was an eventuality that delighted the Broncos and their fans, of course, but ironically it also suited the Patriots just fine. Unlike the Broncos, who were 7–1 at home during the season and 4–4 on the road, the Patriots somehow seemed to prefer playing away from the distractions of their supporting faithful—as if too much cheering in their favor simply threw them off their game. Their 4–4 home record was the worst of any of the league's ten play-off teams, but their 7–1 road record was little short of astonishing. So Sunday's game would be a mixed bag for the red-white-and-blue Pats—it would be a road game, and that much was reassuring, yet it would be played in the only stadium besides their own in which they had suffered a loss this season. Hell, Mile High Stadium was almost as rough as having to play at home.

To help mitigate that disadvantage, and to acclimate themselves to the air they presumed was a little too low on oxygen

231

for their liking, the Patriots arrived in Colorado on the Monday before the game and spent the week breathing and training at the Air Force Academy in Colorado Springs. The Broncos spent the week at home, some sixty miles away, and both teams spent a no-nonsense six days preparing for the game that would end the season for one, and send the other to the AFC championship contest.

Then on Saturday afternoon, their strategies mapped and their butterflies mounting, the members of the two clubs watched with no little interest the Cleveland–New York Jets game that was telecast from Cleveland. The Broncos, to a person, were rooting for the delinquent Jets; if they won, and presuming the Broncos did as well, the championship game would be played in Denver, where the Broncos felt confident they could make amends for the early-season slaughter. (But what appropriate objects could the fans throw from the stands? Skis? T-bone steaks?) The Pats, on the other hand, were solidly behind the Browns. A Browns win, coupled with one by New England, would send the championship game to Cleveland, a secure enough venue, certainly. But if the Jets won, along with New England, the Pats would be forced to fight for the championship at home— obviously not a pleasant prospect.

With four minutes left in the fourth quarter at Cleveland's Municipal Stadium, the Jets led 20–10, and Broncos personnel were canceling their contingency plans for a trip to Cleveland. But the Browns got ten quick points to tie the score before the clock ran out, then they held the Jets at bay through an entire overtime period. The *second* overtime period was getting a little long in the tooth as well when Cleveland kicker Mark Moseley finally kicked the winning field goal, ending the four-hour marathon and beginning plans in earnest back in Denver for a business trip to the sunny shores of Lake Erie.

But first, there was the little matter of the New England Patriots to be gotten out of the way—the current edition of the Patriots club that a year before had won three straight play-off road games to make it to the Super Bowl. In contrast, the last time the orange horses had made the play-offs—two years before—they promptly had lost to the lackluster Pittsburgh Steelers in a game played at Mile High Stadium. In fact, the Broncos were 0–2 in play-off competition under Dan Reeves, and they hadn't won a play-off game in nine years, not since they beat the Raiders on New Year's Day, 1978, to advance to their Super Bowl blowout by the Dallas Cowboys—America's team and Reeves's alma mater.

Despite bright blue skies and temperatures as warm as they were when the Pats came to town in September, forty-four people had the temerity not to show up on Sunday, leaving it to a faithful 76,105 to try to generate a little noise and let the Broncos know that Seattle was ancient history.

Although John Elway was erratic at the start of the game—opening the Broncos' first series with a 25-yard strike to Vance Johnson, then following it with three incomplete passes and an interception, the two teams took turns scoring throughout the first half, and there seemed little reason to panic. Denver got the first lead with a 27-yard Rich Karlis field goal late in the first quarter, then the teams traded punts until midway through the second, when Patriots quarterback Tony Eason found receiver Stanley Morgan with a 19-yard touchdown pass. On the ensuing kickoff, the Broncos moved from their own 18-yard line to the Pats' 22 before Elway, unable to find an open receiver, scrambled into the end zone. Patriots kicker Tony Franklin tied the score at 10 with just two seconds left in the half, but hardly anyone in the stadium noticed. Even the players on the Patriots' bench had their attention focused on what was potentially a far more pressing development across the field. His arms draped across the shoulders of two trainers, John Elway was limping into the locker room.

On the Broncos' final possession of the first half, Elway was hit by linebacker Andre Tippett as he released a pass; the ball landed in the arms of the Pats' Johnny Rembert, and Tippett landed squarely on Elway's left ankle. The quarterback hobbled

233

to the sideline, then was escorted from the field, and 76,105 fans assumed they were seeing the last of John Elway for this season, many of them also assuming they were watching the Broncos' Super Bowl quest come to a crippling finale. So, it would come down to an ankle this year, would it? Oh, the damnable fates of football.

"There was quite a bit of pain, and I wasn't sure how bad it was," Elway remembered after the game. "The medicine man was putting some stuff on it and rewrapping it, and I just thought, this better work."

"When I walked into the room where John was being treated, it looked like a M*A*S*H unit," Dan Reeves recounted, explaining that in addition to his starting quarterback, three other players were receiving half-time attention to injuries. "I didn't know if John would be able to go or not. I told him I didn't want him to go in there if he couldn't play. Then he warmed up on it, and he was hurting, but he said he wanted to try it. He went in, and he never came out."

As if it were a simple matter of suddenly realizing they couldn't depend solely on their superstar quarterback, the Broncos' offensive stalwarts somehow resurrected their running game to open the second half, moving from their own 15 to the Patriots' 5, a gimp-legged Elway completing just two passes, Sammy Winder, Gene Lang, and Ken Bell otherwise advancing the ball on the ground, busting it upfield eleven times before the Broncos were stalled and Karlis completed the drive with a field goal.

Five plays later, the Pats had the ball on the Broncos' 45, and Eason handed off to fullback Mosi Tatupu. Tatupu ran left, then tossed a flea-flicker back to Eason, who launched a 45-yard missile to Stanley Morgan, and New England was back on top. Six plays later, the Broncos had rebounded to the Patriots' 48 when Elway saw linebacker Don Blackmon jump offside and, knowing the penalty would give him a virtual free play, aimed a long pass at Vance Johnson, who was streaking toward the end zone. Defender Ernest Gibson overran the ball, and

Johnson was able to grab it out of the air as he fell backward across the goal line. Now Denver was up by three.

The fourth quarter looked like a punting contest—New England's Rich Camarillo and Denver's Mike Horan (a *punter* this guy, the third one of the season, a bona fide charm) each kicking the ball three times before the Patriots appeared to have one last chance with 1:42 left to play. But on first and ten at his own 10-yard line, Eason dropped into the end zone to pass, and his season came to a thundering close. Broncos' defensive end Rulon Jones raced past Pats' guard Ron Wooten and trapped Eason behind the goal line, recording the fourth safety of his career (an NFL record) and certifiably saving the Broncos' day. Broncos 22, Patriots 17. On the free kick that followed, Camarillo bounced the ball into Steve Foley's enveloping arms, then Elway knelt twice, and the ecstatic Broncos stormed off the field en route to Cleveland, Ohio.

"I've thought about this for six years now—what it would feel like to win a play-off game," Dan Reeves said from his familiar podium. "I underestimated it. I can't tell you how exciting it is."

An exhausted John Elway, his left leg so well wrapped it appeared ready for shipping, rested his head on the podium while his head coach happily answered the endless questions. Then he began to field his own set of inquiries, his toothy smile broadening as he spoke. He explained his injury, and the half-time treatments, and said the pain had continued to subside throughout the second half. "Oh, there's no question that I'm going to play next week," he assured the scribbling reporters.

"I'm more excited than I've ever been in my entire career," said receiver Steve Watson in the locker room, his towel draped around him, his thin torso vivid evidence of why his teammates call him "Blade." "I feel like we've really gotten a monkey off our back by finally winning a play-off game."

"Oh, it's a tremendous feeling of accomplishment," Tom

235

Jackson averred in his role as senior statesman. "You don't get this chance often; it doesn't come around very often. Now there are just four teams left—and we're one of them."

"Seattle?" answered the imposing but still somehow impish Ricky Hunley. "Seattle? Man, where you been? That was *last* year."

January 10

The DC-8 was festooned with orange and blue crepe paper on Friday—the Denver-based United Airlines flight attendants doing their best to send the Broncos to Cleveland in style. The players, as per their custom, were ensconced in the back of the plane, some reading playbooks, some playing cards, some with little headsets stretched across their massive skulls oblivious to all but their seemingly silent music. The owner and coaches and staff occupied the plush leather seats in the first-class cabin, and between the two groups were the working stiffs—television anchors and camera people and producers, radio talk show hosts and sound engineers, still photographers and reporters, plus the senior columnists who were conspicuous by their presence.

Buddy Martin of the *Denver Post* worked for the New York *Daily News* the last time the Broncos were about to play in an AFC championship game. The *Rocky Mountain News*'s Dick Connor was in Denver in those days, but was then employed at the *Post*. It was indeed unusual for the two of them to be traveling aboard the team plane—their newspapers' deadlines normally demanding that they keep to separate schedules—but this wasn't going to be a regular football weekend after all. This was, by general consensus, the last real football game of the year, the last time football truly was the focus before the several-ring Super Bowl circus began. The AFC championship game was as good as football got, so the sporting folklore had it, and at this year's contest, by God, the Broncos would be in attendance. It wasn't exactly a columnist's dream—journeying to Cleveland just as January set in with a vengeance, then having to bang out thousands more words than usual once you were safely there and shivering—but it beat turning your attention to the Denver Nuggets (who were having a truly terrible season), and it meant that you could postpone those obligatory columns about who the Broncos should try to draft to make them perfect, and hell—you could feel it right there in the airplane—this was far more than just another away game.

It was an event of great enough moment, in fact, that KHOW radio's Tony LaMonica was broadcasting our departure live from Stapleton Airport, speaking into a remote telephone as the plane pulled away from the United hangar. "The excitement on the plane is really terrific," intoned the jolly, transplanted New Yorker. "I must tell you, the players are in a very loose mood after practicing this morning at Mile High in sweats and helmets. We're on the active ramp now, and we'll be on the active taxiway in just a minute. The captain has informed me that our DC-8 for today's flight—which has been given the special designation 'Bronco One'—has received a special and complete maintenance check, and I'm told the tower has granted us priority clearance for takeoff. We now have just turned north onto runway 3-5-Left, and we're quickly gaining speed for takeoff and . . . Bronco One is airborne! The Denver Broncos are on their way to Cleveland's Hopkins International Airport and the AFC championship game!"

From across the aisle, KOA radio's Sandy Clough hollered, "Hey, Tony, need an analyst?"—facetiously offering color commentary to complement LaMonica's play-by-play of the lift-off. But suddenly losing his telephone contact, the broadcast finished, LaMonica laughed along with the cluster of people who had heard him, all of whom were similarly employed in the overkill coverage of the football club on whose plane they now were cruising.

Bob Martin, tall and thin and dramatically long of leg, had little trouble filling the coach-class seat that had been assigned to him, a midplane position he has held for twenty-three seasons. The radio play-by-play voice of the Broncos since 1964, the bookish and rather cerebral broadcaster—a warm and engaging shatterer of the tough guy mike-side stereotype—Martin is perhaps more immediately identified with this team than anyone save John Elway. I would give you good odds that in a Broncos-related name recognition poll, he would finish in front of Dan Reeves. He began broadcasting Broncos games way back in historical times—back when the fledgling football horses hadn't yet assumed command of the autumn Sunday afternoon airwaves. For the past seventeen years, Martin has called the Broncos' contests for KOA radio, the 50,000-watt flagship station for a seven-state, forty-odd station "Broncos network." Together with longtime color commentator Larry Zimmer, Martin has become a tradition for at least half the fans at Mile High Stadium who hear him describe the onfield action via their portable radios' headsets each time the Broncos play at home. Huge numbers of the Broncos' television audience have become habituated to silencing their TV sets and tuning him in instead. Bob Martin's mellifluous voice and the Broncos' unpredictable antics hundreds of times have shortened the miles on drives between McCook and Scottsbluff, Nebraska, on Sunday excursions from Shiprock to Santa Fe. And on this Sunday, he said, he would broadcast his 435th Broncos game, his second AFC championship.

"If you had told me in 1964 that I'd still be here in 1986," he said adjusting his seatback, "and that the Broncos would be selling out over 70,000, well, a lot of us would have had a good laugh over that one. Now, KOA purchases one of the highest

238

radio-rights packages in the league, and, if you can believe the research, our listenership percentage is the highest of all the NFL's radio broadcasts."

I asked him to what he attributed that success. "To the growth of the city, and the whole region, I suppose. Denver was just a big regional town when the Broncos were organized, and this was very much a blue-collar kind of operation, and it had a few fans who matched. Then, as the area started to grow very quickly, the Broncos became the alma mater of a lot of newcomers—the team filled that kind of role for them, and it still does. And, as they have become one of the league's elite teams, people have been able to take an enormous amount of pride in them. It's as if somebody finally wrote something about our son that they didn't get off the police blotter. It's that kind of pride."

When I asked him if the broadcasts had ever begun to bore him, he quickly answered that they hadn't. "I'm not much good at repetition and doing things by rote," he said. "And although there is some repetition to what we do, you really don't know what's going to happen each time the quarterback takes the ball. The challenge of play-by-play is getting it right the first time. It's the old line about there being no erasers on microphones. That's the challenge I really enjoy. And I try to keep it all in perspective. You have to remember that it is a totally artificial situation. All of it. It's fun, it's entertaining, it's diverting, but ultimately it isn't *important*. The problem is that the stakes are so high now monetarily, each team such a big business, that people lose sight of that fact."

Despite his happiness with his job, Martin admitted that he didn't suppose he would go on with it forever. "I would guess that I'll be at it just two or three more years," he said, making me suspicious that five hundred games might be a number that has crossed his mind. "But whenever the end comes, I'll feel like I've had a very good run with it."

The last time the Broncos played in an AFC championship game, Martin was ecstatic as he called the final seconds of the 1978 win over the Raiders, shouting above the din: "The players

239

are jumping up and down on the sidelines. The fans respond. Listen to this crowd! The miracle has happened! The Broncos are going to the Super Bowl!" It was an enchanted moment, and Martin remembers it well. "Much had been written all that year about the miracle Broncos, this motley club that didn't really have the talent to get as far as it had. And Jon Keyworth, the running back, had even recorded a song about making those miracles happen. So somehow, it was the appropriate thing to say. I really hadn't rehearsed it." What about Sunday? Did he know what he would say if the Broncos became Super Bowl–bound a second time? "No," he said. "But I've wondered about it. And I'll be mindful of the moment, if it comes. But you never really know."

It was dark by the time the DC-8 touched down in Cleveland and Tony LaMonica phoned in a second live report. As the four chartered buses pulled away from the plane, a carload of Broncos fans somehow transplanted to Ohio waved from behind a security gate, but more than a few airport employees countered their ad hoc welcome with gestures that bespoke a less cordial greeting.

At the entrance to the Stouffer's Hotel downtown, a few blocks from frigid Memorial Stadium, a clutch of Cleveland fans—who were ready to get the goddamn game under way *right now*—taunted the players as they stepped off the buses and into the glare of dozens of television lights—advance crews from the Denver stations filming the Broncos' momentous arrival, each of the Cleveland stations on hand as well to record the enemy's entrance into the city under the cover of night.

More Cleveland fans crowded the lobby; local reporters pushed microphones into the players' faces, often uncertain of whom they were speaking to; John Elway fought off a swarm that surrounded him and backed slowly into an elevator; Tom Jackson, a Cleveland native—who was conceivably coming home to play his final football game—acquiesced to the attention and

240

settled in for the frantic interviews; and the crescendoing chants of *"Go Browns!"* shook the suspended chandeliers.

January 12

The wind had whipped Lake Erie into a roily sea on Saturday; the thick gray skies made the barges, the rusting cranes, and waterlogged docks down on the Cuyahoga appear all the more forlorn; and from the outside, Memorial Stadium looked like an abandoned tire factory, its yellow brick stained by soot and the lakeside weather, dramatic cracks in the mortar snaking up from sidewalks to roof.

It was a wonderful place. Built almost six decades before by the Works Progress Administration in hopes of luring the 1932 Olympics—just one of many dreams to go sour in this much-maligned city—it still seemed like the kind of stadium where football ought to be played, where the weather ought to be lousy, and where the players' jerseys ought to end up gloriously soaked with mud. With its two broad tiers of seats, covered high above by a steel latticework roof—support posts spoiling the view from at least a few seats in every section—it was an icon of an earlier NFL, one without imitation grass or temperature-controlled comfort. And although it was almost empty now, it was obvious that it was the place where all of northern Ohio planned to redeem its dreams on Sunday: Standing on a tall ladder in the west end zone, a stadium employee was coating the goalpost with furniture polish in an effort to make it so slick that celebrating fans would not be able to tear it down once the

241

Browns had defeated the Broncos thirty hours hence. Waiting in the baseball dugout which led to the Broncos locker room, a photographer for the Cleveland *Plain Dealer* was explaining that she would be leaving for Pasadena on Friday—feeling no need to preface her plans with a maybe.

The Broncos—the Browns' unfortunate sacrificial horses—bundled in parkas and topcoats and gloves, ambled out of their locker room a little before noon and nosed around, getting the feel of this ponderous place. Tony Lilly peeking under the massive tarp to try to see if the field was as muddy as the soggy sidelines, Vance Johnson running a stride or two on the tarp, Louis Wright throwing his head back and laughing at his team's looming predicament, Karl Mecklenburg squinting his eyes and nervously pacing the mud.

This was Saturday practice, but the defensive players didn't bother with any volleyball; the offensive players didn't fiddle with any run-throughs; Dan Reeves didn't call out the special-teams squads, and Rich Karlis kept his shoe on. The weather was simply too cold, the drizzle too damp to fire the usual Saturday shenanigans. Nobody felt like doing much but milling, stepping carefully to keep the slop off their snakeskin boots.

Tom Jackson couldn't help but pan the empty seats that surrounded him, remembering the sections where he had sat as a boy, remembering the games he had watched with his father. "It's such a big place," he said, looking up to the roof, his voice like a soft, Lake Erie fog. "I remember when I was a kid it seemed bigger than life. My dad would bring me here to see the Brownies and to see Jim Brown, who was every kid's hero then. On third-and-two situations we never wondered what the Brownies would do. We *knew* they'd give the ball to J.B. Like every other kid, I grew up wanting to be a running back, to be like the great J.B. But I lasted about ten minutes as a running back in high school. I fumbled the ball a couple of times, and the coach put me over with the linebackers, and that was that."

Jackson grew up on Cleveland's southeast side and graduated from John Adams High School in 1969, lettering in football, baseball, and wrestling. Although his high school coaches praised his ability and were impressed by his unflagging desire, Jackson, at five-feet ten and a hundred and ninety pounds, was considered too small to have much of a shot at a collegiate football career. But the football staff at the University of Louisville decided to take a chance on him, and he became one of the school's all-time stars, twice being named Missouri Valley Conference Player of the Year.

The Denver Broncos knew they were taking a similar chance when they drafted Jackson in the fourth round in 1973, and Jackson himself was crushed by their selection. "Before the draft, my hope was either to be drafted by the Browns so I could go back to my hometown, or by some team in a warm-weather city," he told me in the players' lounge at the Broncos' practice facility a week before this trip. "When I got a call from the Broncos saying that they had drafted me, I looked on a map in my dorm room to see where Denver was. It looked like it was way up in the Rocky Mountains, and I remember saying to my roommate, 'What amazing bad luck. I've been drafted to the Rocky Mountains. It's going to be freezing and blizzarding for my whole career.' I was very displeased. But after I'd spent one season here, I moved out here permanently, and made it my home. Now, I don't think I've ever been anywhere where I'd rather live than Colorado."

Jackson became a defensive starter at the beginning of his rookie season, and was part of the Broncos' mid-seventies line-backing corps which included Randy Gradishar, Joe Rizzo, and Bob Swenson, and which was widely considered the best in football, a group that succeeded with speed rather than size. "Unlike Dick Butkus or someone, I didn't ever run through a lot of people to get to the football," Jackson told me. "I tended to run around people. I'm sure that's one of the reasons I've been able to play as long as I have. My body hasn't had to take that kind of abuse—although any position in football takes a toll. And I definitely don't recover from games as fast as I did even three or four years ago."

Named as the Broncos' most valuable defensive player three times, Jackson was also selected to the AFC Pro Bowl squad in 1977, 1978, and 1979. Following the retirement of Barney Chavous at the start of this season, he became the longest-tenured player on the team, surviving to date for fourteen grueling seasons. Sunday's game would be his 193rd as a professional, more than any other player in Broncos history. "I hope that when my time comes to quit I can show as much class as Barney did," he said. "But there is only so long that you play this game. And my dad has always reminded me that I should make the very most of these years I have to play it, and play it as long as I possibly can, because after that it won't be an option anymore. He's right. Even though I know I'll retire before too long, it isn't something I look forward to."

Jackson suffered a knee injury—the first serious injury of his career—during the 1985 season's training camp and had to undergo arthroscopic surgery, missing four games at the start of the season. Although he eventually returned to the starting lineup, his knee plagued him throughout the season, and there was wide speculation that this oldest linebacker in the NFL was finished. "I heard a lot of talk last winter and last spring," he said, "people saying I couldn't play. I wanted to come back at least one more year and show myself that my problems last season had nothing to do with lost skills, but with the injury."

At the start of this season's camp, Jackson told Broncos linebacker coach Myrel Moore that he wanted to be treated like a rookie. "The last few years, Myrel had started giving me some afternoons off to make things a little easier on me. But this year, I didn't know how my leg was going to respond. What I wanted from Myrel was for him to make me work really hard. I didn't want him to give me anything. And he didn't."

"Myrel means a lot to you guys, doesn't he?" I asked.

"He's like a second father to all the 'backers. He's careful to know each of us as a person. He knows what keys you, as opposed to what keys another person, and he focuses on that. Yeah. I really love Myrel."

If Myrel Moore plays a paternal role for the Broncos' linebackers, Tom Jackson in turn has become a similar kind of figure for his fellow players—those who work on both sides of the ball. They have voted him the team's most inspirational player each year since that award was created, and virtually all of them would agree with their head coach when he says, "Shoot, Tom Jackson *is* the Denver Broncos." The inspiration Jackson offers his team is far more than an incessant kind of cheerleading, however. It is something he described to me as simply his being "into the game all the time, always into the game. We can be down by twenty, and in my mind I'm thinking of ways we can win. If you truly believe it, maybe one out of a hundred times something like that will happen, and then, of course, you say, 'Hey, I knew we'd win it all along.' But the award, no, it only really means something because it comes from the other players. They know that I'm more than just a rah-rah ball player. They know it's real."

Then I asked him again about retirement. Would he call it quits at the end of January? If it came to that, would he play his last game in the stadium where he had first watched Jim Brown? "If we win the Super Bowl, there's no doubt in my mind that I'll retire," he said. "But if we get real close, but not quite there, it will really throw a wrench in the way. You wouldn't want to retire thinking the team was just this far away from it. You wouldn't want to watch everybody else go the following year."

As he surveyed ancient Memorial Stadium on Saturday, I asked him, if indeed tomorrow was his last game, what aspects of his football career he would be most proud of in the end. He thought for a moment, then his dark, expressive face flashed the emotion that is such an integral part of him. "I'm just real proud of the way I've played this game," he said. "I feel like I've put a lot extra into it. Merlin Olsen gave me this thought when I asked him something similar once—he said that when you're through playing, it isn't the awards, or the records, or the championships that you remember. You're just thankful that you played the game and played it well. I think when I'm finished—whenever that is—the thing I'll be most proud of is that I went out every Sunday and played the game. Just that I played the game."

Close behind Tom Jackson on the Broncos' longevity list is guard Paul Howard. Although Howard was drafted in 1973—one round before Jackson was acquired—and is the oldest player on the team, he missed the 1976 season with a back injury, and for that reason has played one fewer season than has his fellow old-timer. Howard had suffered only the second serious injury of his career—a torn anterior cruciate ligament in his left knee— near the end of the Patriots game a week before, and the grizzled, 260-pound lineman's absence seemed conspicuous there in cold and cavernous Memorial Stadium. He had had surgery on Tuesday and would have to watch tomorrow's game from his hospital bed in Denver. "It hurts us bad," Dan Reeves had said about Howard's loss. "But hopefully, the times we've played this year without Paul will be a benefit to us now." When it came time to suit up tomorrow, the players said, it would sure seem strange not to have the old man around.

Howard's roster position was officially filled Saturday morning when Dan Reeves informed league officials that the team was reactivating Clarence Kay, his four weeks of drug rehabilitation completed. Kay had returned to Denver on Tuesday and had begun practicing with the team again on Wednesday, following a private morning meeting in which he discussed his treatment and his current condition with his coaches and teammates. "I told them what I went through and what was going on," he told the reporters who were anxious to talk to the new-leaf Clarence Kay. "I think it was pretty much accepted. I was honest with them. I told them how Clarence Kay was and what I went through." When he was asked if returning to the team

246

was a challenge, he smiled wanly and said, "Everything is in black and white. I've got to maintain and do what I'm supposed to do, that's all. Clarence Kay has got himself together."

Following three days of practice, Reeves and his assistant coaches had agreed that although Kay understandably was a little rusty, he seemed to be in shape, seemed to want to play football, and given Paul Howard's absence, they were certain that Kay's blocking ability, plus his rediscovered self-confidence, would be invaluable against the Dogs of Cleveland.

Cleveland had become a wild-eyed football town in the weeks since Christmas, since the Browns cornered the AFC Central title with the handiwork of a twenty-three-year-old, home-state quarterback named Bernie Kosar, a legendary tight end named Ozzie Newsome, a no-name backfield as uncelebrated as Denver's, and a corps of expert defensive backs who call themselves "the Dogs." The Browns had finished the season 12–4, trouncing interdivision rival Cincinnati 34–3 on the next-to-last Sunday of the season to clinch the crown, then disposing of San Diego a week later to secure the home-field advantage throughout the play-offs.

The swell of civic pride in the Browns crescendoed when the New York Jets arrived a week ago, but by the time that game—the Browns' heart-stopping, come-from-behind, double-overtime victory—was over, the city of Cleveland simply went over the psychic brink, and Ohio's north coast lapsed into perfect ecstasy. All of a sudden, the Cleveland Browns were synonymous with the city's and the region's renaissance; if the Browns were winners, then everyone else was a winner as well. The Cuyahoga hadn't caught fire in more than a decade; the bravest strains of fish were swimming in Lake Erie again; Cleveland would soon be home to the country's Rock and Roll Hall of Fame, and those Mistake-on-the-Lake jokes would have to be shelved forever, surely. To top off all the excitement, the long-suffering Browns were now bound for the Super Bowl. If the goddamn Jets couldn't stop them with a ten-point lead late in the fourth quarter, then no one could. The Browns, it seemed certain, would bowl over the Broncos, then smash hell out of whatever NFC team dared to show up for the Super Bowl, and all of America would at long last get off Cleveland's case. It was going to be beautiful.

By the time the Broncos arrived on Friday night, GO BROWNS signs covered every flat surface in town. The statues in front of the Federal Reserve Bank were wearing huge papier-mâché Browns helmets; St. John's Cathedral was displaying a banner wishing godspeed to Bernie Kosar; a U.S. district judge was telling a group of seventy newly naturalized citizens that "the Browns symbolize America"; Mayor George Voinovich was sporting a Browns jersey bearing Kosar's number 19; supermarkets were reporting that dog bones—unofficial souvenirs of the Dogs, or rather *Dawgs,* on the Browns' defense—were in very short supply; bridal salons were offering specials on burnt-orange and brown gowns; hair salons were specializing in hairdos highlighted by shaved patches in the shape of a dog bone or in letters that spelled out GO BROWNS; television anchors were outfitted in Browns colors for their newscasts—which dealt, of course, with little but the fervor surrounding the football game; and the Cleveland *Plain Dealer* was screaming from its brown-accented front page, COLOR THIS WILD TOWN BROWN. Everyone was having a whale of a time, and it was hard not to get caught up in all the revelry—unless, say, you were a Denver Bronco, trying to get a little sleep on Friday and Saturday nights, but listening instead to the honking horns of the parade of cars that cruised all night through the streets surrounding the Stouffer's Inn on the Plaza downtown, listening maddeningly to the devoted fans who somehow stole past the hotel's security guards (Browns partisans themselves, perhaps) and ran up and down the corridors till dawn barking and baying like dogs—like *DAWGS!*

"I don't think this town can be made fun of again," said Ron Bilek, news director of WKYC, Channel 3, a station that had done an entire "Today in Cleveland" broadcast from the kitchen of Pat Schottenheimer, wife of the Browns' head coach. "Yes, the Browns mania doesn't solve poverty, but it certainly gets people revved up. It has nothing to do with trivialities. It's solidified the fact that Cleveland's on the rebound."

Plain Dealer sports columnist Bill Livingston had little trouble agreeing, asking his readers rhetorically, "Isn't it nice to hear Cleveland being mentioned in a positive light because of the Browns?" But as far as Livingston was concerned, he couldn't wait to get beyond the semi-pro attention that the AFC championship brought the city to the big time, bells and whistles, front and center attention that the city would receive with its team in the Super Bowl. Oh, the Browns would be in the Super Bowl, all right. EXPECT BROWNS' VICTORY, Livingston's pregame column was headlined. That much was plain, purported Livingston, and he dealt it out this way:

> I see Elway scrambling around, trying to buy time. I see the lingering effects of last week's injury slowing him just enough to become defensible. . . . I see Kosar taking that Denver defense and withering it with the sheer power of the fellow's brain. . . . Perhaps most of all, I see a Browns team that simply does not believe it can be beaten. It was said during the Steelers' Super Bowl years that they loved nothing more than facing a team from some posh, trendy place like Dallas or L.A. I think the Browns are like that. I think the Dawgs can't wait to fasten their teeth on Johnny E.'s cuffs.

And if you might be tempted to call Livingston a "homer" for picking the Browns simply because they were so near and dear to his heart (the poor man assuming the sheer power of Kosar's brain could pull off things even Shirley MacLaine can't yet accomplish), the *Plain Dealer* included a list of the prognostications of twenty-nine sportswriters from around the country—*twenty-two* of whom favored the Browns. Michael Knisley of the *Denver Post* guessed it would be Browns 23–20 in another

249

double overtime; Steve Caulk of the *Rocky Mountain News* called it Browns, 22–19; Mike Spence of the Colorado Springs *Gazette-Telegraph* chose Cleveland as well, 24–21—no homers in that crowd, for heaven's sake. "The Broncos won't stand in the way of the Dawgs of Destiny," opined Vic Carucci of the *Buffalo News*. "The Browns are not to be denied. Browns, 21–17." And Ed Beitiks of the *San Francisco Examiner* summed things up succinctly for Livingston and his fellow fans: "Everyone from Denver is a fake. Elway will throw three interceptions. Nobody, but nobody, wants to see Denver in the Super Bowl. Browns, 30–10."

Wasn't it something? The Browns were Pasadena-bound, Cleveland was suddenly Camelot, and the Cuyahoga was aflame with hope. "Hey, everybody needs a love affair," said the Browns' owner, Art Modell.

Arguably the only people in all of Cuyahoga County who didn't really care how the game came out were the 120 members of the NBC Sports crew (75 engineers and 45 production people) who were on hand to beam it back to the Rockies and from sea to shining sea—AFC and NFC championship games tending to do very well in the ratings, even if, as in NBC's case this year, the participating teams weren't exactly from cities at the epicenter of American life.

It would be CBS's turn to broadcast the Super Bowl two weeks hence, so the Cleveland-Denver contest would be NBC's final football game of the season, and executive producer Michael Weisman and his crew were pulling out all the stops. First-string announcers Dick Enberg and Merlin Olsen would call the game, of course, assisted with pre- and post- and mid-game gab by NBC's Bob Costas, Ahmad Rashad, Bob Griese, Paul McGuire, and Frank Deford, and with the special guest analyses of Miami Dolphins' coach Don Shula. The operation would require three production trucks instead of the usual one; twenty-one cameras would be aimed at the field instead of the everyday six or seven; by game time, twelve miles of video cable would be strung

250

through Memorial Stadium. "Now we just need a good game," Weisman commented on Saturday afternoon, standing near the lavish pre-game set his crew had constructed on the sidelines, pronouncing his network's preparations almost complete. And he was pleased by the forecast that called for cold weather, gray skies, possibly a snow shower or two tomorrow. "The gray skies give us sharper colors, and with the natural grass, the players will get dirty, mud will fly in the air, we'll see their breath. It'll be perfect. What we want is another Cleveland-Jets situation—double overtime. But we're not greedy. We'll settle for one overtime."

The bookies and betting services all week had been taking wagers on the Browns by three, but the spread might have shot up to ten or more had they heard the incessant car horns and the bellicose, barking fans at the Broncos' hotel on Saturday night. Then the Sunday weather—colder, windier, snowier even than Saturday had been—seemed to seal the Broncos' fate. The Clevelanders looked like roustabouts from Alaska's North Slope as they converged on the stadium in the spitting morning snow, their stocking-capped heads turned away from the lake-borne gale. But it was perfect weather for football, wasn't it?—for a win by the Browns that would send them to sunnier climes. THIS GAME IS GOING TO THE DAWGS, assured a banner that was hung from the rail of the upper deck. NO MORE CLEVE. JOKES, demanded another. "Elway sucks," was the chant that rang out of the stands as 79,915 delirious fans pelted the field with dog biscuits.

. "Wonderful," thought Michael Weisman as he panned the color monitors in NBC's central production truck, watching the frozen ball sail off Rich Karlis's foot and into the sullen skies.

This was going to be a good football game, that much seemed certain by the time the Browns had taken a touchdown lead on a textbook 86-yard drive. And you had to wonder if it indeed might not be a great one when Broncos linebackers Ricky Hun-

251

ley and Jim Ryan pulled two of Kosar's passes out of the air on two successive possessions. The Broncos got Karlis close enough for a field goal early in the second quarter, and the Browns responded by fumbling away the ball as soon as their offense returned to the field. The Broncos were right back in scoring position—the ball on the Cleveland 38—when John Elway, his ankle obviously surviving the strain, took the snap on first and ten, looked for his targeted receivers, then thought better of the plan and ran to the 3-yard line—precisely the kind of a scramble Browns' coach Marty Schottenheimer had seen in his sleep all week. But the horses had little more power, gaining only two yards in three plays before they faced a fourth and goal at the one, as well as a devilish kind of decision. Another field goal would leave them behind by a point, yet the yard for the touchdown seemed anything but a certainty. On the sidelines, Dan Reeves opted for the gamble and the chance for the lead, and Gerald Willhite, sweeping right, somehow stretched the ball across the goal line as he was tackled by Cleveland's Chris Rockins. Karlis's point-after was perfect and the Broncos led by three.

In the final seconds before half-time, Kosar completed a 42-yard strike to Clarence Weathers, and four plays later, the Browns similarly needed only inches of grass for a go-ahead touchdown. But on third and goal at the 2, Kosar—seeing nothing but looming trouble—intentionally grounded the ball and the penalty set the Browns back to the Broncos' twelve. The touchdown denied, Mark Moseley kicked a field goal to tie the score as the period expired. The first half was history; the score was tied; and Ohio State University's Marching Buckeyes did their best to grind the new onslaught of biscuits into the turf.

I watched most of the rest of the game from a cramped seat in the baseball press box—directly behind home plate, had this been the summer game, and just beyond the west end zone in frigid January. The third quarter was quiet, offering little to see from that vantage point except Karlis's 26-yard field goal, which split the polished uprights and sailed end-over-end toward me. As the Browns opened the fourth quarter, Mark Moseley lined up two yards away from the spot where Karlis had stood three minutes earlier, then booted a 24-yarder that was every bit as true. Browns 13, Broncos 13, the season still in doubt.

But with just six minutes to play, I watched it all come to a sobering end, watched as Bernie Kosar backpedaled from the Broncos' 48 and underthrew a long ball aimed for receiver Brian Brennan. Seeing that the football was short, Brennan checked his stride and came back for it, twisting Broncos Dennis Smith to the ground in panicked pursuit in the process, Brennan then cradling the ball between his numbers and doing a deft sidestep around the kneeling Smith, who could do little but beg for another chance. The Browns led by a touchdown; the fans still had enough body heat to begin a tumultuous celebration; and the old stadium seemed assured of seeing its first championship since 1964.

On the ensuing kickoff, Denver returner Ken Bell bobbled the ball at the 2, falling on it and controlling it an instant before it was stripped away, ending the Broncos' six-month quest with a rookie's glaring misjudgment, and I made my way down to the field, wanting to see how the Broncos who had hoped for so much now accepted their fate. Dennis Smith stood far back from the sideline, absently pacing, painfully aware of his role in the Denver defeat. A dozen players in blue ponchos with hoods that covered their helmets shouted vain encouragement onto the field. Tom Jackson, his career just minutes from ending, was anguished but somehow gallant as he glanced at the clock, its numbers briefly stopped at 5:32, the veteran linebacker unwilling yet to surrender. Pat Bowlen, draped in his long mink coat, his trousers stuffed into the tops of his boots to keep them out of the mud, stood at the end of the line of players who were pressing close to the field, the owner doing his futile best to appear impassive. Dan Reeves, at the center of the long blue and orange row, seemingly had yet to hear about the impending defeat, unaware that his hope was lost. He sent in a play, then put his hands on his knees, the better to direct, by gum, what was about to happen.

In the huddle in the west end zone, the eleven Broncos were deafened by the jubilant crowd for whom the stadium was suddenly Oz. But they could see the 98 yards of mud, grass, and crushed biscuits between the ball and the distant goal line; they could see by the clock the few minutes that remained to them; and they could see by the streamers on the uprights the taunting wind that whipped in their direction.

"We got these guys right where we want 'em," observed Keith Bishop in his slow, West Texas twang, and ten Broncos began to titter. "We all just giggled when he said it," tackle Dave Studdard remembered after the game. "I about fell out of the huddle," added guard Mark Cooper, playing in Paul Howard's stead. John Elway flashed a confident smile, then went to work, throwing a 5-yard pass to Sammy Winder to get the horses under way. Elway handed off to Winder on the three successive plays, the small back churning for 3 yards, 2 yards, then 3 again before Elway rolled out of the pocket and scrambled for 11 yards of his own. With a third and one and little breathing room at the 26-yard line, Elway fired a 22-yard pass to Steve Sewell up the middle, followed it with a 12-yard toss to Steve Watson, and the crowd grew markedly quiet. But their spirits waxed bright again when the Denver quarterback turned cool at midfield, throwing two incompletions and suffering an 8-yard sack.

It was third and eighteen from the Browns' 48, and the Broncos seemed at an impasse. But with his ankle holding up and his confidence cresting, his big number 7 smeared by mud, Elway dropped deep and launched a 20-yard rocket to Mark Jackson, who had cut free from "head Dawg" Hanford Dixon at the 28. The Browns' fans grew faint of heart again just as the Broncos' bench erupted. You could *feel* it now; suddenly there seemed to be little doubt about it—the Broncos were headed straight for the cheap seats in the east end zone, headed for the section that had dubbed itself the Dawg Pound, and there wasn't a way in the world to stop them.

The Broncos moved to the 14 with a second completion to Sewell, moved to the 5 when Elway scrambled and raced toward the sideline, then went in for the score as Jackson stretched out and contained a low Elway fastball, rolling with it onto the biscuit-strewn grass of the end zone. The Dawgs in the Pound did their best to distract Rich Karlis into muffing the extra point, but their shouts went flat and sour till next season as the ball sailed through the uprights and tumbled down toward them. Denver 20, Cleveland 20. Ninety-eight miraculous yards in fifteen inspired, impossible plays. Not a dog barked in all of ancient Memorial Stadium

The Browns had thirty-seven seconds left to try to win the game; failing that, they could still secure the win in overtime, but by now that was merely theoretical. A tangible, palpable kind of chill—the coldest yet of the day—seemed to convince the Clevelanders otherwise. Kosar and company went through the motions, endeavoring to do no more than hang on to the ball in the final seconds, then, winning the overtime coin toss, they took the ball again and moved it all of eight yards before they had to punt it back to the Broncos. Camelot was collapsing, the love affair turning cold and cruel, the Super Bowl slipping away on the winter winds.

This time it took the Broncos nine plays to gain the 60 yards that took them to the Cleveland 15, Winder running and Elway passing to pull them off in clumps with a kind of passion now. As Rich Karlis came onto the field to finish the day, NFL and NBC officials were frantically moving the championship trophy from the entrance to the Cleveland locker room, where it had been waiting since midway through the fourth quarter, to the Denver locker room, where it now appeared ready for a more permanent home. Michael Weisman had gotten his overtime game, but the winner wasn't going to end it by the script. Keith Bishop snapped the ball back to Gary Kubiak, who set it down. The Cleveland defenders desperately dove into the air to try to block it, but Karlis got it up quickly, the ball hooking just inside the left upright, close enough to it that 80,000 people held out a final, momentary, heartbroken hope before they got up from their seats in silence, their renaissance shattered by the Broncos' sudden offensive brilliance, their dreams destroyed by an arcing barefoot kick.

"Karlis's kick is up; it's good!" Bob Martin shouted into his microphone from the KOA booth atop the stadium. "The Broncos again are going to the Super Bowl! But it's no miracle this time. This time they earned it!"

Rich Karlis's primary concern in the seconds that ensued, he later told the crush of reporters, was that he would die of suffocation, his face pressed into the turf and held there by a pile of very large men in very bright orange jerseys. Memorial Stadium was strangely, deathly quiet except for that mound of jubilant Broncos, and Karlis's shouts that he couldn't breathe were muffled in the turf. "It felt great to have made the field goal," he said, "but a couple of seconds later, I thought I was going to die."

By the time Karlis escaped from beneath the pile, the trophy had made its way down the dank corridor to the Denver locker room and AFC President Lamar Hunt had presented it to the Broncos' owner, whose jaws quivered with emotion, and whose eyes betrayed an uncertainty that his team had truly done it. "I was standing there on the sidelines," Bowlen said, "expecting to go congratulate Art Modell in a minute. I was damn near sick to my stomach. You never want to doubt that it can happen but . . . well, it didn't look good for us there for a while." But then his team had miraculously tied the score, marched down the field a second time, and Rich Karlis was lining up to try for the winning field goal. "I couldn't watch Rich kick that field goal," Bowlen confessed. "Those moments are almost too excruciatingly painful. But I knew we must have made it because you could hear a pin drop in that place."

Dan Reeves could hardly contain himself in the tent outside the Broncos' locker room, where he addressed the swarming press. "It's the biggest thrill in my coaching career. It's almost

256

like a Hollywood script—it comes out just like you want it to." What about The Drive, the reporters wanted to know—the 98-yard march to tie the game, already epic only minutes after it occurred. "Yeah, I was a little discouraged when we had to start there on the one- or two-yard line," he admitted. "It looked bleak, but we knew we had a chance. I've been around the game twenty-one years, and I've *never* seen a drive like that. But I'll tell you what. With the pressure on him, I'd rather have John Elway playing for me than anyone I know."

Opposite Reeves in the confines of the tent, Elway, stripped to a T-shirt and already wearing a Super Bowl cap, was doing his best to field the shouted questions. A reporter reminded him that on their two previous possessions in the fourth quarter, the Broncos hadn't been able to generate a first down. What was it that made their final offensive spurt possible? "For some reason, we seem to play better with our backs to the wall," Elway responded. "And right then, our backs were about as close to the wall as they could get."

"Hey, John, what's it feel like to be going to the Super Bowl?" someone shouted.

"It hasn't sunk in yet. I don't know," he replied. "I guess I'm going to have to slap myself."

Rich Karlis stood on the third podium, a dog biscuit tucked into the waist of his uniform pants. "It's a collector's item now," explained the Salem, Ohio, native, telling the reporters clustered around him that the extra point to tie the game worried him much more than the field goal. "On the field goal, I was totally relaxed. As hard as those guys had just worked, the last thing I could afford was to go out there and miss it." Fifty of Karlis's family and friends had driven up to the big city to see the game, and as he spoke, his mother struggled her way to the podium and embraced her son, the football hero. With tears streaming down his face, Karlis introduced his mother, telling the reporters that she was his biggest fan. "I don't know if I can find the right words," he said. "There's no place I'd rather win it than here. I know our fans in Denver would have rather had the game there, but I just felt like it was my destiny to win it in Cleveland. I feel bad because this city has waited so long for a championship. Cleveland really has a lot of nice things in it. It's really a great place, but . . . I don't know. This is just wonderful."

In the streets outside the stadium, the fans finally felt the cold. Most said nothing as they walked away, but some were angry, not at the Browns, who so cruelly had let them down, but at the visitors, who had stolen the spotlight they had sought for so long. "Denver sucks!" a group of young men screamed into the media tent. "You suck, you bastards!" When police pulled them away, they surrendered their fight, and two of them started to cry.

NBC's coverage of the game had long since ended, but in the Broncos' tiny locker room, the camera lights of the Denver stations still blared. From a high wooden platform, Channel 4's Ron Zappolo was conducting a marathon of live interviews, his crew sending a succession of players in shoulder pads, players in street clothes, a few players only in towels to join him in the bright light. For forty-five minutes without a break, Zappolo asked how tough the Browns had been, whether the game had seemed truly lost, how The Drive was inspired, what this triumph meant to them. Karl Mecklenburg, Louis Wright, Steve Foley, David Studdard, Mark Jackson, Jim Ryan—one after one they did their best to describe what couldn't be put into words properly, and Zappolo did a remarkable job of eliciting their responses. In the celebratory excitement, everyone was loquacious, everyone was in love with his job and his fellow teammates, and everyone sent joyous greetings back to family and friends and the legions of fans in Denver. It was live television at its informal, emotional best, and you knew that back in the Queen City, few channels had been changed to that other game.

In a corner of the locker room, a small television set was tuned to the CBS broadcast of the NFC championship game—the New York Giants shellacking the Washington Redskins. No one was very interested, save a reporter or two who seemed strangely glued to the blowout. "Hey, who we going to play?" Ricky Hunley asked as he sauntered near the set, his words aimed at Vance Johnson, who was fingering his moussed flattop into place. "Who gives a fuck about the Giants and the Redskins?" Johnson retorted. "Shit, baby, I just know this time we're going to be in the sun, man. Wear Bermuda shorts instead of this shit. It's going to be great. What's the matter with your voice, anyway?"

"I'm hoarse from eating dog biscuits," Hunley deadpanned. "I can still bark. I just can't talk."

John Elway had finally made his way back to the locker room from the tent; he had spoken at length with Ron Zappolo and with all of the Colorado beat reporters, but still a few others trailed him, trying to get one last quote, another twist on the story he'd been telling repeatedly for the past hour and a half. Finally, Jim Saccomano intervened, stepping between the quarterback and the reporters, explaining that Elway had a plane to catch, Elway taking quick advantage of the interference and slipping away to the shower. Then seconds later he screamed— screamed at the top of his lungs as cold water poured down on him from the showerhead. "Jesus," he shouted, his head peering around the tiled wall. "Isn't there any hot water left?"

"Not for about half an hour," came the reply.

"I love this town," he said, flashing the same grin that had started The Drive.

At last free of the attentions of the six hundred reporters who had descended upon this championship game, Reeves, Elway, and the rest of the Broncos boarded four buses that would take them to the airport, where their chartered plane awaited them. But on bus number three, there seemed to be one last bit of business before the Broncos left the waterfront. "Let's go by the hotel and honk the goddamn horn," Dave Studdard hollered from the back of the bus. His idea was an instant hit, and, despite understandable Cleveland loyalties, the bus driver saw no reason not to comply. He gave the big air horn a few hard honks in front of the main doors of the Inn on the Plaza, the players stuck their heads out the windows and barked into the dusk, then the entourage left for the airport.

But it wasn't going to be that simple to get out of town. When the equipment crates were finally loaded in the underbelly of the DC-8 and everyone was on board, the captain announced that the United operations office in Cleveland had just received a bomb threat. A bomb had purportedly been placed aboard the plane, and although the likelihood of the call being a hoax was enormous, there was little choice but to take it seriously. In consultation with Bowlen and Reeves, the flight crew decided to remove everything from the baggage hold and send it on a separate plane tomorrow. The players, coaches, and media people were requested to search the overhead bins above them, then to relax. They would remain in Ohio at least another hour.

"Let's get *out* of this fucking town," Tom Jackson shouted in the midst of the wait, pacing the aisle, looking like a banker in his gray suit, smoking a post-game cigarette. "Man, if we'd have known this, we'd have beat them worse. I don't want anything to do with this damn place," he said, embarrassed for his hometown, embarrassed to think that some crank would want to further tarnish its image.

At 8:45, four and a half hours after the game had ended, Broncos One at last rolled down the runway en route to Colorado and to a welcoming party that was reported already to be 6–8,000 people strong and growing by a thousand people an hour. Then somewhere west of the Mississippi, 30,000 feet above the Iowa cornfields, it was finally time to celebrate. "Listen up, y'all," Reeves drawled into a flight attendant's microphone. "We've got some champagne on board, and there's no question that we've got something to celebrate. We're the AFC champs. But I want you to remember a few things. We've all got to drive home. I want you to make sure you can drive. And another thing, there are about 10,000 people waiting for us at the airport. Some of you are going to have to talk. So enjoy yourselves. You've earned it. But let's wait till the night after the Super Bowl, and then we'll have a real party."

Reeves needn't have worried; it was already too late, his players too tired to initiate anything raucous. Some champagne was consumed, and hugs and slaps on the back were liberally traded among the passengers, but it was a polite party at best, Reeves himself the center of attention as he paraded the aisle with the shiny new trophy in tow. When linebackers coach Myrel Moore wandered back from the first-class section, Tom Jackson, a bottle already in hand, found glasses and told his mentor it was time for a toast. "This is the guy I've got to toast," Jackson said of the man he had called his second father. "This is the guy that I owe it to."

But Moore insisted on proposing the toast himself. "Here's to what football's all about," he said as Jackson poured a swallow into his glass. "Here's to what coaching's all about—Tom Jackson." Tears suddenly streamed down Jackson's face, and he embraced his coach as warmly as he could, kissing his cheek, holding him tight for a long time. The two men—one white, one black, one a gruff and grizzled coach, the other just a guy who played the game—said nothing more before they finally sipped their champagne in triumph.

Tony LaMonica was on the radio again, doing a live report as the plane angled out of the sky: "We're traveling at a speed of about 150 knots now, landing east to west. The aircraft continues to settle on its approach, landing gear down, and . . . touchdown." The players cheered as they felt the tires lunge onto the tarmac, and as the DC-8 taxied toward the United hangar, they peered through their windows to try to see just how big this crowd really was.

Television crews recorded the players' descents down the stairways and their reunions with their waiting families, and searchlights lit the United service lift that had been moved alongside the high fence holding the crowd at bay—15,000 fans, 20,000, no one knew in the darkness. When Dan Reeves and Pat Bowlen joined Denver mayor Federico Peña and Colorado governor Roy Romer on top of the lift, the crowd surged into pandemonium. They had waited for three hours, some of them, and this, at last, was bliss. Bowlen told them they were the greatest fans in the world, Reeves told them he loved them. Then John Elway stepped to the microphone in the midst of a wild and tumultuous cheer. "Wow! Wow! Wow!" he shouted into the sea of faces, entranced by the welcome, the crowd screaming with delight in response to his chant. "I'll tell you what," he said when he could finally be heard again, "it was a great win for us today. It not only exemplified our team, but all of Colorado." It was the first time in all the months since I had begun to observe him that he seemed to truly enjoy the fans who so adored him.

When it was Tom Jackson's turn to speak, he was soft-spoken and subdued in contrast to all the shouting. "There was a lot written this past week about my playing this game back at home," he told the quieting crowd. "Well, I just want to tell you that I'm *home* now. *This* is home. *This* is home," he said.

January 18
—

Dan Reeves sat in front of the Pepsi machine in the Broncos' press trailer, as he had for eighteen previous weeks, his season extending for one more football game. "You know, I never thought I'd say this," he told the roomful of reporters, "but I sure am glad to see you guys. This is an unbelievable feeling. You want to wake up and see if it's real. But I'll tell you, it's a nice way to stay awake. During the season, you try not to say 'Super Bowl' 'cause it might be kind of a jinx. But, yeah, it feels kind of weird to be talking about it, to be saying 'We are going to the Super Bowl.' "

This would be Reeves's sixth Super Bowl as a participating player or coach. The five previous, however, came during his career with the Dallas Cowboys. "I haven't been there in a long time. I think '79 was the last time I went, and it's turned into a lot bigger event since then. The attention the Super Bowl gets now is pretty unbelievable." Someone wanted to know how Reeves would begin to prepare his team for all the attention, the celebrity, the hoopla and seemingly endless hype. "Well," he responded, "I think the first thing we have to do is get out of the ticket business as quick as we can—get all the phone calls from aunts and uncles and long-lost cousins out of the way so we can concentrate on football. I had some lady I didn't even know knocking on my door at 7:30 this morning wanting Super Bowl tickets. Shoot, we were barely back from Cleveland."

What was the moment of victory like yesterday? The question came from a television reporter—it was the kind of question that the TV talent always asked—but somehow it elicited the kind of personal response that this very public man seldom gave. "When Rich kicked the field goal, it was over so fast, and it was for real, but I remember wishing I could slow it down," he said. "It was such a great feeling. You wish it would last forever, but it's gone so fast. The thrill of winning is so quick, and then you just have to go on with everything. You don't have time to enjoy it because now, well, you have to get on with the Super Bowl."

The New York Football Giants defeated the Washington Redskins 17–0 in a windblown blowout that ended at about the time the Broncos were finally airborne Sunday, and by the time they landed in Denver, the Las Vegas and Atlantic City betting services had already posted them as eight-and-a-half-point underdogs to the formidable Giants in the January 25 Super Bowl, and it was easy to understand why. In their previous meeting this season, the Giants had beaten the Broncos 19–16 in the Meadowlands in a close and evenly matched contest. Yet since that game, the Broncos had lost three more, while the Giants were undefeated. The Giants, in fact, hadn't lost a game since October 19, way back in the halcyon days when Denver was six and one. So far in the post-season play-offs, the Broncos had beaten their opponents by a total of eight points; the Giants had been victorious by a total of sixty-three. And in the "intangibles" category that bookies and talk show callers like so much to consider, while it was true that the Broncos would love to once and for all shake their hayseed, unchic *orange* image by winning the big one, the Giants, orphaned from the city of New York and a virtual football laughingstock for the past two decades, hadn't played in the NFL's biggest game in twenty-four years. They hadn't *won* it in thirty—and they and their fans were thirsty.

The Super Bowl belongs to the league. Unlike every other game during the professional season, in which one team plays host to another, the league itself is the Super Bowl host and the two participating teams only appear in a kind of command performance. The game site is selected years in advance—always either in a warm-weather city or in a dome somewhere up in the snowbelt—and the league arranges for everything from hotel rooms to press passes, from tickets to the television coverage that sends the game to sixty nations around the world. The league picks up the two teams' expenses (not one smidgen of which is spared) and it pays the players handsomely for postponing their winter vacations—$36,000 to each member of the winning team, $18,000 for the losers. The one thing the NFL is unable to control about the game, however, the one variable in an ocean of pre-game preparations, is who, in fact, will line up for the opening kickoff. On that matter, the league simply pays its money and takes its chances—as do the television networks for whom the game means an awesome amount of revenue.

On the Monday morning after the AFC and NFC championship games, the league and CBS Sports breathed sighs of relief that could be heard all over midtown Manhattan. While it wasn't going to be a dream Super Bowl in terms of its participating teams, it wasn't going to be bad. The best matchup imaginable in terms of attracting viewers, advertising dollars, and ratings points would pit, say, these very Giants against the Los Angeles Raiders, or the Los Angeles Rams against the New York Jets. The annual hope, you see, is that the participating teams will represent two of the nation's largest television markets, as well as providing for a bit of geographic diversity. For reasons that should seem obvious, league and network officials have nightmares about the day when the St. Louis Cardinals will meet the Kansas City Chiefs in what grandly has come to be known as "the ultimate game." The theoretical prospect of the Miami Dolphins versus the Tampa Bay Bucs sends similar shivers up hundreds of spines.

This year, the Giants will immediately attract the nation's largest television market (and betting market, for that matter—the two not coincidentally going hand in hand) and they nicely represent the urban East. The Broncos, to be sure, are representative of the Wild West, but unfortunately, they are not quite west enough. If they were the Burbank or Santa Barbara Broncos, all would be well with the world, but coming from Denver (isn't that where they *ski*?) means that they represent a region with far too few people to make them the perfect foil for the Giants. As far as officialdom is concerned, the two teams make a good match, but somehow not quite great.

If you had polled the Broncos and their fans this week, you'd have found that they see the game scheduled for Sunday next as somehow rather appropriate. The only team in all of the National Football Conference that they would have rather played—ain't life repetitious?—would have been the Dallas Cowboys, but the Cowboys' jerseys have been cleaned and pressed and put away since well before Christmas. In their absence, the Giants will do just fine. It is the Giants who beat the Broncos two months ago with a fluke pass interception and a momentary Denver defensive seizure. It is the Giants who play in a stadium in a New Jersey swamp where the Broncos have experienced nothing but disappointment. It is the Giants who are a bunch of city-bred street toughs who lately have been playing some remarkable football, and who, by game day, may well be ten-point favorites. Hey, the Broncos have got these guys right where they want them.

But there has been some carping in the Queen City this week. The problem is that the People Who Wear Orange seem to think that the People Who Don't Wear Orange are not getting into the spirit of things. We are talking about the *Super Bowl,* after all, and some people are not wearing the proper color clothing. Some of them have yet to place signs in their office windows; others have cars without a single Broncos bumper sticker; there are those who insist on naming their newborns Jason instead of the obvious John. Longtime Broncomaniacs are claiming that it just doesn't *feel* like it did when the 1977 team went all the way to the final Sunday. Where are the orange hairdos? they want to know. The orange houses? Are so few willing to wear horse costumes for two short weeks?

The argument from the other side is that nothing is as marvelous and as memorable the second time around, which isn't to say that this Super Bowl trip is somehow old hat. It's just that the first time you paint the poodle orange, it's lighthearted fun. The second time you do it, you start to appear a trifle unstable. Besides, doesn't the banner on the state capitol building already read, COLORADO BELIEVES IN THE BRONCOS? Isn't every schoolchild in the region writing an essay about The Drive? Haven't colored ice sculptures of Rulon Jones and Tom Jackson begun to pop up in people's yards? Didn't 63,246 men, women, and children in orange snowsuits descend on Mile High Stadium at 1:30 this afternoon to cheer themselves speechless at what may have been the largest pep rally in the history of the planet?

January 20

For the first time all season, the Broncos boarded their plane on Monday without wearing coats and ties. Perhaps it was because they wanted to fit right in when they landed in casual southern California, perhaps because an informal forty-third birthday party for Dan Reeves had been scheduled for the flight. En route over the desert southwest, they dined on birthday cake, did a mediocre job of serenading their coach, and joked—not a little apprehensively—about the week of hype and media madness they had been told would await them. But before their attentions were firmly focused on the next game, more than a few of them still wanted to savor the stupendous win in Cleveland, reading *Sports Illustrated*'s account of the Broncos' "GETTING THERE THE HARD WAY"—the issue with Rich Karlis on the cover.

"It's great," Karlis commented about the photograph of him and holder Gary Kubiak jumping for joy in Cleveland, which appeared on the cover of the nation's premiere sports journal. "After first hitting the biggest kick in my career in a fairy-tale game, this is like two fairy tales in one week for me. It's incredible." Did Karlis worry about the legendary *Sports Illustrated* jinx, the one that supposedly imparts immediate bad luck to anyone who graces its cover? "No," he said. "The way I figure it, if the jinx was true, you'd have to ruin about fifty-two people's lives per year." Besides, Karlis is employed as a place kicker in the National Football League, a job that demands a strange addiction to pressure, extreme self-confidence, and a cast-iron gastrointestinal tract. Anyone whose palms have ever sweated or who is even vaguely superstitious need not apply—a kicker who was dependent on a rabbit's foot, or on wearing the same undershirt week after week, or staying off the cover of *Sports Illustrated* would be as handicapped as a jockey who was afraid of horses. "I fully expect to make every field goal I try," Karlis had told me earlier in the season. "If you aren't dead sure you can do it, you shouldn't be a kicker."

Karlis, a twenty-seven-year-old native of small Salem, Ohio, began his professional kicking career by making the first eleven field goals he tried—just as if there were obviously nothing to it. He completed the strike-shortened 1982 season with eleven completions on thirteen tries, an .846 completion percentage, a remarkable feat for his bare size-eight foot. In his four subsequent seasons, Karlis has remained an excellent kicker, but, almost inevitably, he has been unable to match his rookie-year numbers. During the 1984 season, his game-tying field goal attempts hit an upright and bounced away wide at the conclusions of two consecutive games. And last year, when his missed field goal was ultimately the margin of defeat in the Broncos' home loss to the Raiders, which cost them the AFC championship, police in Mile High Stadium had to protect Karlis's wife from a group of demented fans who were cursing her husband, threatening to kill him.

Comparing that kind of insanity with the adulation that followed last week's game-winning kick in Cleveland, I asked him what it was like to live in such a love-hate spotlight. "There's a percentage of society that lives off other people's failures," he said. "They don't have to feel so bad about themselves if they think somebody else is an even bigger failure than they are. Kickers are highly visible. We either succeed or fail on our own—it isn't a team effort. So it's easy for fans to focus in on you. And that's the nature of the beast—what can you do for me today? But actually, I think I'm harder on myself when I miss a kick than anybody else is. It's a very specific craft, kicking a field goal, and I fully expect to make it every time I try." To date in the 1986 season, he has made twenty-five field goals in thirty-three tries, a .758 percentage, and his game-winner in Cleveland was his ninth field goal in a row.

Off the field, Karlis is perhaps the most active of all the Broncos players in terms of time devoted to community service and charitable endeavors—although he would be quick to name ten other players who are as active. Nor does he shirk from requests for paid public appearances, where his presence at the grand opening of a tire store or carpet outlet can virtually guarantee big crowds. "It's all because of television," he explained. "Via television, athletes and other well-known people are just illusions. They aren't real. When people have an opportunity to see you in person and get your autograph and talk to you, they're fascinated to find out that you're just a regular person. Without television, I don't think there is any way that players would be the celebrities that they are. I was in a Marie Callender's restaurant the other night, and a man at the cash register told me I looked familiar. He asked me if I used to work there. I told him I hadn't, but he just couldn't figure out where he'd seen me. So I told him who I was, and then he was so embarrassed that he hadn't recognized me that he wouldn't let me leave without taking a couple of free pies. That kind of thing happens a lot."

In addition to garnering free food, Karlis has used his local celebrity to raise thousands of dollars for The Family Tree, a metro Denver organization that provides shelter for women and children who are victims of family violence. His own "Points for People" program, in which he and over four hundred other individuals pledge specified dollar amounts for each of his successful field goals throughout the season, has raised nearly $300,000 since its inception in 1984, the proceeds going directly to The Family Tree. "I had wanted to focus my community work in a specific area," he said. "I think you can often be more successful if you don't spread your efforts too thin. Both my sisters had experienced family violence, so it was something I knew about first-hand and something that really concerned me."

I asked him if he viewed his service work as a kind of obligation. "As a well-known figure," he responded, "especially as a Denver Bronco in this city, you have the opportunity to be a positive force. You can use that celebrity, or whatever you want to call it, to try to achieve some worthwhile things. I think everyone has to decide what's right for him, but for me, yes, it's a kind of recommitment to things that I believe are important, things outside the sometimes-strange world of football."

And what about the Super Bowl? Would he prefer an easy Broncos victory, one that left him standing on the sidelines, or did he dream about ending this season by kicking a winning field goal? "Well, basically, I just want us to win," he said. "But sure, I'd love to go out on the field with us tied or down by a point or two and kick a field goal to win it. That's what kickers live for."

The greater Los Angeles area is perhaps the perfect place to stage a Super Bowl. Somehow, this extravaganza disguised as a football game seems to belong in the nation's glitz and glad-handing capital. And make no mistake about it. Although the Broncos and Giants will play the game—four short hours or so at the climax of this lunatic week—in Pasadena, the Super Bowl is unfolding from one end of this smoggy seaside basin to the other. The Broncos, for instance, landed Monday at Long Beach; they're staying in Newport Beach down the coast in Orange County, practicing in Irvine, meeting the press in Costa Mesa, traveling to Pasadena, *sixty miles* away, to play the obligatory football game, returning to Newport Beach for a post-game party, win or lose, then leaving Monday from LAX in Los Angeles. During the week the team will spend here, they will devote no fewer than eleven hours to bus rides. By the time it's all over and they get to go home, they'll feel like a semipro team on a very nasty road trip.

Just to help spread the Super Bowl's impact—and to try to reduce the gasoline glut—the national media on hand for the festivities are being housed in darkest Anaheim; NFL commissioner Pete Rozelle is hosting his annual gathering for a few thousand of his closest friends at Universal Studios in exotic Hollywood; and the Broncos' and Giants' fans who are beginning to pour into the region like latter-day dust-bowl drifters in matching T-shirts are filling motel rooms from Azusa to Oceanside, from Oxnard to Colton and West Covina. You can't tell the players without a program. You can't make the venues without a map.

The scene resembled a catfish farm at feeding time early this afternoon—hundreds of members of the frenzied fourth estate (newspaper reporters, magazine writers, producers and talent for TV stations from Trenton to Tokyo) descending on fifty-odd football players, eleven coaches, and an owner in an orange sweater scattered around the football field at Orange Coast College in Costa Mesa, the intrepid sports journalists swarming into the little stadium as the chain-link gates were rolled back, charging to secure a position within earshot of John Elway, scanning the field for the jersey numbers of another player or two who might have something of vague interest to say, each of the scribblers, each of the camera crews hoping to get the quip, the quote that would satisfy some editor back home who had no idea how impossible this was.

Media Day is the NFL's rather inflated term for two-hour-long sessions on the parched Orange Coast College turf, one in the morning featuring the New York Football Giants, the second, following the sportswriters' obligatory free lunch, featuring the far less sought-after, somehow less newsworthy, less appealing, underdog Denver Broncos. While upwards of 1700 people with press credentials stormed the field to take on the Giants this morning, a mere thousand or so stuck around till the early afternoon to engage the Broncos in the ten- and twenty-on-one interviews that reporters rather indelicately refer to as "gang bangs."

The problem with the Broncos, as the national (and international) sports media see them, is that they are a one-man band—John Elway and forty-four stumbling idiots, a no-name team with an all-world quarterback, a group of guys who ought to be out of work right now, plus the genius who pulled off The Drive. "The Denver Broncos? Forget the Denver Broncos," wrote Jim Murray, nationally syndicated columnist for the *Los Angeles Times*. "They're just the piano in this recital. They just have to stand there and hum." According to Michael Katz of the New York *Daily News*, "If you take John Elway away from this team, they're 5–11 or 6–10—just an ordinary team. Denver is probably somewhere in the top ten—but near the bottom of it." To add to the ignominy, Giants coach Bill Parcells says the Redskins were a tougher opponent than the Broncos during the regular season, and the point spread has widened to a fat nine and a half. Which makes you wonder why they are going to bother to play the game on Sunday, and why in the world all those people with stories to write and tidy little segments to edit were wasting their time on the Broncos today.

Yet Media "Hour" wasn't quite as Elway-focused as you might have guessed it would be. Yes, he was pinned against the rail in front of the first row of the stadium's bleachers for all of the allotted minutes, and yes, he spoke repeatedly about growing up the son of a football coach, about his refusal to play in Baltimore, about his relationship with Dan Reeves, about his scrambling abilities and his arm, and—need I mention it?—about the phenomenon that was The Drive. "I'm pretty ordinary, to tell you the truth," Elway said seven or eight times during the session, each time the remark coming hard on the heels of a particularly adulatory kind of question, Elway absently brushing his fresh haircut as he spoke. But there *were* others who were questioned, other Denver personnel who spoke right into the microphones.

In the stands on the same side of the field, Dan Reeves, wearing his cheerleader's sweater, talked about pre-game anxieties. "Sure," he said, "the anticipation is great, the butterflies are great, but once you kick off, it boils down to just another football game—only with a whole lot more people watching." He did variations on that theme for thirty minutes.

Opposite Reeves and Elway, Tom Jackson, Karl Mecklenburg, and Rulon Jones were positioned in the western stands—the three of them presumed by the NFL's legion of PR people to be the team's defensive draws. The reporters wanted to hear Jackson talk about the old days, to compare this team with his first Super Bowl squad, to explain his role as a motivator. "Every time you guys mention my name," Jackson joked with them, "do you *have* to call me 'the oldest linebacker in the NFL'?"

Stories about Mecklenburg had been appearing in the national magazines all season, so the scribes circling around him already knew what they were after. They just needed a few quotes to fill out their half-written stories on this undersized linebacker from Minnesota who was so intelligent he could remember the many hundreds of play assignments for seven different defensive positions, so talented that in 1985 he became an All Pro in a season he began on the bench. "Well, basically, I'm an inside linebacker, but I have a lot of rover responsibilities where I play some defensive end, some nose guard, some outside linebacker. Generally, Joe Collier tries to put me where he thinks the ball's going to go," Mecklenburg said—over and over again.

Jones, also a second-year Pro Bowler, a tall, blond, introverted rancher's son from Utah who somehow turns into serious trouble on a football field, was known as the Broncos' single-handed sack attack, and the reporters wanted to know what he saw as the requirements of the coming game. Never long-winded, and always a little shy, Jones spoke to his shoes and said what he always said. "We're just going to have to pin our ears back and go at them and play our best game of the year"—everyone within earshot scribbling the "pin our ears back" part, if nothing else.

Down on the field, in the midst of the rest of the Broncos players and the media people who skittered around them like shoppers at a clearance sale, Pat Bowlen spoke to the three reporters who happened to know who he was, and talked about his attraction to the game. "Guys like me are just jock-sniffers at heart," he said. "A lot of us live vicariously via the team." He explained that he would make an appearance at the commissioner's party on Friday evening, but that those events weren't really his style; he said he was well pleased that the Broncos were considered substantial underdogs; then he took a moment to complain about the sportswriters and broadcasters who surrounded him. "The media has been treating us as sort of a ragtag operation. It's the same old deal. We're just the guys in the funny orange shirts from out in the Rockies."

I knew exactly what Bowlen meant, yet it seemed ironic to hear him say that the Broncos were being snubbed at a moment when a thousand journalists had them covered like a dirty sheet. But just then, a loudspeaker voice announced that the session was over, and the Broncos—their faces lighting up as if they suddenly had been paroled—made a beeline for their buses, Bowlen and the coaches quickly following, a few reporters tagging along for some final comments, but most of them, their pads open and their Minicams cranked up, turning their attentions to each other. The media madness that this Super Bowl week engendered was a story in itself, and editors were always impatient.

January 24

The trouble with the Super Bowl is that it is simply a football game—sixty minutes of sport which is, some people like to pretend, the axis around which the earth spins. But the gap between the reality of the gridiron and the absurdity of the hype is enormous, and there is probably no way in which the game can ever live up to its lead-in. By the time Sunday's game is finally played, more than three thousand people will have received some sort of media accreditation, each one trying to outmythologize the other. To read about it, or to hear the television tell it, Super Bowl XXI is the biggest story since World War II, the principal difference between them being that during the earlier conflict, no one was trying to get tickets.

For their part during the course of the week, the Broncos basically have done what they would do to prepare for any game. Their days have been occupied with long team meetings, snappy practices, and three square meals, their evenings free till a midnight curfew. When wives and children and girlfriends and mothers and fathers and friends started to arrive on the scene on Thursday, it began to seem as though the week's main event might be a big wedding come Saturday afternoon. The weather has been warm and spirits have been high, the pace certainly less than frantic. It's been okay. All of it, in fact, has been fine—except for the Media Day onslaught on Tuesday and those harrowing seventy-five-minute interview sessions on Wednesday and Thursday mornings—the combined two and a half hours comprising the players' and coaches' only mandatory contact with reporters all week. For most of the Broncos, the three sessions amounted to a diversion, a curiosity at best, a pain in the ass at worst. But despite the fact that the reporters were desperate for stories and that they sat rapt in the midst of the most ridiculous kind of drivel, at least one player worried that two and a half hours simply weren't enough.

"I decided last week," Vance Johnson told the pack of reporters who tried to shoulder their way close to him in the ballroom of the Newporter Resort on Thursday, "Vance, if you ever want to be famous, this is the week. I want to be famous. I want to be famous as hell. I can't tell you how famous I want to be. Listen, man, I'll talk to anybody, whatever you guys want to know. The Vance can talk about anything. He's got a lot of character."

Vance Johnson *is* a character, this week playing the role of an elfin football ingenue, the country boy entranced by the bright lights, the once painfully shy kid from Tucson, Arizona, who now talks so incessantly about himself that it's impossible to know whether he believes a word he says. VJ, "The Vance," who had his ears pierced to celebrate the trip to the Super Bowl, whose four-inch flattop has to be held in place by a preparation of decidedly industrial strength, whose sartorial tastes tend toward shirts, jackets, and trousers, for that matter, festooned with dangling fringe, who even garnered a late-night appearance on Joan Rivers's show—is currently the Broncos' closest facsimile to the kind of personality that the Super Bowl media go crazy for, a welcome relief from the focus on John Elway, who, frankly, is just too much white bread and too many teeth to be able to support more than seven or eight stories per reporter. When the Chicago Bears' Jim McMahon and William "The Refrigerator" Perry became brief superstars during last year's Super Bowl frenzy, Johnson, the Broncos' second-year wide receiver sensation, was paying close attention. "It used to kill me not to have any friends when I was a kid," he told anyone and everyone who would listen. "I was too shy, too afraid. I used to say to myself, I'll show you guys. One day I'll be famous. And here I am. It's happened. They'll see me here in the Super

Bowl, see me on the Joan Rivers show tonight, and they'll think, 'Man, that's that little dude we used to shit on.' "

The Vance owes much of his celebrity this week to Mike Downey, a sports columnist for the *Los Angeles Times*. He would have attracted some interviewers anyway, and the booking on the Rivers show has been secure for several days, but it was Downey's long profile of The Vance in his paper's Wednesday editions that caught his hundreds of colleagues' eyes and convinced them that here, at long last, was another Bronco with some bite, with enough color to sustain, say, seventeen or eighteen column inches. Downey spent his Media Hour on Tuesday standing beside The Vance on the field at Orange Coast College, listening to the ebullient young black man talk an orange-and-blue streak, and the writer came away well convinced that in two days' time he would hold his own against the talk-show host. "Memo to Joan," Downey wrote, "There is no need to ask: 'Can we talk?' He can talk. He wants to talk. He lives to talk. Joan, he's the male *you*. He makes Dr. Ruth look meek. He makes the Gabor sisters seem mute."

By Thursday morning, when 1,200 or so reporters followed their free breakfasts with a little more than an hour of free access to the Broncos, who were seated around the ballroom beneath carefully calligraphed nameplates—The Vance was in major demand. Downey had discovered him, but all's fair in love and Super Bowl reportage, and five hundred more stories on The Vance were certain to appear between then and Sunday. The reporters stood seven deep around him; photographers had to lift their still cameras and Minicams blindly into the air, then hope their aims were accurate; Clint Sampson, Johnson's fellow wide receiver, used his cardboard nameplate to fan his friend on whom the hot lights were focused; and The Vance held court in high style, saying "I think The Vance will have a great game on Sunday," saying "I'm not intimidated by anybody," saying "If I can be a celebrity for a few days, that's fantastic," saying "Hopefully, when I die, people will have something nice to say about me," adding "I haven't really listened to myself too much in this interview." Somehow, there was some charm sprinkled on his self-indulgence, and through it all, The Vance seemed not so much boorish as simply boyish. You didn't want to slap his face so much as tousle his hair and tell him to go on, get outta here.

When the reporters were interrupted and told their time had expired, when The Vance was finally speechless, Linda Barragan, public relations director for the Newporter Resort, stole into the room to ask him for a favor. If the opportunity arose during his conversation with Joan Rivers that night, would he be kind enough to say something complimentary about the hotel? "Sure," said The Vance, surprised that the favor was so simple. "This is a great place. Hey, sure, I'll tell her anything. I'll say 'Joan, can we talk?' "

The Newporter Resort, the Broncos' headquarters this week, is one of those palm-shaded places where elegance is the watchword and pastels are the colors of record. The bayside, Moorish-styled buildings are covered in a pale salmon stucco; the concierge wears a light peach suit; the matchbooks are a tasteful creamy turquoise. It does not at all seem to be the kind of establishment that would gladly hang a gaudy orange banner reading WELCOME AFC CHAMPION DENVER BRONCOS above its valet entrance, nor would you suppose that the four big, boxy satellite up-link vans parked nearby would be seen to be setting the proper tone. But it's the Broncos souvenir stand in the lobby which convinces you that the hotel's management has simply thrown up its hands for this week in the interests of making some very big money.

In addition to the Broncos players, coaches, staffs, and their families, the Newporter is also playing host to the massive media contingent from Colorado—the nineteen staffers sent southwestward by the *Rocky Mountain News*, the *Post*'s similar contingent, task forces of two dozen or more from each of Denver's network television stations, the whole payroll at KOA radio, and many dozens of lesser lights representing every news medium from the Rocky Mountains that can afford the breathtaking room tariff.

And there is another contingent making the most of these hardship-post surroundings. Colorado governor Roy Romer and Denver mayor Federico Peña are the cornerstones of a carefully orchestrated effort to turn the Broncos' appearance in the big game into a marketing extravaganza for the state and the city. To hear them and their subordinates tell it, it was absolutely critical to make the Super Bowl trip, despite the costs and the scheduling complications. "We've been inundated by calls," explained Peña, who is favoring the relaxed look of orange cardigan and pullover sweaters as he stands at the public relations frontlines this week. "I can't tell you what this is meaning for Denver. We are showing the national media, and a lot of other people as well, that Denver is a dynamic, exciting city, and that the state of Colorado has a terrific future ahead of it." Of course Mayor Peña would have preferred to watch the Super Bowl on television back home in dynamic and chilly Denver, but *somebody* had to do this, and he already owned the sweaters.

January 26
—

Saturday was the lull before the Sunday storm, a day for writers to prepare the flood of pre-game features that would fill their papers' Sunday sports sections, a day for television crews to put the finishing touches on Saturday night pre-game specials, and it was a landmark day for the members of two football teams. Saturday marked the final, the absolute, shout-it-from-the-rooftops last practice of the season, and that fact alone—quite apart from the certainty that now the *game* at last could be played—put ninety professional football players in very good moods indeed.

At the Newporter, most Broncos players had lunch with their families, then spent some time lounging with them at poolside, or oceanside, or bedside before, late in the afternoon, they boarded buses, bound for a destination they didn't know. The league had gone to great security lengths to provide both teams with secret Saturday night lodging; no honking horns or screaming fans would disturb their slumber if the National Football League had anything to say about it, and its decision that the players themselves couldn't be trusted with the information about their location seemed only prudent. It would be a quiet Saturday night, to be sure, but after all, tomorrow would be a work day.

The Rose Bowl is perhaps the most well-known football stadium in the nation, but although Sunday's game was the fourth Super Bowl it has hosted, it is seldom the scene of a professional football contest. It does provide the home field for the UCLA Bruins each autumn, and each New Year's Day, the Rose Bowl is the sight of, well, the Rose Bowl, the granddaddy of the seemingly limitless number of collegiate bowl games which are played around the country during every holiday season. In fact, if it weren't for the stadium and the game called the Rose Bowl, the NFL's extravaganza would probably be known by a more prosaic name, something, say, like the National Football League Championship Game. It's only because of this lovely, sixty-five-year-old, elliptical stadium, squeezed between Pasadena's residential hills, that the word "bowl" has ever become synonymous with football.

The Rose Bowl exits from the Pasadena and Foothills freeways were jammed by 10:30 Sunday morning, still five hours before the game got underway. Jammed with Giants fans in rented cars, jammed with a car or two, it's true, with a recent orange paint job, yet much of the traffic was made up of people who would have been there regardless of the game's combatants. Those people were converging on the Super Bowl because it was the centerpiece of a dream vacation, the prize in a package tour for sales leaders from dozens of different companies, the ultimate freebie for a legion of advertisers and event sponsors and official concessionaires. Fans they were not; most of them were there simply because it was the place in all of America where millions of other people wished they could be that day. The cachet attached to a Super Bowl ticket was worth much more than money, and they were part of the glittering scene.

For its part, the new low-budget CBS was avoiding ostentation. True, the network was expecting somewhere in the neighborhood of 130 million American viewers for its Super Bowl broadcast, and it was selling a single thirty-second commercial for $600,000, a 12 percent increase over the $555,000 rate NBC secured last year. But these were belt-tightening times at the network, and besides, CBS wanted to redirect attention to the game. "We plan to concentrate on the core coverage," producer Doug Richardson said before the broadcast. "It will be a nuts-and-bolts telecast. The pageantry and hype will be less important than the game itself." To that end, the network planned to use only fifteen cameras, five fewer than it used to record Super Bowl XIX two years ago, but, with the assistance of ten video-tape machines with slow-motion capability, two graphics generators, one telestrator—which would allow game analyst John Madden to draw illustrative circles and arrows—and one still picture–storage unit, executive producer Ted Shaker was confident that viewers wouldn't notice the Spartan approach. And he was confident, too, that even the most rabid fans in New York, New Jersey, and Colorado could withstand a pre-game show that began *two hours and fifteen minutes* before the kickoff.

281

Finally, at precisely 3:15, at the moment the CBS producers commanded it, with the floorshow over and the field finally cleared of pop musicians and pubescent dancers, the Giants' Raul Allegre put his foot into one of the Wilson balls that had been engraved with the official Super Bowl XXI insignia.

Paul Zimmerman sat in the middle of the Rose Bowl press box—his stature among the nation's football writers and his senior position at *Sports Illustrated* earning him a coveted front-and-center seat. The storied Dr. Z, who back in August had correctly predicted each of the NFL's six divisional champions and had picked the Broncos and the Giants to be the two teams who would survive to play here today, was excited about the prospects for this game. He admired the two coaches—Bill Parcells, the chubby guy from New Jersey in the baggy warmup jacket who had always known he wanted to coach the New York Giants; Dan Reeves, the country boy in a CEO's suit who had lived his life for football. Zimmerman liked the Giants' awesome linebacking corps and its old-fashioned, stick-it-in-their-craw kind of offense; he liked the complexities of the Denver defense and its high-tech, high-art offense built around John Elway's arm. He was impressed, way back at the end of summer, by the Giants' hunger, their sense of mission, and by the Broncos' imitation of a well-oiled machine. He guessed then that if the two teams did meet in the season's final game, the Giants would win a close one. This hefty football scribe in a rumpled blazer and high-water, pale blue chinos, his dark moustache seemingly mounted onto an ever-present short cigar, the yellow pad in front of him ready with hand-drawn grids to record the numbers, anxiously watched the opening kickoff fall out of the California sky, silently rooting, despite his determined impartiality, for the Giants, to make him look like a football genius.

Zimmerman wasn't surprised, however, when the Broncos completed their first possession with a 48-yard Rich Karlis field goal, his tenth in a row now. But the early Denver lead did strike some concern among the millions who had never considered that this would be anything other than the Giants' day. Then New York countered with a scoring drive of its own, 78 yards in nine plays, quarterback Phil Simms completing each of six pass attempts, including a short 6-yarder for the touchdown. Three minutes later, the Broncos were back on top, Elway running a quarterback draw from a shotgun formation at the 4, diving into the end zone to make it seem in its early minutes that this was going to be that rarity among Super Bowls—a tight and plainly terrific game.

The Giants got nothing going the next time they had the ball, and following Sean Landetta's punt, the Broncos proceeded to chew up the field again, moving into scoring position for the third time in as many tries, Elway dazzling the 101,000 who sat inside the bowl and the rest of the television-watching world with a 54-yard strike to the newly famous and always fleet-footed Vance Johnson, who was tackled at the Giants' 29. In six more plays, the ball was positioned on the one-yard line—first and goal for the Broncos. Elway rolled right, but before he could find a receiver or an opening to run into, Lawrence Taylor trapped him for a 2-yard loss. Second and three to score. Gerald Willhite tried a quick trap up the middle, but was caught by Harry Carson for no gain. Third down and 3 yards out. Now it was time to get serious, but on a sweep to the left, Sammy Winder was smothered by Carl Banks for a loss of 3 more yards. Fourth down now, and the Giants had pushed the ball back to the 6. The team that had sculpted The Drive in Cleveland two Sundays before somehow couldn't earn the final yard on this drive, which could have produced a commanding 17–7 lead. But at least there would be the field goal, everyone on the planet assumed, until Rich Karlis's kick sailed wide to the right of the yellow uprights. *He had missed it.* He had pushed a virtual gimme, and the Broncos had gotten nothing. Karlis hung his head as he made the long walk back to the bench, and the defenders breathed a giant sigh of relief as they turned the ball over to their offense. Denver 10 still, New York 7.

Again the Giants had to punt, but in the process of stopping them, the Broncos had lost Tom Jackson, who had sprained his knee and had to be helped from the field. Landetta's punt pushed the Broncos back to their own 15, then Elway was sacked for a loss of 2. But he got the Broncos out of their hole when, on second down, he hit Clarence Kay with a 15-yard pass up the middle.

It was a first down for only a fraction of a second. An official was suddenly signaling that the catch was incomplete, Kay was protesting that, my God, he had definitely caught the ball cleanly, grabbing it four or five inches off the ground, and the instant replay system went into use for the first time ever in a Super Bowl. After a long two-minute wait, the decision of the officials in the instant-replay booth was that they were deferring the decision back to the field. They saw nothing on the videotaped replays which conclusively showed that Kay caught the ball, nor anything showing conclusively that it had first skidded onto the turf. Under the terms of the replay rule, the call would simply stand. Incomplete pass. Third and twelve at the 13. Elway dropped back again to pass, but before he found a receiver, defensive end George Martin found him and smothered him in the end zone for a safety. Things were beginning to go awry, and Denver was left with a fragile one-point lead.

Following the Broncos' free kick, the Giants' offense sputtered again in just a single series, and before the half-time whistle, Denver quickly rebounded, moving to the Giants' 16, Elway finding Steve Watson on a 31-yard sideline pattern. It looked, momentarily, like the Broncos were back in business. But with thirteen seconds to go in the half, Karlis pushed his second kick of the quarter hauntingly wide to the right.

The stadium's public address system played John Denver's "Rocky Mountain High" as the teams trotted into their locker rooms, but the syrupy song seemed to mock the shaken Broncos. Their defense had played brilliantly so far, holding the Giants

284

to a single touchdown, and Elway and the offense had been able to do everything they wanted to do but score. After a first quarter in which they had looked like Giant killers, the second quarter had resulted in two missed field goals, which were without apparent explanation, a disputed call that denied a first down, then resulted in a safety, a worrisome injury to Tom Jackson, and not a single point. The Broncos still led 10–9, but somehow they didn't feel like singing.

It wasn't the Walt Disney Productions half-time show—featuring 2,000 high schoolers in satin and sequins and appropriately entitled "The Land of Make-Believe"—that set the stage for the second half. It was Old Blue Eyes instead, the familiar voice of Frank Sinatra booming out "New York, New York" as the Giants came back onto the field to the wild cheers of 60,000 or so of their devoted fans. They weren't even leading the game, and their offense had scored but seven points, yet somehow you could feel the certainty in the warm afternoon air—some extraordinary football was about to be played, and the Giants were planning to play it.

When the smoke had cleared early in the fourth quarter, the New York Football Giants had scored 24 unanswered points. In the nightmarish fifteen minutes of the third quarter, Phil Simms completed seven of seven pass attempts, one of them for a touchdown; running back Joe Morris fought for 32 bruising yards and a touchdown; and Raul Allegre hit a chip-shot field goal—the Giants amassing 163 yards of offense while the Broncos mustered a total of *two*.

The Broncos might as well have stayed in the locker room and watched it on TV—the third quarter was plainly and decisively the province of the Giants. Denver did have the ball briefly when the fourth quarter opened, but Elway, fighting off the Giants' defenders who were now blitzing him with a giddy fury, threw an interception to cornerback Elvis Patterson. The Giants had the ball at midfield; Simms and Morris went to work again, and no one doubted that they would promptly score. But when Simms's end-zone pass to tight end Mark Bavaro bounced off him and into the serendipitous arms of receiver Phil McConkey for the touchdown, the Giants seemed utterly incapable of making mistakes. It was their game now, their afternoon, their season. Only mediocre in the first half, the Giants had come to frenzied, firecracking life, and the Broncos had fizzled in response. It was New York 33, Denver 10—the same slim ten points the Broncos had scored back when hope burned bright in the first quarter of play.

They shouldn't have bothered to tick down the final ten minutes and forty-eight seconds, but the commercials had been bought and the stadium was rented for the entire evening, so it seemed like the proper thing to do. The score changed to 39–20 before the gun sounded, but by then the numbers were unimportant. Following two quarters in which the Super Bowl looked like it somehow might live up to its super billing, it ended in its by-now traditional rout, the Giants looking indisputably as though they were the best team in the National Football League, the Broncos reeling, shell-shocked by Frank Sinatra. God *damn* these New York/New Jersey football teams! The Broncos were now 0–3 against them on the year, and the year had just come to a shuddering close.

On the sidelines, Dan Reeves pulled his headset away from his ears and gave up the fight, his face etched with aching disappointment. Tom Jackson—who had spent the last half of what likely was his final football game standing in a warmup jacket on the sidelines—put his arm around an anguished John Elway, the young quarterback who had played his heart out but come up short. It wasn't supposed to end like this, but the lesson of football was that you couldn't depend on the outcome. All you could do was play the game.

It crossed my mind that I might have seen my final football game as I stood in the knot of several hundred people who were pushed and pressed into a concrete tunnel beneath the stadium. And being trampled to death by reporters chafing for post-game quotes seemed like an ignominious way to die. But at last the Pasadena cops, who were big enough themselves to catch the eye of an offensive line coach, opened the barricades and the reporters spilled into the interview areas like water from a breached dam, and I moved with the flow till it seemed certain I would survive.

Phil Simms, the Giants' quarterback, had played a magnificent game, completing 22 of 25 passes and throwing three touchdowns. He had been voted the game's Most Valuable Player, and he would meet the crushing press in an area cordoned off specifically for that purpose. From a group of podiums nearby, the Giants' Lawrence Taylor, George Martin, Phil McConkey, and the almost mute, Rambo-esque Mark Bavaro would relay their impressions of their victory. Bill Parcells would participate in Pete Rozelle's presentation of the Vince Lombardi trophy to the Giants' warring owners, Wellington and Tim Mara, in front of the CBS cameras, then he would go to his own specified podium to express his great delight.

The NFL's PR people had arranged it all and, yes, the losing team would be heard from, too. Dan Reeves would speak at the opposite end of the separate room where Parcells was interviewed; John Elway would be positioned down the hall near the several Giants players; and sure, the men in dark suits with UNLIMITED ACCESS passes dangling from a buttonhole would try to get Rich Karlis. They understood the compelling journalistic need to ask him how he felt about his failures.

Elway was wearing a terry-cloth robe as he fought his way through the throng of reporters to his appointed podium and, as he had for eighteen previous games this season, tried to explain the job he had just done, the job he endeavored to do. "I felt I did everything I could," he said honestly, forgoing a modesty that would have been false. "I gave a hundred and ten percent. I think I got everything out of myself that I could."

It was an accurate appraisal. Elway had played brilliantly, running for a touchdown, throwing for a touchdown, leading the team in rushing with 27 yards, passing for a total of 304, including the 54-yarder to Vance Johnson that was breathtaking in its beauty—the pass which led to the Broncos' goal-line collapse and Karlis's first achingly errant kick. But the Broncos had depended on Elway for too much. The running attack that had sputtered all season was stopped with a crashing finality there on the Giants' one-yard line, then, as if the team confessed its tragic flaw, it did not even try another running play from that moment midway through the second quarter until the game had long since been surrendered in the fourth. "If you want a turning point," Elway told the reporters, most of whom just wanted a quick word or two from him before they turned their attention to the Giants, "that was it. When we didn't get into the end zone on that first and goal, it hurt. It really hurt."

As Dan Reeves made his way to his podium, there were few reporters to block him—when your team loses the Super Bowl, you are very quickly yesterday's news. Reeves faced the group of two dozen journalists, the smallest post-game press corps he had spoken to since the beginning of the season, and he appeared terribly defeated, this fiercest of competitors having to bear his loss so publicly. "We've got to get better," he told them. "That's about all there is to say. Apparently right now we aren't good enough."

When they pressed him, Reeves agreed that his team had to be a fairly good one to have even been able to suit up for this game. "Certainly it's an accomplishment to get here," he agreed, "but we just didn't play well enough to deserve to win it. And that's what we're in business for. We try to win the games we play. But I want our players to remember how this feels. I expect to be back here many more times, and I want them to know how much better it'd feel to win."

As Bill Parcells was completing his press conference, he walked to the opposite end of the room, trailing a knot of reporters, then interrupted Reeves, giving him a big bear hug and saying "God bless you" to the coach he had faced from across the field. It was the kind of gesture that Reeves himself might have made if he had been the victor, but it was painfully hard for him to accept it in defeat. He felt hollow and hurt and somehow horribly embarrassed, and he was only able to whisper, "God bless you, too. You did a great job."

Rich Karlis had obviously been crying, but he was composed as he talked at length about his tormented afternoon. "I've always prided myself in being able to deliver in the big games," he said, his voice flat, his eyes red and swollen. "But today I let a lot of people down. I feel responsible. My misses hurt our momentum, and I think if I'd hit them, it might have been a different ball game. I just see those misses as one of the deciding factors in the game."

Karlis had exulted in the excitement and the attention that his game-winning field goal brought him two Sundays before, and now he was willing to accept the opposite condition. His words weren't a means of excusing his performance; instead they were a kind of penance, one he wanted to make. "I didn't get my hips completely around," he explained to the now-growing corps of reporters who wanted to hear his frank remarks. "If you don't get completely around and if everything doesn't break at the right time, the ball goes into the woods. After I missed the kicks, I thought about all the people I let down, all the guys who had put their hearts and souls into this game, guys like Tom Jackson, who'll probably retire and will never have another chance at a Super Bowl. All week I had dreamed about kicking the winning field goal, but this pretty much wipes out my dreams."

The locker room was already quiet. A few players had showered and dressed and gone to the sanctuary of the buses, where they could sit in the darkness and not have to say anything to

289

anyone. Others patiently entertained the questions of the Colorado reporters, speaking in a kind of quiet trance from the benches in front of their lockers. Elway was dressing now, but was still the subject of much attention. "Well, for the eightieth time," he said, finally weary of all the inquiries, "yes, I'm very disappointed. But I'm also very proud of our football team."

Karlis had returned from the interview area, but still he spoke about his failures, still he wanted to assume all the blame. "No, we lost this as a team," Rulon Jones said to the reporters standing near him. "Well, we'll just try again next year," said Jim Ryan, already acknowledging that life most likely would march on. "Maybe in a few weeks Vance'll be able to look back and think, yeah, I caught a touchdown pass in the Super Bowl," said a subdued Vance Johnson. "But man, it's hard for him to think that way now." Keith Bishop still wore his terry-cloth robe as he sat in front of his locker, in little hurry to dress and leave and be done with it. "I just wish we could have won it for everybody back home," he said passively, spitting tobacco juice into a plastic cup.

Bishop, Jones, Elway, Karl Mecklenburg, Dennis Smith, and their families would fly out of Los Angeles early in the morning for a week in Hawaii and the Pro Bowl next Sunday; for the five of them, there was a bit of football left. But as Denver Broncos, their season was now finished. It had been six months to the day since the Broncos' veteran players had had to drive to Greeley to go to work, and now the work was done.

Tom Jackson's knee was obviously swollen, his trousers stretched tight around it, and he was ready to leave the locker room when a reporter stopped him to inquire about his retirement. Was this his final football game? What were his plans? "My plans? My plans are to go get some scotch," he said, mustering a bit of a grin, his anguish somehow more obvious when he smiled. For fourteen years, he had begun each season hoping he would be part of a team that would make it to the very top of the heap. Twice now his teams had come very close. This year, for the first time in all those years, he was not on the

290

field, playing the game, giving it a bold and gallant shot, when the effort came up short.

Jackson limped out of the locker room. Beyond the door, he stopped and hugged Dan Reeves's wife, Pam, holding her but saying nothing because nothing could be said, then he joined the Broncos on the bus.

Epilogue

The plane we were scheduled to board was fogbound in San Francisco, and we stood on the hot Tarmac at LAX while United Airlines scrambled to find another 747—there were so many wives and children, parents and all kinds of kinfolk, politicians and reporters, players and staff returning to Denver that only the big wide body could accommodate us. The long faces had long since vanished by midday on Monday, but no one felt particularly festive while we waited. Conversations were quiet and cordial and everyone was obviously tired, as though we all had been on a lavish company holiday that had lasted a few days too long.

There had been a party of sorts at the Newporter following the game—the going-through-the-motions kind of affair that half the candidates who run for office preside over on election nights—then Dan Reeves had gotten up early on Monday to meet with reporters for the last time this season, telling them there was much work to be done. The Broncos defense had to be examined intensively, and somehow a running game had to be procured. Draft day was only three months away; training camp would start in six. "We've made strides," said the head coach who had now completed his sixth season, "but we're not where we want to be."

All talk of football was finished by the time we were finally airborne. People slept, thumbed through issues of *Business Week* and other magazines that seemed certain not to have sports sections, and half the players were occupied with their infant children, who happily knew nothing about the loss. Only a few people bothered to look when the captain pointed out the Grand Canyon, but he got everyone's attention near the end of the flight when he announced that he had just received a radio warning about severe turbulence over the Front Range foothills west of Denver. He told everyone, including the flight attendants, to be seated and to buckle seat belts *immediately*. Something in his voice convinced everyone to take him seriously. We were assured of making it back to Colorado, at least, but getting all the way to Denver suddenly seemed problematical as the huge aircraft began to buck, its fuselage groaning with the strain, the wings seeming certain to snap from the violent force of the air. In the rear of the plane, where the players and their families and the media taggers-on were seated, there was a little nervous laughter, but no one said anything until KHOW radio's Tony LaMonica hollered, "This wouldn't have happened if you'd have won the goddamn football game!" Now we could all laugh, despite the buffeting and the fear, and I turned to see Vance Johnson and Mark Jackson grinning broadly and holding their hands above their heads, as if this were nothing more than an amusement park roller coaster ride. And soon everyone had joined their act, hands above heads, laughing and talking now, suddenly confident that we could ride the son of a bitch down to the distant runway.

It had been a roller coaster kind of season. It had begun with the hot promise and the heady predictions of training camp, followed by the assurance of four pre-season games that nothing was going to be easy. After a sublime skin-of-their-teeth victory over the Raiders to open the season, the Broncos were brilliant for five more games before they met the Jets and collapsed in a barrage of bagels. But they rebounded—beating Seattle and the Raiders again in successive weeks, those two games providing the margin that would ultimately give them the AFC title. Yet beginning with the following game against San Diego, their only loss at home all season, the Broncos initiated a strange and unshakable pattern—for seven successive weeks, they followed a win with a loss, a loss with a subsequent win, until in Seattle, on the final weekend of the regular season, they simply and spectacularly fell to pieces. In 1985, the Broncos had finished the season with an 11–5 record, but had missed post-season play. This year, 11–5 was good enough to send them—their confidence quaking—into the vaunted play-offs.

Despite a hobbled quarterback, or perhaps because of him, the Broncos ran their way to victory over the New England Patriots and on to Cleveland, where, it seemed certain, the roller coaster ride would stop. Then, with the Cleveland fans already celebrating and the Broncos' season only five minutes from coming to a perplexing and disappointing close, this team entered the football folklore. The Drive was played on a lofty level where athletes, or any of us, almost never perform. For a few brief minutes on a frozen field 1,400 miles from home, the Broncos were a perfect football team.

The ride did end in Pasadena, as it would have ended, win or lose. It was the second time in its history that the Denver team had survived a long and bruising season to play in the NFL's Mardi Gras, the second time that Fat Sunday had been followed by an ashen Monday. It was the Broncos' twenty-third game since Greeley, and now all their games had been played.

Barney Chavous had been a member of the Broncos' miracle Super Bowl team, but his football career had ended as this Super Bowl season began. Following its conclusion, three more stalwarts from that legendary team—Rubin Carter, Paul Howard, and Tom Jackson—would probably decide to retire, the three men still in their mid-thirties but already too old for this combative kind of employment. Carter and Howard had been placed on injured reserve, and although both said they would love to play again, the odds seemed stacked against them. Jackson's injury was minor, and he could return and try once more to win it all, yet he knew his playing time inevitably was short.

Yet if those four had played their swan songs this season, a group of young players, including Ricky Hunley, Orson Mobley, Vance Johnson, and Mark Jackson, had begun to appear by the end of the season as though they would have similarly long and illustrious careers in the funny orange shirts. Keith Bishop, Mike Harden, Rulon Jones, Karl Mecklenburg, and Gerald Willhite were among many whose prime seemed destined to endure a while. Following his three superb play-off games, it seemed certain that John Elway already was one of the game's great players, and that regardless of the money he earned to do so, he would play it remarkably for many years. Clarence Kay, one hoped, had much to look forward to.

I came away from a season spent in their proximity envying very little about the lives of these young men. The routine, the pace, the pressure, and the uncertainty of their work held little appeal. From the time he was five years old, Tom Jackson told me, he had lived his life by someone else's schedule. The best thing about retirement, he said, was the prospect of shaping his days himself.

The fickle celebrity and the strange adulation that accompanied the simple act of putting on the uniform; the demands of the fans who wanted to touch you but not necessarily to talk; the constant requests from reporters, promoters, and political hucksters—all seemed to weigh heavily against pursuing such a volatile line of work, one which so many young men aspire to, but which is impossible for all but a few. And there was the certainty that even if you were somehow good enough to play the game for even just a few short years, you would be physically reminded of it forever—by your knees, your neck, your back.

Yet undeniably, there was this about being a professional

football player: You did earn your living by playing a game, the same game you once had played for nothing but delight. And you did know—in ways that very few of us are able to share or understand—the rarefied pleasures of comradeship, of setting goals, and aspiring to attain them as a team, people with common purposes fully dependent on each other. Those, it seemed likely—quite apart from all the money and the disproportionate mystique—were the things that would keep you committed to the fray.

For their part, the coaches seemed to devote their lives to the sport simply because they couldn't help themselves. Whether they had ever been athletes of renown themselves, they had all played the game and, somewhere along the line, had become spellbound by it. For Dan Reeves, Joe Collier, Myrel Moore—and even for a man like Pat Bowlen—it was the *game*, with its strategies and challenges, the sacrifices and demands of the most intense kind of competition, that had become addictive, life somehow seeming flatly lived without the struggle. When Reeves paced the sidelines apprehensively at the end of a game, when he bent, put his hands on his knees, and focused intently on the final seconds, then hobbled on his football knees to the center of the field to commiserate with the losing coach, he was gloriously and completely happy. Those moments were so precious that they were even worth the anguish when, inevitably, the man he faced from across the field was the victor when they met.

The parade had been planned ten days before the Super Bowl—a victory celebration scheduled for Monday afternoon, and it would be held even if the Broncos somehow lost the game. City officials and the parade's corporate sponsors knew that regardless of the outcome, a large number of fans would want to welcome the Broncos home.

As the plane was taxiing to the United hangar, everyone safe and sound and on the ground, Reeves announced over the intercom that all the players would be required to participate in the parade. They were exhausted, depressed, and they wanted to do nothing except escape the crowds and go home, and their coach knew exactly how they felt. But word had already been received that the crowd was growing very big indeed and there was simply no way in which the team could snub its supporters. So they had lost a football game; that had happened a time or two before, hadn't it? And had it ever before caused a breach between the team and this football-focused town? The parade, plus a quick physical on Tuesday morning, would be the final demands of the season.

Reeves encouraged the players' families to join them for the trip downtown, and the large entourage sped away from the airport in buses led by a flashing and wailing police escort. At Wazee Street in lower downtown, the large windows were removed from the three buses before they joined the tail of the parade, turning onto Seventeenth to follow the yard-wide orange stripe that had been painted down the middle of the street for the length of the parade route. But the stripe was difficult to see. Crowds of people standing twenty, thirty, fifty deep surged from the sidewalks onto the pavement, filling it from both sides. The military color guard, the high school marching bands, the Budweiser Clydesdale horses, and an orange bus filled with the slightly awestruck residents of a nursing home were able to squeeze their way up the center of the street, but before the Broncos' buses could begin to advance, mounted patrolmen had to try to clear a path—the uniformed men and the horses with the shaggy winter coats leading those horses of a different color through the deep canyon formed by the office towers, through the midst of thousands and thousands of people who were hailing their defeated heroes.

Although I had been afflicted with the strange and contagious affection for the Denver Broncos for many years, I had never been one of the People Who Wear Orange, and it's hard to know if I would have been one of those who made the special effort to line the parade route. I did buy a cap once in some surge of parochial pride, but I had never worn it, not even in front of the television on an anxious Sunday afternoon, the autumn awash with passion. Somehow over the years, I couldn't help but detect a suspicious kind of neurosis, a zealotry that I wanted nothing to do with, in the fans who wore their fantasies on their sleeves, who found community in the color orange. Yet I suspected that the problem was much more mine than theirs. It was easy to decide that someone like The Barrel Man was skating on very thin cerebral ice until you met him and discovered that his peculiar avocation actually had enriched his life.

At the end of the twentieth century, this society tends to shun ritual and to turn away from collectively shared myths and aspirations, and it's probably to our detriment that we do so. Perhaps we all need a mythic benchmark or two in our lives— the reassuring anchors that are bound up in the ritual expressions of ideas and hopes otherwise hard to define or to understand. Whether we find them in religion or the natural world, the pursuit of money or a professed devotion to a team that plays a game, they are important because they can be depended on. In Colorado, each Broncos season has become a kind of constant now, and whether you wear a barrel or defer to something a little more demure, you can be sure that the team will accept your allegiance. The beauty of it all is that anyone can be a Broncos fan, and anyone can share the team's uncertain fortunes.

"It seemed to me, back when we had the team," the Broncos' former owner Gerald Phipps had told me midway through the season, "that to keep the fans with you, you had to prove to them that you were trying to provide a winner. You didn't have to win—we proved that for quite a few years, didn't we?—but you had to show them you were trying your best. And I think that in a funny way, trying to win, doing everything that you can, is more important to them than winning is itself."

I was reminded of what he had said as I stood in Civic Center Park on that Monday evening, the January weather surprisingly balmy, the snow turning to slush, waiting in the midst of a sea of fans for the parade finally to reach us. The City and County Building was lit with orange light and a huge banner secured to it read DENVER BY A MILE. News helicopters fluttered overhead, searchlights crisscrossed the darkening sky, but the crowd was surprisingly calm. Had the team won the game the day before, the fans who were there might have been wild with celebration, but their purpose that evening was something different. They were there, it seemed, to reassure the team and to say thank you for the season.

When the buses at last made their way down Broadway toward us, people surged into the street to try to reach out to touch players' hands, to blow them kisses, to wave and smile, tears streaming down their faces. By the end of the parade route, the players had seen more than 100,000 people, and the numbers alone were enough to overwhelm them. They were astonished at the reception and most responded by brightening their own spirits, returning broad smiles to the crowds that crushed in around them. Vance Johnson and Mark Jackson, boyish as ever, their hearts no longer broken, stood in the tall spaces where the buses' windows would have been, holding on with one hand and leaning out into the street, laughing and delighting in this strange new life, this phenomenon of sports celebrity. But Rich Karlis couldn't escape his sense of failure, his conviction that he had let so many people down, and despite his efforts, his waves and his thin smile bespoke his sadness. Dan Reeves, sitting in the front of the lead bus, looked exhausted at long last. He could hardly muster any kind of acknowledgment, and it seemed that this outpouring of emotion had rekindled the pain of yesterday's loss. His face seemed to say that he and his team didn't deserve this kind of greeting. Their goal had been to win the Super Bowl, and surely their failure didn't warrant this kind of welcome, the expression of this much affection. Like Bill Parcells's gesture the day before, he found this one hard to accept.

The players and coaches finally made their way to the platform that had been erected on the plaza in front of the building, and people who had watched along the twenty blocks of the parade route streamed toward them now, fans racing through the side streets, everyone converging for a final glimpse of the team.

Bob Martin and Ron Zappolo were the masters of ceremony for the brief rally and the crowd erupted when Martin's voice filled the park. "The way I see it," he said, "the 1987 season has just begun. The Broncos are 2–1 and they'll get after it again in September." The two men in turn introduced Pat Bowlen, Dan Reeves, the players, their wives and girlfriends. Bowlen promised that the city one day would have a world championship; Reeves could only say how moved he was by the reception, then he was at a loss for words. "You can't know how much this means to us," Tom Jackson told the 100,000 people below him who were now only a moving, loving mass in the darkness.

It struck me, standing among them, that these were the same people who had faithfully gone to Greeley during the hottest days of the summer to see the players in person and to express to them their hope. Young and old, they were, for the most part, people without the means to make a trip to California, let alone participate in the extravagance of the Super Bowl as well. Few of them were season-ticket holders, I suspected, and surely half of them had never seen the Broncos play in person, but at least there was this. At least they could come out on a warm winter evening and assure these young men who were their heroes that everything was going to be all right, assure them that winning wasn't the only issue. If you won it all, in fact, what then would you strive for? For football to mean anything, didn't it have to be played with the sense of something to gain? Besides, just imagine what the coming season would bring. The Broncos would be the most marvelous team imaginable, and the fall would be filled with delight.

I returned to Denver briefly at mid-March, just after the team had tentatively accepted the NFL's offer to play in an exhibition game in London's Wembley Stadium in early August. The league

301

had hoped that it could provide the suddenly football-mad Britons with a Super Bowl rematch, the Broncos versus the New York Giants. But the Giants, world champions now, had declined, saying the trip would interrupt their summer training. Not everyone in the Broncos organization was thrilled about the prospects of the whirlwind trip either, but somehow, acceding to the league's wishes seemed like the proper thing to do.

At the Broncos' offices in north Denver, Dan Reeves and his staff were preparing for the end-of-April draft they hoped would garner them a bighearted power fullback; Jim Saccomano and his staff were preparing the 1987 Broncos media guide that would herald the defending AFC champions; and alone in the cavernous weight room, Paul Howard, his leg still in a heavy cast, was working to keep himself in shape, hoping he had some football yet to play. Tom Jackson, writing his autobiography, was leaving the question of his retirement dramatically unanswered.

The Denver Nuggets were having a terrible season, and the town still didn't have a major league baseball team in spring training down in Arizona. The Broncos beat reporters were taking a break, and the callers on the sports-talk shows had little to talk about but the football team. They still wanted to know what had happened to the defensive secondary at the end of the season; they speculated about whether a Pro Bowl player or two might be traded to try to shore up the running game, and they were of mixed opinion about this London business.

The snow sculptures had long since collapsed on the dormant lawns; the flags and pennants had been taken down and stored, and the lights in the downtown buildings no longer read GO BRONCOS by night. But despite the slush and the incessant traffic, the orange stripe still survived on Seventeenth Street. It was faded now, but it still stretched from Wazee to Broadway, then turned south to the heart of the city.